Y0-ACD-609

Modernist Cultural Studies

UNIVERSITY PRESS OF FLORIDA

Florida A&M University, Tallahassee
Florida Atlantic University, Boca Raton
Florida Gulf Coast University, Ft. Myers
Florida International University, Miami
Florida State University, Tallahassee
New College of Florida, Sarasota
University of Central Florida, Orlando
University of Florida, Gainesville
University of North Florida, Jacksonville
University of South Florida, Tampa
University of West Florida, Pensacola

UNIVERSITY PRESS OF FLORIDA

GAINESVILLE

TALLAHASSEE

TAMPA

BOCA RATON

PENSACOLA

ORLANDO

MIAMI

JACKSONVILLE

FT. MYERS

SARASOTA

Catherine Driscoll

MODERNIST

CULTURAL

STUDIES

Copyright 2010 by Catherine Driscoll

Printed in the United States of America. This book is printed on Glat-
felter Natures Book, a paper certified under the standards of the Forestry
Stewardship Council (FSC). It is a recycled stock that contains 30 percent
post-consumer waste and is acid-free.

15 14 13 12 11 10   6 5 4 3 2 1

Library of Congress Cataloging-in-Publication Data

Driscoll, Catherine.

Modernist cultural studies / Catherine Driscoll.

p. cm.

Includes bibliographical references and index.

ISBN 978-0-8130-3424-9 (alk. paper)

1. Modernism (Literature) 2. Modernism (Art) 3. Culture. I. Title.

PN56.M54D75 2009

809'.9112--dc22   2009025057

The University Press of Florida is the scholarly publishing agency for the
State University System of Florida, comprising Florida A&M Univer-
sity, Florida Atlantic University, Florida Gulf Coast University, Florida
International University, Florida State University, New College of Florida,
University of Central Florida, University of Florida, University of North
Florida, University of South Florida, and University of West Florida.

University Press of Florida
15 Northwest 15th Street
Gainesville, FL 32611-2079
http://www.upf.com

For Norman Clare Talbot,
who first gave me *Finnegans Wake*.
I miss you.

Contents

Figures

Preface and Acknowledgments

In 1992, I arrived at the University of Melbourne fresh from a very traditional literary undergraduate education. I arrived in a department that had recently changed its name from the Department of English to the Department of English with Cultural Studies. At the time it was by no means agreed upon, even among scholars who affiliated themselves with the term, that cultural studies was a "discipline," or even that it should be one, and my comprehension of what cultural studies did or referred to was at best sketchy. As a Joyce scholar, I vaguely suspected that it would not like me very much. In fact, my first encounter with cultural studies in practice was not a very reassuring one. At the welcoming party for new (post)graduate students, a not entirely sober student with an awe-inspiring two years of seniority accused me, much to his amusement and my confusion, of being an "unreconstructed Leavisite." So my first exploration of cultural studies was designed to discover what an "unreconstructed Leavisite" might mean and whether I wanted to be one. Sixteen years later, I am still not entirely sure.

As I write this preface, the department where I first met cultural studies has changed its name to the School of Culture and Communication, and I am now chair of a department that has only recently managed to wrest the title "Cultural Studies" from years of negotiations over who does cultural studies and whether or not it is (still) worth doing. The negotiations traced in these shifts provide a crucial context for this book and lay out the audiences for whom I have written it. I do now see "cultural studies" as the field from and to which I primarily write. But I have never found my training in modernist literature to be anything but an asset to research and teaching in cultural studies.

I feel very strongly that practitioners of cultural studies should better understand the modernist context in which the key tools and many of the canonical works of their discipline emerged. And more scholars working on modernism should be able to both think critically about how and why they use that term as a description of something that has now past and understand how particular theories about culture that they share with cultural studies ground their work. This book is thus both an account of modernism for cultural studies and an account of cultural studies for modernist studies. I think this aim alone would be worthwhile because it seems to me that these fields still routinely and willfully misunderstand one another. But I have a further aim—to make a case for the importance of understanding ourselves as modernist. Even for those who find claims about our "postmodernity" passé, opaque, or otherwise frustrating, this might seem a counter-productive aim. But I not only want to understand what modernism and cultural studies mean to each other but also to insist on their ongoing importance for cultural analysis today.

This book has been a long time in the making and many people have helped in ways I could not have done without. Thanks to David Bennett, Melissa Gregg, Meaghan Morris, Elspeth Probyn, Russell Smith, and especially Ken Ruthven. Thank you to my students, past and present, and to my colleagues and staff in the School of Philosophical and Historical Inquiry and the Faculty of Arts at the University of Sydney. This project was also supported by the Australian Academy of the Humanities, and by the literature program at Duke University where I spent a sabbatical. I must also thank the University Press of Florida, especially Amy Gorelick, for wanting to publish this work, and Penelope Cray, for her careful reading and advice. Finally, no book appears without many kinds of personal support for which it is especially hard to give adequate thanks. Reams of gratitude are due to Judith Driscoll, Sean Fuller, Morgan Howard, and Ruth Talbot-Stokes.

Introduction

The Critical Attitude

What difference does today introduce with respect to yesterday?
Michel Foucault, "What is Enlightenment?"

There is an enormous amount of literature on and around the subject of "modernism." In academic books and articles, reviews and magazine columns, exhibition catalogues and liner notes, and elucidating comments across many media, references to modernism tell a story that is broadly consistent, however many fine distinctions and heated debates follow from it. In this story, "modernism" is a movement that began in the early twentieth century, generally reaching a crescendo between the two world wars, in which "modernists" radically transformed the ways in which all forms of art were produced and understood. In modernism we thus find radical aesthetic movements like Cubism in painting or the skyscraper in architecture. Sometimes that story extends beyond aesthetics to politics and science, for example, or to less specialized aesthetics, like advertising or fashion.

This story is worth knowing, publications on the topic generally agree, because modernism had such broad and lasting impact on what Western culture thinks is valuable, beautiful, culturally inevitable, and socially important. For example, modernism reinvented art as something worth doing and talking about in revolutionary terms. But this story about "modernism" describes something that happened in the past, even if its after-effects continue to be important. According to this story, modernism was displaced, or at very least radically transformed, in the years after World War II. Since then, new forms of art and media have emerged that, while developing out of modernism, are better understood as belonging to "postmodernism." An associated story about postmodernism has thus emerged, in which, for example, "art" is no more important than any other kind of cultural activity, including the most popular and the least specialized, such as sport or television. This is the case because no shared overarching understanding of "art" or its uses is now possible. And as the changes called "modernism" included new ways of thinking about culture—like German critical theory or formalist literary criticism—"postmodernism," too, advances its own kinds of cultural analysis. "Cultural Studies" exemplifies this "postmodern" cultural analysis, supposedly abandoning value distinctions between different kinds of culture to manifest a scholarly field that deems everything equally worthy of analysis.

I summarize this well-known story in these crude terms not to begin yet another book on how modernism is hard to define, or, for that matter, easy to define. Nor is this a book that aims to redefine the distinction between modernism and postmodernism. Many scholars have shown how the roots of modernism reach well into the nineteenth century, and even farther back. Many others have questioned whether the definitive postmodern break or turn frequently proposed in the 1980s and 90s ever actually transpired. While I refer to many of these arguments, my aim here is quite different. I do want to argue that modernism is not a thing of the past, but I want to do so by showing that cultural studies as a discipline—and before that as an interdisciplinary field—might well be considered a modernist project. I think that understanding the modernism of cultural studies is both necessary for seeing and sustaining the value of cultural studies and reinvigorates the importance of modernism today.

This argument is less a plea for (slightly) more established disciplines to take cultural studies seriously than it is a plea for contemporary humanities and social sciences, including cultural studies, to take modernism seriously. I thus want to intervene in the now habitual association between the "new humanities" and postmodernism, a move that sets cultural studies and modernism in opposition to one another, with modernism being situated as the kind of serious cultural project that cultural studies has either abandoned or was never able to access. The effect of this association is to make cultural studies seem superficial and modernism seem redundant; these are the claims against which this book is opposed. That tidy story about modernism as a past movement obscures many things, including the extent to which the famous debates and motifs of modernism are both familiar and important to us today. Thus, even as *Modernist Cultural Studies* mounts an argument about the history and content of cultural studies, it speaks equally to what has been monumentalized as modernism by decades of textbooks, lectures, and catalogues.

The following chapters thus revisit modernism in the light of contemporary cultural studies, looking for how cultural studies might understand modernism differently. Each chapter has more or less the same purpose, discussing the interdependence of modernism and cultural studies from a series of different perspectives. Taken together, these perspectives, or lines of inquiry, assemble a rather different story about modernism than the one I sketched above. In this alternate story, modernism is defined by the way it understands and articulates both "culture" and the subjects that perceive and manifest culture. In this way I propose that cultural studies is a crucial continuation of modernism into the present. I will leave an overview of each chapter's line of inquiry to the end of this introduction, however, because something else is necessary first. Given that I want to make an argument for a particular way of thinking about modernism, I cannot proceed without first offering a more careful definition of modernism than the broad-strokes story with which I began. And so the next section engages with one of the most slippery questions for modernist studies: what is "modernism" anyway?

The Problem of Definition—Modernism

One of the first things that modernism and cultural studies have in common, and this is not at all a peripheral or minor similarity, is a persistent problem with definition. In considering the characteristic ways "modernism" and "cultural studies" refuse definition, this introduction also establishes how I will use these terms throughout the book. After all these years and all those books about modernism, we cannot simply ignore the story they hand down to us. Therefore, I need to find a way of engaging with it while assembling that alternate story of my own.

First of all, I will not consistently capitalize "modernism." Despite the ease with which the term is used, there is little consensus about modernism except at the broadest level. Instead I will use two different terms: Modernism and modernism. I use "Modernism" to refer to the now institutionalized assemblage of generally aesthetic forms and practices that appeared (roughly) in the early twentieth century. "Modernism" in this sense is both the object and the product of all those readers and textbooks. While we might dispute the characteristics of this Modernism—which novels, which architects, which tendencies it should include—we cannot dispute that it exists. I use Modernism with a capital M to refer to that certain object, but I use the uncapitalized "modernism" to refer to an attitude to modernity that has much less temporal or formal coherence. This may seem unnecessarily complicated, but the distinction is important. Unless I find some way of marking this difference, every time I write "modernism" readers will read "Modernism" and yet no other term can now capture the attitude to modernity to which we continually refer. This pragmatic distinction therefore allows me to use "modernism" to name and discuss something almost permanently in dispute and "Modernism" to name the category that not only textbooks but also public and popular culture use as if it were agreed upon. By accepting that the canonized object (Modernism) and the ongoing critical attitude (modernism) can neither be reduced to the same thing nor separated entirely, perhaps we can move on to some other kind of discussion. Such a tactic is urgently needed because how to define modernism has come to absorb an inordinate amount of critical energy within modernist studies.

Many texts begin, to take Peter Childs' *Modernism* (2006) as an exemplar, with "Answering the Question: What is Modernism?" (1). This question is almost always understood to be a periodizing one. Different authors and texts propose numerous beginning points for Modernism, making reference to different disciplines, figures, or themes. In literature, for example, we might begin with scandalous mid-nineteenth-century texts—*Madame Bovary* (1857) or *Les Fleurs du Mal* (1868)—or we might take a tighter historical view and begin with some stylistic exception like Joseph Conrad's *Heart of Darkness* (1902). Some such examples have become key to debating modernism, but acknowledging their role as place markers does not resolve the question of how to periodize modernism. For example, the social impact of the French Revolution of 1848 might be considered a crucial precursor to modernism by some scholars and a beginning point by others, while the influence of F. T. Marinetti's "The Founding and Manifesto of Futurism" (1909) might be positioned as either a beginning point or a crescendo. These two examples demonstrate that, while there is much disagreement about the periodization of modernism there is nevertheless solid consensus that, some time between the beginning of the twentieth century and World War II, Modernism definitely happened.

Nevertheless, very few elements of modernism are particular to Modernism whether they emerged, like manifestos and experimental photography, in the eighteenth and nineteenth centuries or, like cinema and popular music, they dramatically appeared or changed direction in the Modernist period but reached no apotheosis there. Virginia Woolf's famous assertion, often employed to signal a beginning point for Modernism, that "On or about December 1910 human character changed" ([1924] 1990: 634) indicates several crucial problems with attempts to periodize modernism. Her reference to the London exhibition "Manet and the Post-Impressionists" (1910) points to dramatic changes in early twentieth-century Western painting and attributes to them real insight into what had changed in the world. Woolf's claim is reinforced by her and her associates' significance to such discourse on "modern art" (the exhibition was, after all, curated by fellow "Bloomsberry," Roger Fry). But Woolf's claim is actually a retrospective one, made in May 1924 when life surely must have seemed different than it had in 1910. Woolf's statement is also an ironic one, and not only because of the war that dominated the intervening thirteen and a half years. Its claim to certainty in fact communicates both uncertainty about the present and anxiety about the future.

If Woolf's account of the Impressionists is taken to describe a Modernist vanguard, then Woolf herself joined the movement rather late. The paintings that struck her so forcibly as new were all nineteenth-century works, including paintings by Vincent Van Gogh, Paul Gauguin, and Paul Cézanne. Woolf herself belongs to a thread of modernism sometimes called "High Modernism," which refers to a coherent and spectacular form of Modernism between the wars. But debate persists even over what constitutes this apparently central phase of Modernism. For some writers, 1922 is the pinnacle of High Modernism, while for others the interwar period generates "heroic" modernism and High Modernism refers to its canonization after World War II. Woolf's statement neatly captures not only the radical difference attributed to Modernism—its definition as a break with the past—but also the limitations of any such definition. Thus, for our purposes, Woolf's famous comment is telling in several respects. It helps us to not only define Modernism as that subject of exhibitions, anthologies, and magazine articles framed as a concrete historical phase, but also to recognize the limits of what such periodization can tell us. It helps us define modernism as a critical attitude—as a mode of inquiry that escapes any such categorical dating.

The task of defining modernism is additionally complicated by other terms tangled up with it: modernity, late modernity, and modernization. As the title of the now influential journal *Modernism/Modernity* makes clear, for modernist studies today the concepts of modernity and Modernism need to be addressed together. But this has not involved giving up canonical Modernism. As Rita Felski argues, jettisoning the definition of "aesthetic modernism" by its use of "self-consciousness; simultaneity, juxtaposition and montage; paradox, ambiguity, and uncertainty; and the dehumanization of the subject . . . is to render an already vague term effectively useless by robbing it of any meaningful referent" (1995: 25). Instead, Felski uses the term "modernity" to indicate the broader temporal frame in which this aesthetics emerges and to which Modernism responds. In another context, Felski describes the failure to distinguish between these terms as a "symptomatic confusion of a historical period (modernity) with an artistic movement (modernism)" (1994: 191). But this entanglement is complex. As Felski notes, "our own view of what modernity *is* has itself been influenced by the cultural power, prestige and visibility" of Modernism, and the Modernist "canon, paradoxically, is seen to provide a heightened perception of a historical reality that it has itself helped to construct" (191).

It is in the context of Modernism, then, that "modernity" generally refers to the emergence of a secularized human-centered world shaped by the scientific revolution, modern democracy, and the Industrial Revolution. Modernity thus comes to name a far greater breadth of time and range of objects and practices than Modernism, but only if we begin with a discourse on modernity that must itself be called modernism. Modernity might variously begin with the "Renaissance," mean everything after "the Middle Ages," begin with the "Enlightenment," or involve all developments spawned by the modernization of politics and economy. It is certainly not helped to certainty by the evasiveness of all the terms by which modernity is itself periodized. But while modernity and Modernism are equally difficult to pin down to dates or events, and nevertheless impossible to distinguish entirely, the two are not synonyms. Indeed, Modernism has generally been seen as a historical break within the broader span of modernity—so that, for example, whether or not they are included in Modernism, the society *Madame Bovary* offended and the art both before and after the Impressionists were certainly part of "modernity." It is in this context that the phrase "late modernity" has come to seem useful for talking about modernity during and after Modernism.[1]

"Late modernity" can be used to describe a shift in modernity's conditions of production—one that marks the radical difference between a steel mill and a radio station or modern democracy as defined by Jean-Jacques Rousseau or by Ronald Reagan. The central distinction made with this term is usually an economic one: late modernity is the era of commodity capitalism rather than of the Industrial Revolution. But "late modernity" is also a problematic term, for it attempts to push aside the importance of modernism to our contemporary discussions of modernity even as it intimates that the questions and changes that define modernity are ones now trailing off, fading away, or being displaced. "Modernization" seems to convey exactly this sort of progress narrative. Proceeding through industrialization, urbanization, and secularization in an unending line, modernization seems to demand a linear understanding of modernity. There may be crescendos and intermittent periods of slowness, but modernization appears to be an ongoing technologically determined process. And so it is. Given a sufficiently broad understanding of technology, modernization means the technologically determined progress of modernity. But grounded as it is in modernity, even modernization never manages to be simply linear. Only within modernity do we understand technological change as modernization. While the wheel, the aqueduct, and mathematics each constituted a technological change, they did not constitute modernization. Change is transformed into modernization by a shared sense of urgency and fear of redundancy in the face of the ever-changing experience of life today.

Becoming Modernist

Although I do not intend to write yet another survey of theories of modernity, to better grasp the tangle of definitions at hand it is useful to observe how contemporary modernist studies handles them. Susan Stanford Friedman's 2001 essay, "Definitional Excursions: The Meanings of Modern/Modernity/Modernism," provides a useful beginning point. That a relatively coherent discipline of modernist studies exists to which this essay can address itself further demonstrates that Modernism names an object with at least pedagogical and scholarly coherence. But Friedman characterizes modernist studies as "filled with contestation over the very ground of study" (493). The essay's central call for consensus about modernism seems at odds with Friedman's acknowledgment that "Definitional activities are fictionalizing processes, however much they sound like rational categorization" (493). But it helpfully singles out two themes as integral to defining Modernism: revolution, on the one hand, and reason and progress, on the other. While Friedman might have called the first Modernism and the second modernity, she does not want to assign separate terms to these themes because the border between them is unclear and, in any case, they seem to depend on one another. Friedman is right on both counts. Her proposed solution is instead to define Modernism according to the gulf between these themes.

This is certainly a provocative strategy, but one that ultimately remains stuck in the shadow of spectacular Modernism. Despite the range of texts from which Friedman takes her examples, some are much more clearly installed in Modernism's canonical space than others. As Felski suggests, attempts to detach the term "Modernism" from the history of its use will not help us clarify its relation to modernity. My insistence on maintaining two terms comprehends Friedman's themes very differently. For me, Modernism refers to a set of modernist artifacts as an aesthetic revolution that, because like all revolutions it had to happen at a particular point in the progress of history, can now be installed as something we have moved beyond, while modernism names an attitude to a modernity that comprises both progress and revolution. Friedman rightly has difficulty reconciling Alice Jardine's characterization of "modernity" as a critique of the Enlightenment with Jean-François Lyotard's characterization of "modernity" as the project of the Enlightenment (Friedman 494), but this becomes less problematic if one acknowledges that Jardine and Lyotard both use the term "modernity" to identify a critical attitude to the history of the present.

A number of Friedman's questions are also raised by Fredric Jameson in *A Singular Modernity* (2002). Jameson's definition of modernity as "worldwide capitalism itself" (12) has some force. It establishes a singular trajectory for modernity, coherent in its causes and its effects. This is particularly interesting because Jameson was influential among those scholars in the 1980s who posited that dramatic changes to capitalism had transformed modernity into "postmodernity." But *A Singular Modernity* appears in a very different critical context than that surrounding Jameson's *Postmodernism: the Cultural Logic of Late Capitalism* (1991). In particular, *A Singular Modernity* counters a now dominant mode of modernist studies that distinguishes between types and experiences of modernism: "the affirmation of the 'modernity' of this or that generally involves a rewriting of the narratives of modernity itself which are already in place and have become conventional wisdom" (Jameson 2002: 35–36).

Jameson begins by distinguishing between "new" and "modern," the latter being "grasped in connection with a series of analogous phenomena and contrasted with a closed and vanished phenomenal world of a different type" (18). Jameson stresses that modernity consists in "an awareness of history invested in the feeling of a radical break" from the past (21). Like many before him, Jameson credits Charles Baudelaire with inventing our concept of modernity through the "category of the classical," which is "the birth of historicity itself" (22). But Jameson's argument adds something crucial.

Modernism is difficult to periodize precisely because it is always claiming to break with something, and Jameson's claim that "We cannot not periodize" (29) itself depends on a modernist sensibility. It is another way of expressing the critical attitude that constitutes modernism—reflection on the difference of today with regard to yesterday.

Jameson aims to offer a clear way forward from Friedman's "definitional excursions" while rejecting simplification. He asks, "Why not simply posit modernity as the new historical situation, modernization as the process whereby we get there, and modernism as a reaction to that situation and that process alike" (Jameson 2002: 99). It is not this simple, he argues, because such an approach does not account for the contradictions that attend different usages of the terms "modernity," "modernization," and "modernism." At the same time, Jameson also recommends the exercise of replacing the word "modernity" with the word "capitalism." While clearly this exercise would do even less justice to the complexity at hand than the terminology he had previously dismissed, it is designed to acknowledge the ideological content of the concepts "modernity" and "Modernism" and thereby to reveal what critics want from such terms (215). What we want, according to Jameson, is "utopia"—something we can find through an "ontology of the present" (the subtitle of *A Singular Modernity*). Such an ontology might, however, be best understood through the very terminological schema Jameson had previously dismissed and for which imagining "utopia" is also a "therapeutic" simplification (215). That is, modernism may well be a response to modernity—but it is certainly a particular one. It encompasses that drive to periodize within which we have invented "Modernism" as the finite past revolution to which we respond and thus distinguished it from the attitude it otherwise describes. I want to suggest, following Michel Foucault between the lines of Jameson's philosophico-aesthetic account, that an ontology of the present is in fact a good description of modernism's critical attitude.

Jameson recognizes that the theoretical, political, and artistic preoccupation with breaking free from "modernism" has ironically produced a resuscitation of modernism in a re-packaged form. According to Jameson, even Lyotard, who became famous for his account of *The Postmodern Condition* ([1979] 1984), is a quintessential modernist, reliant "on what remain essentially modernist categories of the new" (4) and "the supreme value of innovation" (5). Sensing that the "break" of postmodernism was no break at all, Jameson turns to describing our contemporary situation as late(r) modernity. He finds support for this in Anthony Giddens' insistence that "It is not sufficient merely to invent new terms, like 'post-modernity' and the rest. Instead, we have to look at the nature of modernity itself, which, for fairly specific reasons, has been poorly grasped in the social sciences hitherto. Rather than entering a period of post-modernity, we are moving into one in which the consequences of modernity are becoming more radicalised and universalised than before" (Giddens 1990: 3; Jameson 2002: 11). For Giddens, modernity is an "idea of the world" that is centered on "human intervention" and gives rise to "a complex of economic institutions, especially industrial production and a market economy" and "a certain range of political institutions, including the nation-state and mass democracy" (Giddens and Pierson 94). Given this definition of modernity, it seems we certainly have not moved beyond it; what, then, is modernism's relation to this modernity?

For Jameson too, these terms are hard to pin down; he compares attempting to define modernity to simultaneously looking at and through a pane of glass. But Jameson's solution is quite different to Friedman's. While he also finds himself negotiating between two things that can neither be reconciled nor separated, Jameson is generally satisfied, in a move similar to Felski's, to distinguish between modernism (that perspective on modernity) and "artistic modernism" (Jameson 2002: 95). The first half of A Singular Modernity, "The Four Maxims of Modernity," focuses on an ongoing dialectic of break and continuity that Jameson understands as part of a fundamentally irresolvable "wider dialectic of . . . Identity and Difference" (23), while the second half focuses on a concrete historical pastness he calls "The Ideology of Modernism." For the purposes of my argument, this distinction needs to be even sharper. Modernism with a capital M is not simply the aesthetic formation of modernism, but the institutionalization of a certain representation of modernism.

It also seems useful to juxtapose the work of Friedman and Jameson with Raymond Williams' under-recognized essay, "When Was Modernism?" (1989). Like Friedman and Jameson, Williams too is searching, in the wake of new conversations about postmodernism, for some useful consensus on modernism that might avoid unhelpful pluralization of its meaning. My distinction between modernism, a critical attitude to modernity, and Modernism, an institutionalized assemblage of generally aesthetic forms and practices of the past, is a helpful way to explicate Williams' argument. As no characteristic of modernism is specific to Modernism, Williams argues that modernism can never be grasped by a list of its historical contents; therefore, something else must provide it with consistency. This something else is, ultimately, the critical stance we take toward modernity. Williams is quick to assert that, whatever ideologies it deploys, the periodization of Modernism is necessarily retrospective. What this installation risks, therefore, is relegating the critical force of modernism to the past. Such a relegation always remains incomplete precisely because it is a historical fiction. If canonized Modernism has indeed lost its anti-bourgeois stance, and this is Williams' focus, then this same loss has necessitated a sort of afterlife for Modernism as a representation of modernism. It has demanded a modernist attitude to Modernism, including the ongoing renovation that has allowed works originally left out of the ideologically inflected Modernist canon to retrospectively enter it.

Thus I find the clearest support for my distinction between modernism and Modernism in Williams' recognition that the ideological construction of Modernism as a past object does not exhaust modernism as an ongoing critical attitude toward modernity. However, I have in fact taken my title for this introduction, and the refrain it establishes for the book as a whole, neither from Williams nor any other famous scholar of Modernism, but from Foucault. In reclaiming the term "modernism" as a necessary critical force, Williams meets up with Foucault's claim, in "What is Enlightenment?," that modernity is an attitude rather than an epoch. At the conclusion of an essay that addresses figures from Immanuel Kant to Baudelaire, Foucault asks: "I wonder whether we may not envisage modernity rather as an attitude than as a period of history. And by 'attitude,' I mean a mode of relating to contemporary reality; a voluntary choice made by certain people; in the end, a way of thinking and feeling; a way, too, of acting and behaving that at one and the same time marks a relation of belonging and presents itself as a task. A bit, no doubt, like what the Greeks called an ethos" ([1978] 1984b: 39). Foucault's status as the "little black dress" of contemporary cultural theory (see chapter 5) always risks losing the significance of his points in the familiarity of his reference. Nevertheless, I risk using Foucault yet again because his analysis of how categories bring into being (sometimes for the first time) what they claim to categorize is too important to omit in this context.

Modernist Cultural Studies is not a theoretical primer in any sense. Instead it is an overview of how cultural studies might provide a new perspective on modernism, of modernism's significance to cultural studies, and of the modernism of cultural studies itself. Making this argument does require spinning a web of theoretical connections between Modernism, modernism, and cultural studies, but I have generally sacrificed detailed engagement with the projects of particular theorists or philosophers for a broader focus. That said, to give substance to my claims, I foreground some exemplary writers and texts. Modernist artists like James Joyce, Dziga Vertov, and Woolf, and Modernist theorists like Theodor Adorno, Sigmund Freud, and George Simmel—as well as figures less often included in the Modernist canon like Chanel, Martin Heidegger, and Williams, or less neatly collapsed into periodized Modernism like Matthew Arnold, Foucault, and Gilles Deleuze—provide a sense of how intensely alive the connections between modernism and cultural studies remain. In each of my occasionally brief discussions of figures and ideas that thread through and between modernism and cultural studies, I aim to locate each within what Foucault might call the "network of analogies" (Foucault [1973] 1966: xi) that binds them together. At times, this breadth of reference seems to crudely work against the radically specific contributions made by particular figures. My aim, however, is to attend to a continuity that does not exclude the importance of radical innovations within it. Having cited Foucault somewhat as a defense, let me now make him an example.

Foucault may be best known for his discussions of epistemic shifts—the broad changes that ground distinctions between, for example, classical "similitude" and modern "representation" in *The Order of Things* (1973) or the Greek "care of the self" and Christian confession in "Technologies of the Self" (1998). But discontinuity at this epistemic level also stresses epistemic continuity across discourses and institutions that otherwise seem quite different. While *The Order of Things* traces the emergence of modernity and "Technologies of the Self" closes with reference to the difference between modernity and both the classical and the medieval, Foucault's essay on Enlightenment shows that, for him, what modernity encompasses is very broad indeed. From Kant to Baudelaire to "ourselves" in 1978, Foucault recognizes a familiar ethos or attitude. Undoubtedly there are important, even spectacular, differences between Kant and "ourselves," and undoubtedly what Kant and Baudelaire meant to their contemporaries is not the same as what they mean to us now. Yet the continuities seem so significant to Foucault that these differences do not substantiate a new ethos. As he puts it at the end of *The Order of Things*, "in the midst of all the episodes of that profound history of the *Same*" only a "change in the fundamental arrangements of knowledge" allowed the "man" of modernity to emerge (422). Across his writings, and despite attention to crucial discontinuities in particular fields like medicine and discourse on the self, Foucault insists that since the birth of modernity he can "no more than sense the possibility" (422) of something significant enough to mark another epistemic shift.[2]

Foucault's approach thus avoids periodizing by dates or great names as singular instances and finds common ground between Enlightenment thinkers and Modernists without ignoring discontinuities. I certainly do not wish to pretend that attention to the particularities of time and location are not crucial to the way that cultural studies at its best proceeds. Particularity matters, as does the difference of here and now. I conclude this book with a chapter on popular music, and it is clear that even the relatively small space of five years can radically reconstitute that field through, for example, new modes of distribution or the re-assemblage of an old genre for a new audience. But even insistence on particularity is part of the homology between modernism and cultural studies. Both cultural studies and Modernism have been understood overwhelmingly in terms of discontinuity, and both specialize in reinventing themselves as radically new. My contention here is that a genealogical approach to cultural studies that considers what it continues as well as what it disrupts is timely, and that what such an approach reveals about the relation between cultural studies and modernism is particularly useful for rethinking why we still care about Modernism in the way that we do. To return once more to Foucault's essay, to see ourselves as "historically determined, to a certain extent," by modernity is not to foreclose on the present: "Such an analysis implies a series of historical inquiries that are as precise as possible; and these inquiries will not be oriented retrospectively toward the 'essential kernel of rationality' that can be found in the Enlightenment and that would have to be preserved in any event; they will be oriented toward the 'contemporary limits of the necessary,' that is, toward what is or is no longer indispensable for the constitution of ourselves" (43).

Modernist Cultural Studies

Using the term modernism to negotiate between modernity and Modernism, this book traces the emergence of cultural studies through modernist reflection on culture. Less a history of ideas than a provocation, *Modernist Cultural Studies* is a challenge to contemporary practitioners of cultural studies and modernist studies to look at what might be familiar about that which we often discuss as new as well as at the ongoing relevance of what is often left behind by new discoveries and critical turns. The terms I more or less leave behind to assemble this story are "late modernity," with its presumptions about immanent transformation of the life-world, and, to a certain extent, "postmodernism." I might even seem at times to be arguing that, pragmatically speaking, there is no such thing as postmodernism. It would be more accurate, however, to say that I think postmodernism is—or was (in typically modernist fashion, it is no longer so in vogue)—a name for some threads of modernism that were unable to be integrated into its institutionalization as Modernism and for some of the desire to reclaim modernism's critical force in its wake. Yet I must say something more about what I mean by "Cultural Studies" when I claim it is modernist.

From this point on, to refer to an academic discipline now practiced with considerable coherence, I will consistently capitalize "Cultural Studies." This capitalization not only helps avoid confusing the academic discipline with less specialized uses of the terms "cultural" and "studies," but also acknowledges the discipline's present recognizability. Cultural Studies has the same kind of coherence I have imputed to Modernism in that, while its borders and precise contents are endlessly under debate, a by now institutionalized set of conventions gives it both coherence and core content. Newspaper pundits, educational administrators, students and academics, activists and institutions might not agree about what Cultural Studies is, but, even in their disagreement, they nevertheless refer to, affirm, and disseminate a set of acknowledged parameters.

The work of defining Cultural Studies is not as obscured by the fog of old debate as that of defining modernism, but the definition is nevertheless no simple matter. Some accounts begin with figures like Arnold, who insisted on a new "cultural" approach to education in the mid-nineteenth century, and others with institutions like the Centre for Contemporary Cultural Studies (CCCS) at the University of Birmingham (aka "the Birmingham School") that began calling their work Cultural Studies in the 1960s. But it is also possible to start elsewhere, arguing that Cultural Studies takes different forms in different places and thus that, for example, a U.S.-centered Chicago School history is needed to complement the Birmingham School one. It is also possible to argue that Cultural Studies can only be understood by unpacking the idea of "culture" on which it relies, beginning perhaps with the Enlightenment, perhaps with the Romantics, or perhaps with the Frankfurt School.[3]

The most common beginning point for introductions to or definitions of Cultural Studies is still "the Birmingham School." I discuss the Birmingham School's relation to modernist ideas about culture in chapter 8, but here I want to consider how some texts with different relations to the CCCS's mode of institutionalizing Cultural Studies frame the critical attitude of the discipline. I return first to Williams, who is widely credited with exerting a major influence on Cultural Studies, if not having "single-handedly invented" it, to quote the blurbs on his books with Verso. At the very least, Williams acts as a singularly canonical intersection between modernist studies and Cultural Studies. His often reprinted essay, "Culture is Ordinary" (1958), which Henry Jenkins, Tara McPherson, and Jane Shattuc call "the symbolic beginning of what has become 'cultural studies'" (35), provides an excellent place to begin. In this essay, Williams explains that there are two dominant images of culture—on the one hand, culture as the arts and learning and, on the other, culture as the common meanings of a whole way of life— and that he wants to insist on "both . . . and on the significance of their conjunction" (Williams [1958] 2002: 93). Williams locates culture and its analysis at the intersection of the everyday, the institutional, the historical, and the material—as, in phenomenological terms, "the life-world." It is this dimension of Williams' work that is often seen as grounding the claims of contemporary Cultural Studies.

When Williams wrote "Culture is Ordinary" there was no discipline of Cultural Studies with which it could engage, critically or otherwise (Williams certainly did have critical things to say about Cultural Studies later in life). While Cultural Studies might be at work in Williams' essay, there were no departments, no readers, no conferences, no curricula, and no rankled media pundits defining it. Like modernism in relation to modernity, Cultural Studies is self-consciously made possible by an object it can never quite define—culture. And, like modernism, it is continually challenged by the effect of institutionalization on its critical attitude. The bulk of the essays published in Lawrence Grossberg, Cary Nelson, and Patricia Treichler's canon-forming collection, *Cultural Studies* (1992) were presented as papers at a 1990 conference. As a collection, these papers both feel out the parameters of Cultural Studies as a discipline and regret the looming limits of too much disciplinary conventionality. In fact, the introduction stresses that Cultural Studies is both hard to pin down and not defined by any one method: "The choice of research practices depends upon the questions that are asked, and the questions depend on their context" (Grossberg et al. 2).

By the time Meaghan Morris, one of the contributors to this collection, published her essay "A Question of Cultural Studies" in 1997, the debates about whether Cultural Studies should be a discipline or not had largely been set aside, just in time to help ground the renovation in modernist studies to which this book speaks. Assessing what Cultural Studies is now, as well as what it should be, Morris insists on the centrality of "power" to Cultural Studies' focus on "the pressures that limit choices, constrain semiosis and shape experience—constraints and pressures that are produced by human institutions and that can, and sometimes should, be changed" (Morris

1997: 50). In this way, Cultural Studies is consistently held to a promise it is presumed to have made at a confluence of modernist influences, including ideology critique, the close descriptive practices of ethnography and semiotics, and the educational agendas of writers like Williams.

One central argument in this book is that Cultural Studies continues the key conceptual framework of modernism. Cultural Studies has thus never been a terribly coherent practice despite some general assumptions; it has never been completed or stabilized by any particular method or by any object more specific than "culture" itself. This instability is familiar to most practitioners of modernist studies, as is the concern that forming a canon of "classical" texts would shut down critical experiments in the field. So Clement Greenberg's concern in 1939 that, even as Modernism was being first defined, it was growing "more and more timid every day" (20) is echoed decades later in 1990 by Cultural Studies scholars who feared what institutionalization would mean for their critical edge.

In each of the following chapters I consider examples of contemporary modernist studies approaching modernism in ways generally aligned with the breadth of interest, interdisciplinarity, and attention to the everyday and popular, as well as the political and economic, that have come to be associated with Cultural Studies. I am interested in drawing out how Cultural Studies influences modernist studies as well as how Modernism impacts Cultural Studies. These chapters are grouped into three parts, each of which approaches the juxtaposition of Modernism, modernism, and Cultural Studies differently. A brief overview will provide a useful close to this introduction.

Part 1, "Modernist Modernity," includes three chapters that use the critical framework of Cultural Studies to test the boundaries of what counts as Modernism. Each chapter pushes this approach a little further beyond the expected boundaries of Modernism, demonstrating that to be opened up to Cultural Studies analysis the Modernist canon requires expansive contextualization, as well as a very flexible approach to genre, field and value. Chapter 1 takes up the once controversial claim that the revolutionary impact of Modernist art might as easily be found in cinema as in "higher" arts like literature, painting, and music. This chapter also extends the inclusion of cinema in canonical Modernism to consider both how cinema helped constitute Modernism itself and how discourse on cinema, serving as an index of what had changed in modern life, produced the kind of comprehensive narrative about culture now integral to Cultural Studies. Chapter 2 turns to a central Modernist figure, James Joyce, and uses his fiction as a prism through which we might see emerging the cultural category of the adolescent, complete with the models of psychic and cultural identification used to explain the modern emergence of a visibly different adolescent life. Chapter 3 unites a series of Modernist reference points with a broad sample of cultural contexts for their distribution and reception to show how an idea of "modern love" was both a crucial condition for and an apparent product of Modernist art. Cultural Studies' more expansive approach thus provides a refreshed perspective not just on the content and contexts of Modernism but on the extent of its impact.

While part 2, "Refashioning Modernism," acknowledges a trend in contemporary modernist studies toward a more Cultural Studies–inflected approach to modernism, this is not its explicit focus. Instead, "Refashioning Modernism" focuses on Modernism's influence on Cultural Studies, exploring the modernist emergence and Modernist refinement of key Cultural Studies tools and concepts. Part 2 specifically foregrounds three concepts produced through the interplay between modernization and modernity as it engages the entangled influence of urbanization and industrialization on modern culture: everyday life, style, and the contemporary. These concepts are central to Cultural Studies, and yet the discipline has mostly ignored their Modernist elaboration and refinement. Chapter 4 focuses on the figure of the shopgirl to explore the modernist invention of the everyday as well as Modernist reflection on everyday life, including in new modes of social theory and in the work of artists like Marcel Duchamp and Jean Rhys. Chapter 5 explores the modernism of both fashion and style through the figure of Chanel and demonstrates how expertly Modernist commentary on these subjects foreshadows contemporary Cultural Studies. Chapter 6 takes Woolf's last novel, *Between the Acts* (1941), as a starting point for considering how modernist ideas about history and temporality formed not only the necessary conditions for Modernist experimentation but for the emphasis on critique of the contemporary world that dominates Cultural Studies as well.

Part 3, "The Specter of Modernism," focuses on both the modernist emergence of Cultural Studies and the problems with its categorization as postmodern. Locating the formation of Cultural Studies in the same period as the formation of Modernism itself, part 3 represents Cultural Studies as a mode of Modernism as well as a continuation of modernism. Chapter 7 uses Heidegger's essay on "The Age of the World Picture" as a prism through which to consider the new ideas about world, subject, and knowledge that characterize modernity and are also the conditions from which modernist and postmodernist ideas about culture emerge. Chapter 8 traces the emergence of Cultural Studies itself from a web of new modes of cultural expertise. Here I explore the idea that it was the canonization of Modernism as something now past that created the gap in which the discipline of Cultural Studies could appear and be named. Chapter 9 considers the modernism of contemporary Cultural Studies through both histories and critiques of the discipline and through the example of Cultural Studies approaches to researching and teaching popular music. Finally, in the conclusion, I return to the question of how and why it matters that, given all of this intimacy with Modernism, Cultural Studies came to be associated with postmodernism.

Cultural Studies comprises a set of attitudes and practices with a much longer history than the named discipline. The relationship between modernism and Cultural Studies is much more specific than sharing in a broad Western tradition and much stronger than any intellectual inheritance. If we have indeed not yet gone beyond modernism, it is not because of the continued relevance of any particular tool or text but instead of the critical attitude that binds them together. Cultural Studies adopts that critical attitude to the present that, as Jameson, Williams, and Foucault each quite differently insist, we cannot "go beyond." Understanding modernism as a critical attitude allows us to see modernism as simultaneously a representation of modernity and an experience of modernity and to locate Cultural Studies as an important modernist genre.

1

MODERNIST MODERNITY

1

Moving Pictures

Cinema as Modernism

An "age" does not pre-exist the statements which express it, nor the visibilities which fill it.

Gilles Deleuze, *Foucault*

For years the above epigraph has been one of my favorite accounts of Michel Foucault's understanding of discourse. It seems particularly valuable here as a cue for thinking about the relation between modernism and cinema. To explore what approaching modernism as an attitude might mean, this chapter takes up the dramatic shifts in the fields of art, science, technology, and popular culture that can be captured by the label "cinema." Here I consider the canonical Modernist period from the perspective of cinema, seeing in cinema statements about the age that make that age possible. I also find in cinema a range of ideas and debates that continue in the critical perspectives of Cultural Studies. In order to also focus on what Cultural Studies can say about Modernism, I will begin my discussion with the pivotal Modernist tension between mass culture and revolutionary art, considering, on the one hand, avant-garde film and, on the other, auteur cinema, which has both popular and avant-garde forms.

Film Art and the Auteur

While a public discourse on the "serious" adaptation of literature and history to popular film was well established by the 1920s, it was nevertheless widely presumed in newspapers and the new film and "style" magazines that the aesthetic potential of film was clearly distinguishable from film popularity. The most famous examples of Modernist cinema have long been films that challenged the dominant mimetic conception of photographic representation. These examples are not always works claiming to be revolutionary art, like Salvador Dali and Luis Buñuel's *Un Chien Andalou* (1929), but are sometimes also popular films like D. W. Griffith's *Birth of a Nation* (1915). Such films qualify as Modernist because they are formally innovative, introducing techniques that challenged the possibilities for filmic representation and tendencies of film spectatorship.

Un Chien Andalou also exemplifies Modernist film as an enclosed experimental form of play easily integrated into the field of visual experiments with painting and photography for which the surrealists continue to be famous. The art of *Un Chien Andalou* has a very precise origin, which in fact separates it from cinema as a popular field. From its French gallery release in 1929, *Un Chien Andalou*, made too coherent by its association with artist-producers at the expense of a studio or production team and separated from both corporate commodification and the pre-eminence of performance and the screen star, has not been the same object as "the movies." Film was already a spectacularly successful medium in 1929 and what *Un Chien Andalou* experiments with is not film as artistic medium so much as film as a cultural practice. The ground broken by *Un Chien Andalou* and the film texts surrounding it is that of the "art house film": contributing to the entrenchment of cinema as a set of film styles that work to name different film audiences with different cultural values.[1]

The most usual way to consider cinema as a medium for Modernism has been to separate a certain kind of art film from the majority of popular film in this way. This role for film emerged early in the history of cinema, but was always in tension with other versions of what cinema meant as a form of modernism. In the work of critics such as Walter Benjamin, who wrote about the impact of film both on art and as art; in popular film magazines such as *Photoplay* that held up films, stars, and cinema itself as objects for simultaneous idealization, vilification, and debate; and in the self-reflexive attitudes of filmmakers—whether framed theoretically, as with Dziga Vertov, or not, as with Charlie Chaplin—we find a set of entangled questions about pleasure, art, culture, identity, and modernity that has no single social, temporal, or authoritative location and yet can be called modernist. At this level, the move, since the 1950s, to position cinema as Modernist has meant expanding in a modest way what counted as Modernism. But the real challenge raised by thinking about the relation between Modernism and cinema is that, beyond naming new texts and artists, it inevitably also draws attention to cinema's spectacle of economic, technical, geopolitical, and cultural change.

Just as modernism is not Modernism alone, cinema is not film alone. To think about cinema as modernism means to consider not only particular film artists, styles, texts, and commentaries, but also the changing technology of film itself, the emergence and transnational dissemination of movie theaters along with cinematic conceptions of cultural difference and similarity, the diverse practices of movie going, and changing ideas about the audience for cinema. The field of modernist studies has gradually moved beyond simply being able to see art in film and film in art to recognizing the importance of cinema itself to modernism and modernity. The critical history tracing this shift includes philosophical and political analysis of film and, at the same time, new approaches to cinema that recognize the modernist dimensions of film outside the film text itself.[2] Certainly Modernist studies developed and has long retained an emphasis on the art of film and the filmmaker as artist—what film studies calls "the auteur." But before we presume that the auteur dominates the way modernist studies talks about film because it neatly parallels an existing model of Modernist genius, it is worth giving some context to the changing place of film in the field.

As Colin MacCabe notes, "the efforts of pioneers in film criticism in France, England or America took place outside the groves of academe"(ix). This is, in part, because of an entrenched disdain for the popularity of film presumed to have displaced fiction from its place as an index of mass culture. MacCabe's account of this delay in film scholarship is worth further consideration. He claims, "All this changed in the seventies when the political demand to study contemporary culture and the considerable body of film criticism already established (most notably the work of Bazin and *Cahiers*) enabled the study of film to find a growing place within the university" (ix). MacCabe does not name this context Cultural Studies, although he might have, but instead identifies modernist studies as "one of the few areas of academic scholarship that has begun to investigate this complicated interrelation" between cinema and literature (x).

In this context, David Trotter objects to the dominant mode of understanding cinema's influence on literature through avant-gardism, in particular, Russian montage theory. Instead, to emphasize "parallel" literary and cinematic histories of Modernism, Trotter wants to draw attention to both the impact of popular Anglophone cinema and movie-going on the Modernist icons James Joyce, T. S. Eliot, and Virginia Woolf and the importance of filmmakers like Griffith and Chaplin to that impact (Trotter 3). The "impersonality" of both cinematic and literary modernism is key to Trotter's argument, which concerns the double effect of cinema's and modernist literature's combined transparency and opacity (10–11). Quoting Eliot, who wrote that "only those who have personality and emotions know what it means to want to escape from these things" (in Trotter 10), Trotter paradoxically attributes this impersonality to *popular* auteur cinema. Even if modernist studies now quite often addresses the popular, it still does so most comfortably through an auteur figure—whether in the mode of F. Scott Fitzgerald, Henry Ford, or Chaplin. For Cultural Studies, however, the figure of the auteur is a problematic one. On the one hand it offers an appealingly visible and acceptably valuable example, but, on the other, it draws analysis toward a singularity that speaks less clearly to "culture" than to "genius." Cultural Studies also speaks about art (and always has; see chapter 8), but it usually does so with an emphasis on fields of production, circulation, and reception that decenter the auteur. Of particular interest here is the way such contentions around genius, genre, and the popular are themselves longstanding modernist debates contemporary with cinema itself.

A distinction between art and popularity in film is not necessarily of primary importance to these debates. Benjamin makes a case for Chaplin's significance that seems unconcerned with his popularity either way (Benjamin [1936] 1969: 223; [c. 1928] 1996b: 199–200). Chaplin in fact figures positively and prominently in a number of European writers on film contemporary with him, at a time when there seemed to be a more pervasive discursive distinction between popular and art film in the United States. But this distinction was never as certain as its common deployment suggests. Even when cinema began to differentiate markets and subgenres that foregrounded film art as opposed to film technology, there were always crucial examples, such as *film noir*, that were both popular and taken up relatively quickly as aesthetically important. And artists were very often invested in the popularity of cinema—not merely in abortive plans such as James Joyce's scheme to have Eisenstein film *Ulysses* or the *Destino* collaboration between Dali and Walt Disney; and not merely for financially practical reasons, as with William Faulkner screenwriting career. More substantially, works of art like Marcel Duchamp's *Nude Descending a Staircase* (1912), Joyce's *Finnegans Wake* and Jean Rhys' *Good Morning Midnight* (both 1939) provide starkly opposed examples of the impact of popular cinema genres and cinematic perception on Modernist art. The set of tensions between art and the popular raised by these examples will return throughout this book. They are still so far from being untangled as to demonstrate that the concerns of Modernist film critics remain relevant today.

David Bordwell notes the influence of "art cinema" on the emergence of film criticism, which, he writes, applied "techniques already common in the interpretation of literature and the visual arts" and celebrated the director as "the creative source of meaning." He cites Andrew Sarris on how the powerful influence of "directorial continuity" became accepted "even in Hollywood": "Not only did auteur criticism, the avant-garde, and the art cinema push film writing toward explication but also particular interpretations could appeal to these filmmaking practices as sources of persuasiveness and novelty" (Bordwell 44–45). As MacCabe also suggests, André Bazin is a crucial figure here, emerging with his auteur theory as part of the institutionalization of Modernism and presenting it as a counterpoint to the popular reign of the studio system and its panoply of stars. Yet the stars and the auteur go together in the modernism of cinema, and this is so not only because art and popular culture were mutually redefining one another within Modernism. If Bazin's version of the auteur presumed that the director placed a personal stamp on every film, the auteur is also paradoxically compatible with the impersonality extolled as central to modernist art, a paradox equally present in the figure of the movie star.

In "Tradition and the Individual Talent," Eliot argues for the "continual extinction of personality" as an artist sacrifices himself or herself to a history and a work of art as "something which is more valuable" ([1919] 2005: 154). Eliot's theory of impersonality seems relatively easy to apply to cinema, but the more substantive value of art for Eliot involves the exercise of "talent": "it is not the 'greatness,' the intensity, of the emotions, the components" that makes art great for Eliot, "but the intensity of the artistic process, the pressure, so to speak, under which the fusion takes place" (155).[3] Drawing on such arguments, Trotter's central thesis rests on a convergence of the "impersonality" touted by Modernist critics and the impersonality of the cinematic apparatus. There is, however, more than one version of modernist impersonality. Eliot's theory does not erase personal experience but rather declares it insignificant to the work of art and its reception. But when Benjamin sets out to jettison "outmoded concepts, such as creativity and genius, eternal value and mystery" in order to oppose the fascist manipulation of art ([1936] 1969: 218), he proposed a form of impersonality in which art has its own effects and Eliot's "true poet" has little place. Benjamin's version of impersonality allows for Eliot's insofar as "The uniqueness of a work of art is inseparable from its being imbedded in the fabric of tradition," which is itself "thoroughly alive and extremely changeable" (Benjamin [1936] 1969: 223), but for Benjamin modern life and culture is more broadly impersonal. The apparent personality of art is a misrepresentation, however valuable it seems. This difference is perhaps also marked by Chaplin, for whom cinema offered hope, while the machine and the masses were dehumanizingly impersonal, or by Vertov, whose use of the impersonal suits the "shock" of impersonality in Benjamin but not the classical temper it reaches for in Eliot.

Thinking about impersonality as modernist rather than Modernist also suggests other contexts. A range of critics attribute the first use of modernity in the sense I outline in the introduction to Charles Baudelaire's essay, "The Painter of Modern Life" (1863). This essay presents modernity as being always concerned with the everyday circulation of representations of life. Baudelaire takes the Parisian painter and journalist Constantine Guys as his exemplar of the spirit and technique of the distinctively modern artist. This modern artist takes an interest in the whole world but avoids intellectual and political circles; he is an idle, yet observant and curious, man of the crowd; and his art lies in the ability to classify and harmonize every encounter rather than in thorough knowledge of old masters. Baudelaire famously characterizes modernity by the transitory, the fragmentary, "the ephemeral, the fleeting, the contingent" (Baudelaire 130)—the same elements he believes characterize modern works of art. If we focus only on the iconic events of Modernism, several of these attributes—such as simplicity, transitoriness, and avoiding intellectualism—cease to be generally characteristic or are only associated with certain movements. The element of Baudelaire's painter that meshes most neatly with canonical Modernism is the artist's break with the past, where turning away from the old and toward the present is crucial to adequately representing the present. But the field of cultural production that most nearly maps onto modern art as defined by Baudelaire is cinema: an intensely specific point of view that is nevertheless distanced from the entirely personal.

Baudelaire is central to periodizing accounts of Modernism because he articulates modernism as a critical category and an epistemological (if not an ontological) shift. Linking Baudelaire and cinema in this way makes an argument parallel to Tom Gunning's suggestion that the key precursor of cinema's new point of view is the nineteenth-century Symbolist poet's "systematic derangement of the senses" (2004: 53). While Gunning concedes that this connection may be part of the "contingent crisscrosses of history"

(52), he sees the Symbolists, and the early photographers and cinematographers, as belonging to wider discursive shifts toward the defamiliarization of perception. This shift, evident in the Symbolists, the Impressionists, and elsewhere, is accompanied at all times by its opposite, the cultural production of familiarity. This is another modernist tension that has in no way been resolved and cinema perhaps tells this story as clearly as any other genre. Cinema is not merely a cultural adaptation of a technological innovation, but also a major epistemological challenge. Moreover, as an expanding transnational web of images and practices that have particular impact on how the world can be known, cinema also has particular ontological implications.

Cinema encompasses both popular and theoretical debates about how the modern world and human perception of that world differ from what came before it. Tied to the emergence of Modernism, film was an integral piece of the apparent difference of the present, and its changes made other cultural patterns more obvious. While this cannot be reduced to the difference of mass culture, it is important that cinema involves not only film and its specialized devices but a whole array of systems in which films move. For Theodor Adorno and Max Horkheimer, this systematic dimension of film is crucial. They see in the mass reproduction of culture, of which film seemed exemplary, a "culture industry" that narrows understanding and evaluation to what is most efficiently reproducible and ideologically conformist. In *Dialectic of Enlightenment* (1944), Adorno and Horkheimer claim that, "Because of his ubiquity, the film star with whom one is meant to fall in love is from the outset a copy of himself. Every tenor voice comes to sound like a Caruso record, and the 'natural' faces of Texas girls are like the successful models by whom Hollywood has typecast them" (139–40). The cinematic apparatus, then, also extends to or incorporates people.

Film Machines

Cinema's intimacy with technological innovation makes it an excellent place from which to consider the techno-determinism threading through theories of modernity. The industrial revolution, changes to modes of transport that brought forth modern conceptions of borders and travel (see chapter 7), and the proliferation of technological interventions in the definition and management of human life (see chapter 3) are all integral to modernity. As Gunning acknowledges, "Technology in the modern age has a direct relation to the phenomenon of innovation and novelty, and therefore to what makes the modern age modern" (2004: 39). The late nineteenth century to early twentieth witnesses an extraordinary array of such inventiveness, from the automobile (1885–1902) and airplanes (1890–1906) to X-rays (1895) and the theory of relativity (1905). Often such dates are misleadingly neat, but it is surely more difficult to assign a date to the invention of film technologies than to that of cars and planes, given not only the different key figures who were working independently on such technologies but the very diverse criteria for what counts as "film," let alone "cinema."

The special relevance of the relationship between film and modernism is underscored by the way in which mass-produced cameras (the first Kodak camera was produced in 1888) and then the early versions of cinema (Lumière's cinematograph is usually dated 1895; one of the earliest images is appositely of a train racing a horse) distributed not only new modes of living, but new modes of participating in the representation of modern life. If the same can be said of new publishing genres or new modes of dress, for example, cinema was nevertheless unparalleled as a new popular image of and experience of modernity. This is not because cinema was a greater technological change than, for example, the light bulb or pulp magazines. It is perhaps most of all because cinema encompasses not just film and its systematic distribution but film's discourse on novelty. As Gunning puts it, "Modernity must partly be understood as learning to be surprised by certain innovations, a discourse that valorizes and directs our attention to such changes and the excitement they can provoke" (2004: 44).

No longer the technological marvel of the nickelodeon, by the 1920s cinema began to construct rather than presume its own novelty (see Gunning 1994). Cinema is an exemplary instance of the way popular media technologies are attached to strategies for recovering "original strangeness" once they have been understood and cease to be a wondrous attraction (see Gunning 2004). The significance of such strangeness, however, is not the discovery of recent "new media" scholarship. Gunning links his argument about strangeness to Viktor Shklovsky's famous invocation of "defamiliarization" as the means by which "art removes objects from the automatism of perception" (in Gunning 2004: 45). Gunning stresses that a range of nineteenth-century inventions exacerbated the insistent pressure of modernization by challenging "basic categories of experience" (48) such as time and space, presence and absence, and the ontological status of being, origin, and singularity. In this way, cinema's endless desire for new horizons of cinematic experience—last year's latest special effect displaced by this year's parody of the genre—is a version of modernism's drive toward the new and its attraction

Figure 1. Sergei Eisenstein, *Battleship Potemkin*, 1925, Goskino, U.S.S.R. Film still from the Kobal Collection.

to the experience of limits. Benjamin sees a similar process already underway in photography, which "To increase turnover . . . renewed its subject matter through modish variations in camera technique—innovations that will determine the subsequent history of photography" ([1927–40] 2002: 6). Understanding cinema as modernism thus invites a review of some classic Modernist film texts and texts of film criticism for what and how their innovations were supposed to mean.

A comparison between Sergei Eisenstein and Vertov will be helpful here. Both are formalists who saw the form of their films as conveying their most crucial meanings and especially as serving the means of social change. But they differently understood how cinema knew the world. *Battleship Potemkin* (1925) exemplifies Eisenstein's development of the *montage* style—creating film narrative out of cuts and splices by a series of what he called either "shocks" or "attractions." Cutting shots of faceless Tsarist soldiers descending the Odessa steps together with close-ups of students, pleading mothers, and other victims of their attack (see figure 1) conveys the image of an oppressive regime more vividly than a single wide shot of the scene could have done, and this is exactly why Eisenstein thinks of these cuts as able to induce shock. Using such examples as "a mouth + a child = 'to scream,'" Eisenstein explained that the "*intellectual* contexts and series" of cinema worked like "ideograms." While he argued that montage, like the ideogram, is constituted by images, it "is to be regarded not as their sum, but as their product, i.e., as a value of another dimension, another degree; each, separately, corresponds to an *object*, to a fact, but their combination corresponds to a *concept*" (Eisenstein [1949] 1969: 29–30, emphasis in original).

Such an understanding of film requires an idea of film affect—of the ways in which an image, and the juxtaposition of particular images paced in particular ways, can manipulate the spectator. Montage relies on a succession of signs to create an experience the audience is meant to feel: the sequence of the doctor thrown overboard, the maggoty meat, and the pince-nez communicates an upswell of moral outrage at injustice. But the impact of Eisensteinian montage relies on location shots and other realist tropes as well as manipulative framing and shot composition. Figure 1 is a now iconic example of how even the content of individual shots works by montage. The baby carriage hurtling unprotected down the Odessa steps between the fallen victims of state oppression is a sign saturated with possible significance that opens the film up to potential meanings and affects at the same time as it limits them. It works like the cut between images in which an overwhelming array of connections—though not every possible connection—can be made between the component pieces of the montage. The meaning of Eisensteinian film—drawing on the psychological theories of Ivan Pavlov and Sigmund Freud, C. S. Peirce's semiotics of the relation between the producer and the interpreter of images, and aesthetic theories of art and drama—was always explicitly ideological. The Eisensteinian theory of film, then, is not only a formalist one, but also a cultural theory of cinema that encompasses cinema's distribution, reception, and wider discursive location.

Modernist aesthetics presume that changing modes of perception are evident in changing artistic practices. Douglas Crimp aligns this shift, which I have previously associated with Baudelaire but which is also a recurring theme in Benjamin ([1927–40] 2002; [1936] 1969), with modernism's displacement of art's "'natural' orientation to the spectator's vision" (Crimp 44). It follows that as one learns the language of cinema, what is learned is taken to the rest of life to compile meaning and anticipate shocks—indeed, to experience visual images as an equally if not more direct means of communication than written or spoken language (which, in films like *Battleship Potemkin*, are confined to intertitles). And yet film style can be culturally specific, as both the changes in such styles over time and the differences between the styles of, for example, Soviet propaganda, German expressionist, and mainstream Hollywood film of the same period, make apparent.

Gilles Deleuze argues that, during the period in which cinema developed, art and the performing arts were more generally changing the status of movement: "abandoning figures and poses to release values which were not posed, not measured, which related movement to the any-instant-whatever. In this way, art, ballet and mime all became actions capable of responding to accidents of the environment; that is, to the distribution of the points of a space, or of the moments of event. All this served the same end as the cinema" ([1983] 1986: 7). For Deleuze, this "movement-image" refers to a style in which characters on the screen are faced with certain situations to which they must react. Characters constituted by the movement-image operate within a "sensory-motor schemata" in which they respond to a situation, cognizant of the correct movements to make. Across his two books on cinema, Deleuze traces a shift, which more or less conforms to a break between pre– and post–World War II cinema, toward characters who were less determined by action than they were *seen* to be themselves *seeing*.

Ultimately, the movement-image relies on, and indeed constitutes, the familiar and the habitual, even if a character becomes "reduced to helplessness, bound and gagged" (Deleuze [1983] 1986: 3). We can see in this type of image some parameters of the action film or series as they have continued to unfold. What distinguishes Deleuze's approach to cinema, however, is his emphasis on the tension between movement and time. In the movement-image, the filmmaker highlights either an action that creates a situation or a situation that evokes an action. While optical and sound "images" are components of the movement-image, the spectator necessarily identifies with the character as an "agent." But the cinema Deleuze sees as centered on the "time-image" calls for potential responses from the viewer that do not depend on or wait for a character cue, thereby heralding a "cinema of the see-er and no longer the agent" (2). In both the musical and Chaplin, Deleuze sees the cinematic transformation of movement into "a continuity constructed at each instant" (7). For Deleuze, cinema is an "essential factor" in "this new way of thinking" (8). At the same time, however dramatic the difference in cinematic perception, it did not emerge ex nihilo. Changing cultural experiences—from photography, advertising, and new styles of art to the transformation of urban spaces and modes of consumption—led to and affected the cinematic distribution of movement and time as well as their comprehension.

Deleuze's formulation posits neither a beginning nor an end for cinema as modernism. The shift from the movement-image to the time-image should not be transposed onto a shift from modernism to postmodernism. In fact, Deleuze is accounting less for a displacement of action by vision than for the emergence of a new cinema that differed from the one that brought Hollywood to prominence and yet did not entirely transplant it. Deleuze's distinction does not claim to write a history of cinema ([1983] 1986: xi) or address all cinema at a given time—after the war there continued to be, and still is, a plethora of films in which the hero always knows what to do—but to map a particular stylistic taxonomy. Tom Conley notes that Deleuze's distinction between one form of realism and another is indebted to his close reading of Bazin (Conley 9). For Bazin, these changes to cinema did not produce new modes of perception but rather the means of more perfectly expressing a realism always already desired. By 1939, the year many histories of Modernism end, Bazin imagined that cinema had reached a point of technological completion in which all that remained for film to achieve was the refinement of its subject and its style. Where Deleuze sees the redirection of the cinematic image from action to temporality (see chapter 6), Bazin sees the arrival of *mise-en-scène*. Bazin agrees, more or less, that it is no longer action that tells the story in "mature" cinema. For Deleuze, time-image cinema cannot support "as in the *film noir* of American realism, an organization which related to a distinctive milieu" (Deleuze [1985] 1989: 214). Conley reads this crisis of representation as having a causal relationship to the war: "with the filming of the concentration camps, it became evident that any filmic image was in deficit in respect to what it was showing" (10). But, as Conley acknowledges, the taxonomy of the time-image and the movement-image is not a structuralist opposition insofar as each type of image inheres in the other (10). Thus time does not displace movement in film or even overwhelm it. Bazin's conception of mise-en-scène also relied on earlier developments, such as Griffith's close-ups and Eisenstein's montage, despite his emphasis on a historical break. Even for Bazin, however, while the techniques of mise-en-scène and the long shot diffuse action and stress that the characters' whole world can be seen, including by them, it is not synonymous with the new use of point of view in literature or painting.

As Bazin and Deleuze also suggest, and Trotter insists, we must not reduce Modernist film to Eisensteinian montage. Trotter's counterpoint to montage is the continuity editing of film-makers like Griffith, but the work of Eisenstein's colleague Vertov offers yet another alternative. Vertov can be understood to compose his film by "collage" rather than montage—he

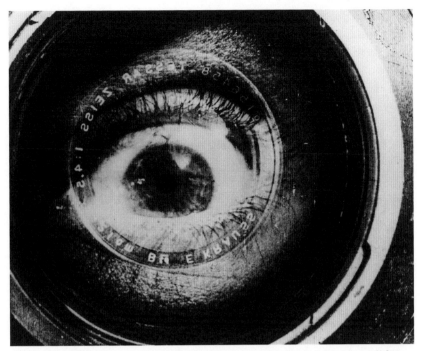

Figure 2. Dziga Vertov, *Man with a Movie Camera*, 1929, Vufku, U.S.S.R. Film still from the Kobal Collection.

avoids the insertion of narrative via point-of-view cuts in favor of overlapping images that compile a narrative sense via repetition and variation. Vertov often used stock footage in his films and composed his films around a pattern of motifs and rhythms. But this does not mean that films like *Man with a Movie Camera* (1929) have no narrative. In fact such patterns of rhythm and motif produce a story reliant on the narrative points of view suggested by figures like, in *Movie Camera*, the editor, the cameraman, the audience, and the camera itself, not to mention the central on-screen girl, all of which an audience already accustomed to cinematic narrative cannot help but attempt to characterize.

Vertov felt that a revolutionary kind of truth was relayed by what he called the "Kino Eye," which refers to the way the edited film, rather than the camera, sees things. For Vertov, this "cinema truth" (*kinopravda*) explicitly countered the manipulation of montage, in particular its use of sentimentality and melodrama, and thus allowed new critique of the ideological structure of popular cinema. He aligned his own films with newsreels rather than "movies," claiming newsreels were "organized from bits of life into a theme, and not the reverse. This also means that Kinopravda doesn't order life to proceed according to a writer's scenario, but observes and records life as it is, and only then draws conclusions from these observations" (Vertov [1922] 1984: 45). Both Vertov's goal of achieving an international language of pure cinema—represented manifesto-style in the opening credits of *Movie Camera*—and his fascination with the life of the city—the structuring frame of *Movie Camera*—are quintessentially modernist. And *Movie Camera*, as much as the work of Buñuel and Dali, is cinema about cinema. It opens with a man climbing out of a camera, establishing an anti-realist frame for the film. The same man then moves behind a curtain, which will become the curtain veiling a cinema screen for an audience that we, as another audience, are watching.

Movie Camera thus consistently claims to expose the mechanisms of film production, but these self-reflexive devices—as in figure 2, the famous extreme close up of the man with a movie camera's eye—are undercut by two equally important elements of the film. First, while *Movie Camera* exposes the mechanics of film it also makes the same documentary claims as Vertov's newsreels. And second, this tension cannot neatly be resolved as an ideological critique of movie-making to which documentary film is an exception because *Movie Camera* also makes a glamorous magical device of cinema: theater seats rhythmically open and close themselves, awaiting their audience to whom cinematic special effects will reveal both what they should know and how they should feel. It is also too simple to interpret *Movie Camera* as being an ideological set piece exposing the means of production. The elaboration of leisure activities in *Movie Camera* represents not just pending rewards for workers, but a field of everyday life that moves from beach holidays and weddings to children's games and death via contemplation of city spaces and their rhythms of shape and movement. The city appears animated and almost alive, not at all consistent with the demystification with which Vertov is usually associated, and the Bolshoi Theatre's folding up at the end of the film is closer to the Modernist manipulations of Joyce than the propagandist clarity of Eisenstein.

While Vertov attacked Eisenstein's melodramatic manipulation and his imposition of character and narrative on film's potential to see the world differently,[4] Eisenstein was almost as critical of the cinematic games—what he called "'formalist' jack-straws and unmotivated camera mischief" (Eisenstein [1949] 1969: 43)—in films like *Movie Camera*. The audience in *Movie Camera* laughs at the special effects of the camera but Vertov, having foregrounded the techniques by which the film is made, frames their laughter as a combination of knowledge and wonder. Not all criticism at this time assumed that immersion in popular cinema required ignorance of the conditions by which it was produced. In "Cult of Distraction: On Berlin's Picture Palaces," Siegfried Kracauer argues that the audience can enjoy cinema as a distraction from something they nevertheless remain aware of. He suggests that audiences consume film formulae without necessarily believing they are true accounts of the world or being thus distracted from reflection on their life-world. Despite the stereotypically shallow images of humanity on screen—"According to the cinematic testimony, a human being is a girl who can dance the Charleston well and a boy who knows just as little" (Kracauer [1926] 1995: 301)—for Kracauer the unreality of cinematic cliché is always visible. This credits the audience with considerably more critical acumen than Adorno and Horkheimer's more famous thesis on the "culture industry," in which cinema "is sought after as an escape from the mechanised work process, and to recruit strength in order to be able to cope with it again. But at the same time mechanisation has such power over a man's leisure and happiness, and so profoundly determines the manufacture of amusement goods, that his experiences are inevitably after-images of the work process itself" (137).

Considering the significance of cinema in general and its relations to art, industry, and its audience in particular—a significance that Cultural Studies, film studies, and media commentary all suggest we are still unpacking—such differences between writers usually placed so closely together are in no way trivial. Despite Modernism's frequent reduction to lists of oppositions with postmodernism—such as Ihab Hassan's paradigmatic list in which Modernism's purpose, form, and boundedness is opposed to postmodernism's openness, play, and process (Hassan 267–68)—even its vaunted emphasis on art over the popular is nowhere near uniform. Modernist opinion on popular culture, to which I will return in chapter 9, differed even across very similar cultural positions and with respect to the same forms. Drawing on this complex history, Cultural Studies is not just another way of insisting that film be discussed in its aesthetic, theoretical, and political contexts. Cultural Studies attends first of all to the dynamics by which common sense categories such as "art" and "popular," "city" and "girl," are established. And while thinking cinema as modernism through Cultural Studies certainly reminds us to consider cultural production and consumption, including what happens to cultural products once they are among their possible audiences, such considerations were also important for the Modernists.

The relationship between mechanization, modernization, and images of modern selfhood was also debated in the spectatorial position implied by texts as successful as *Metropolis* (Lang 1927) and *Modern Times* (Chaplin 1936). Among cinema's consistent tropes in the Modernist period is the ambivalent positioning of the machine as something that could express and convey experience. In fact the human-machine relations both built into cinema and represented in Modernist films was always a complex set of questions rather than an ideological grid in which films and filmmakers should be positioned. The battleship and the baby carriage in *Potemkin* are machines within the cinematic machine, producing variable and distinct effects and signifying a history that can never be completely monolithic and uniform. Vertov's camera stands in for the audience's clever and curious relation to modern life. As my reference above to *Metropolis* and *Modern Times* suggests, this engagement with cinema as ambivalent ideology machine is not about Soviet propaganda or avant-gardism. Hollywood films like Edmund Goulding's *Grand Hotel* (1932) or Orson Welles' *Citizen Kane* (1941), which, with very different claims to make, seek to conceal the camera, also tell their audience what to feel and know. While not all film is equally propagandist, there is no cinema that is not also an experience of both technology and ideology (see chapter 7) and this fact is central to cinema's modernism.

The Subject of Cinema

Despite the argument with which I finished the last section, and despite Adorno and Horkheimer's often insightful critique, the difference of cinema from other modes of cultural production does not lie in its capacity to reproduce (and be reproduced). However, referencing this claim at all invokes another Frankfurt School "classic," a text included in the canons of modernist studies and Cultural Studies alike: Benjamin's "The Work of Art in the Age of Mechanical Reproduction." Benjamin begins this essay with yet another take on the way human perception and art shift together: "During long periods of history, the mode of human sense perception changes with humanity's entire mode of existence. The manner in which human sense perception is organized, the medium in which it is accomplished, is determined not only by nature but by historical circumstances as well" ([1936] 1969: 222). While in the opening of this essay, Benjamin is more interested in the difference between photography and older forms of visual art, contending that the photographic print appears to be the equal of any original photograph and thus not mystified by the authenticity or "aura" of the original work of art, he does ultimately extend this discussion to cinema.

Figure 3. Clarence Sinclair Bull, "Joan Crawford," 1933. Photograph from the Kobal Collection.

Benjamin identifies some key differences between photographic and filmic perception. While, like the painting, the photograph has a consistency from one viewing to the next and thus the ability to cross spatial, temporal, and cultural boundaries, cinema achieves this differently. Film extends the power of technical reproduction first by speed—"A film operator shooting a scene in the studio captures the images at the speed of an actor's speech" (219)—which heightens the realist effect of photography, and then by a super-realism that is able to "capture images which escape natural vision" (220). But the destruction of that dimension of art Benjamin calls its "aura" by technical reproduction works much more problematically for cinema than for photography, which is one reason I chose cinema rather than photography as an index of modernism. While the mass-distribution of photography removed many of the elements of expertise required for artistic endeavor, cinema curtails this erasure of expertise just as it curtails the erasure of the aura in other respects, turning actors, producers, and directors into fonts of genius and conduits of authenticity.[5] Cinema thus captures a relation between expertise and the masses that is crucial to modernism (see chapter 8). In "The Culture Industry Reconsidered," Adorno tries to accommodate Benjamin's discussion of the aura in his reply to critics of the culture industry thesis by seeing in the machinations of the culture industry a weak version of the ritual-mystical uses of art by which "it conserves the decaying aura as a foggy mist" (Adorno [1967] 2001: 102).

As both art photography and the nostalgic deployment of photography in family snapshots evinces, there are many ways the aura can be returned to the photograph. While it is Roland Barthes who most famously makes the link between photography and death ([1980] 1982), this recognition is also key to Benjamin's sense of what could be ritualized in photography (although his suggestion that this may no longer be possible is countered by Barthes and others): "The cult of remembrance of loved ones, absent or dead, offers a last refuge for the cult value of the picture. For the last time the aura emanates from the early photographs in the fleeting expression of a human face. This is what constitutes their melancholy, incomparable beauty" ([1936] 1969: 226). From this potential comes the power of the face and the close-up in silent cinema, which itself feeds the insistent emphasis on the face of the movie star.[6] Figure 3 is a publicity photograph of a young Joan Crawford in the early 1930s, one of many such images that helped to constitute the new popular field of celebrity fandom (see also figures 5 and 10). But as the cascading photographs of Crawford around her demonstrate, the publicity photograph was as self-conscious as a Vertov film. It may also, paradoxically, share certain techniques with Vertov's use of self-conscious-ness to undermine fantasy. As Benjamin insists, the glamorous image of the film star contains a crucial degree of impersonality. "The audience's identifi-cation with the actor," he writes, "is really an identification with the camera. Consequently the audience takes the position of the camera; its approach is that of testing. This is not the approach to which cult values may be ex-posed" (1969: 228). While Benjamin sees that the cinema audience attaches to the actor on screen, for him cinema is both too realistic to allow the ac-tor to be subsumed into character and too mediated to allow the authentic personality of the actor to be communicated. As Miriam Hansen concurs in her discussion of Rudolph Valentino fans, the audience knows that the actor they worship is not really there (Hansen 1991b).

The "person" that is there is the impersonal spectator, suspended in a state of incompleteness because he or she is entirely dependent on what is looked at. Hansen discusses the emergence of the spectator in terms that describe popular as well as scholarly reflection on cinema and modern life at the time. This "historical construction," she argues, will not "necessarily coincide with the invention of cinema." Instead "it is defined by the elaboration of a mode of narration that makes it possible to anticipate a viewer through particular textual strategies, and thus to standardize empirically diverse and to some extent unpredictable acts of reception" (1991a: 16). The star and the spectator together thus form one instance of divided modern subjectivity and the plethora of new film fan magazines in the 1920s was certainly as cognizant of the fact as any later film theory. Of course the magazines did not use the same language as Stephen Heath, who writes, "the spectator is produced by the film as subject in process, in the process of demonstration of the film, with the repetition an intensification of that process" (169). But this repetition can also be perceived in the effects achieved by the star's face, which—not only but most insistently in silent cinema— both performs and *is* their character. Valentino is his smoldering look; in F. W. Murnau's *Nosferatu* (1922), Ellen is her terror and desire and the monster is his hooked shadowy leer; and the moral makeovers of countless screen women play out their transformative identity on and off screen and in and out of the audience.

The star's face—an exchange of looks, despite the obvious barrier of the camera, card, or magazine cover—always also reminds the spectator that others are looking at it too. The mediation that Benjamin claims distinguishes the actor from any authentic aura converts the spectator-star relation into a triangular one, visibly inserting the social into the perception of self and other. It is in this way that the star can literally embody the audience's relation to dominant discourses on the problems and potentials of modern subjectivity. Movie star and fan magazines accelerated and refined the development of modernist celebrity and were often explicit about their "construction" and the process of star-making, which required stars to simultaneously supply realism (revelation) and artifice (glamour). While the person behind the image thus becomes another text to be constructed as revelation, this duplicity does not undermine the star's function as an object of both desire and identification. As an object of desire, the star might be whole and beautiful. But as an object of identification, the star is an image attached to related products, such as films, celebrity, or cosmetics. In this way, the commodities touched by stars also mediate between them and the consumer, who thus becomes something other than a spectator.

In the Modernist period, then, new theories of culture and identity that engaged with modernity found a fascinating example in cinema. While they were far from the only Modernists theorizing film, the writers of the Frankfurt School all employed an intersection of Marxist and Freudian theories to understand contemporary culture, and they have powerfully influenced how cinema has been understood in both Cultural Studies and modernist studies. Moreover, the separate and broader influences of Karl Marx and Sigmund Freud—whose ideas were disseminated in edited form through almost as many channels as cinema was—helped form a terrain that made expertise on cinema seem a public necessity.

In 1929, producer Irving Thalberg claimed that motion pictures were especially equipped to represent "the attitude of modern life, the attitude of children towards parents, the family life or the lack of it" (1964: 46). Popular magazines as much as early "film theory" credited psychoanalysis, in particular, with a privileged place in explaining cinema. Catherine Clément argues that cinema "comes into the world at the same time as psychoanalysis, carried by the same waters mixed with wonder and science. . . . In silent movies and in stories about hysterics, we find the same figures of frightened women, the same frightening vampires; it's the same imaginary" (44). Popular forums like *Photoplay*, as much as avant-garde ones like *Close Up* and most surrealist film-making, take up as a reading practice the aphorism that the movie industry is an industry of dreams, often with specific psychoanalytic reference points.[7] It is interesting in this context to consider Adorno's objection to arguments that surrealism exemplified psychological dream theory. For Adorno, surrealism often worked in ways analogous to dreams, but was always framed by the expectations of art: "in the dream the object world appears in a form incomparably more disguised and is presented as reality less than it is in Surrealism, where art batters its own foundations" (Adorno [1956] 2005a: 1114).

Psychoanalysis has very widely been used to account for the spectator-film or audience-star relation with a theory of identification. Use of this theory has emphasized Freud's developmental story about "primary identification," where the self is constructed in relation to a desirable other; in terms of cinema, this "self" is presumed to be the subject in the audience. But if this developmental story is "ambivalent from the very first" (Freud [1921] 1922: 61), accounting for a difficult if not finally irresolvable process, it nevertheless might be too simple to explain the way cinematic spectatorship is embedded in a wider cultural field. The psychoanalytic model of identification closest to cinema is neither this parent-child relationship nor the relationship between a group and its ideal leader (Freud [1921] 1922: 94), which has also been deployed to talk about movie stars. Instead, it is the contagious partial identification Freud exemplifies by girls in boarding school who catch one another's passions like a "mental infection" (64–65; see also chapter 9). This model better fits not only the new film fan cultures, but also Benjamin's insistence that the movie star is not an object for the spectator. The movie star is neither role-model nor ideal given their explicit artificiality on and offscreen, as figure 3 makes clear, but is instead constituted by shared attachments.

In such ways not only does cinematic authenticity work differently to that which can be invested in the photograph but cinema itself emerged amongst multiple discourses on just that complexity. The total "immersive" experience of cinema that seems to provide an authentically anchored sensory experience and yet was so explicitly constructed as manipulation was a favorite object of, and inspired new directions in, Modernist cultural critique. This is not confined to debates about art and the popular, film form, authenticity and reproduction, or subjectivity and identification, but these are all places to start a history of cinema as modernism as well as Modernist. Cinema also expanded and altered critical discourse on cultural location and identity.

Cinematic representations of spatial, temporal, cultural, or ontological difference—whether via "historical" film, other exotic "locations," or the fragmented representation of an emotion or identity—claimed a new sort of realness; of location. This fact differently exploits what Benjamin calls

> the desire of contemporary masses to bring things "closer" spatially and humanly, which is just as ardent as their bent toward overcoming the uniqueness of every reality by accepting its reproduction. Every day the urge grows stronger to get hold of an object at very close range by way of its likeness, its reproduction. Unmistakably, reproduction as offered by picture magazines and newsreels differs from the image seen by the unarmed eye. Uniqueness and permanence are as closely linked in the latter as are transitoriness and reproducibility in the former. . . . Thus is manifested in the field of perception what in the theoretical sphere is noticeable in the increasing importance of statistics. The adjustment of reality to the masses and of the masses to reality is a process of unlimited scope, as much for thinking as for perception. ([1936] 1969: 223)

The changing form and varying distribution of film clearly distinguishes between different modes of perception. For example, the separation of vision and sound in silent film—where a musical score could be performed live, by separate recording, or not at all—directly shapes the type of experience cinema offered. But Benjamin's insight here moves beyond aesthetics into a different kind of critical frame for cinema.

To summarize my argument thus far, while the Modernists undoubtedly saw the changing field of cinema around them in different terms than we do today, there are two continuities that seem worth stressing. The first is the way in which "cinema" became a name for, and a theory about, the whole of modern life—work it continues to do for Cultural Studies. The second is the way that "cinema" worked as a spectacle of "new" media, a nexus of ideas about technology, experience, and social change that are echoed in important ways in so many examples of "new media," before and after cinema. Cinema as modernism is in this sense not about particular films and how they are produced and consumed, but about how aesthetics, technology, and experience are bound together in a representation of cultural change. Gunning points to continuities between cinema and the Exposition culture that emerged in the late nineteenth century and expanded in the early twentieth—a link also made by Benjamin in his account of the cultural impact of photography (Benjamin [1927–40] 2002: 6). World's Fairs and Expositions, Gunning writes,

> celebrated, represented and explained the agents and effects of the modern world. Their visual displays and verbal proclamations, protocols and practices, announced key aspects of modernity: an overcoming of space and time that allowed a new sense of the global in a world shrunken by new technologies of transportation and communication; a demonstration and, nearly, the deification of new sources of energy and power, especially electricity; a narrative of progress ... and last, but not least, a mode of highly stimulated spectatorship. (2004: 39–40)

The comparison is apt in another sense. While there was a version of the Exposition that addressed agriculture and pastoralism in new scientific and industrial terms—the State Fair in the United States or the Agricultural Show in Australia—like most images of modernity, including cinema, the Exposition was an urban event that represented modernity and modern culture as centered on urban life.

The space of the cinema, figuratively and literally, offered a glimpse of cosmopolitan urbanity even as it sprung up in rural places. The traveling picture show had already been a site of interaction between the urban and the non-urban, and the rural "picture palace" gave this a new home (see

Figure 4. Sam Hood, "The Roxy Picture Theatre, Everard Park, South Australia (taken for BHP, on Adelaide-Whyalla trip)," 1939. Film photo negative from the Hood Collection, The State Library of NSW, Australia.

figure 4). Such mobile cultural trajectories are one of the ways in which cinema maps out the spaces of modernity, running lines from major cities through provincial towns and regional hubs and from major centers of cinema production, like Hollywood or Berlin, out through different cultures and locations. Such lines are always marked by different kinds of translation and are never unidirectional. If early Hollywood films showed in Chinese squares, then it is also true that Chinese cinema soon began to assemble its own genres, experimenting with film well before picture theaters started to spread more rapidly in the 1920s (see Hansen 2000; Lee). And if small Australian country towns impatiently awaited the latest Western movie, these audiences engaged with the rural as much as the metropolitan through such genres.

Figure 4 is a photograph of the "Roxy Theatre" in Everard Park taken for an industrial survey of South Australian towns in 1939. Its imperfect framing, exposure, and condition testify as clearly as its content to its distance from Hollywood or the famous Manhattan theater for which it was named. Stripped of the exoticism by which modernist studies often understands early twentieth-century cinema in "other" places, this image also manifests the way cinema represented modernity and modernization, even within and for modern rurality (see chapter 6). Cinema as modernism was explicitly manifest in translation for Australian country towns celebrating New York as much as for shopgirls watching Joan Crawford or for the hybrid forms of Shanghai silent film. While much has changed in the context of film today, a context that some film critics call "post-cinema," this process of translation has not been rendered obsolete. What the modernity of the rural means has both changed and varies, but it is still impossible to imagine a homogenously urbanized mono-cultural world in any other way than as a decidedly modernist utopia.

Kracauer's essay on the hotel lobby, which is centrally arguing for the significance of detective fiction, offers a telling comparison to cinema and one that draws close enough to his more famous essay on picture palaces to suggest that what seemed notable about cinema as a space was not confined to it. Kracauer reads both lobby and genre as "spheres of lesser reality" where "consciousness of existence and of the authentic conditions dwindles away in the existential stream."[8] But, he adds, "The *aesthetic* rendering of such a life bereft of reality, a life that has lost the power of self-observation, may be able to restore to it a sort of language" ([1922–25] 1995: 173). The "togetherness" that characterizes the hotel lobby is empty and its detachment "from everyday life" is not a process of reassurance, like a church congregation. It is a "space that does not refer beyond itself" and in which "the aesthetic condition corresponding to it constitutes itself as its own limit" (176–77). The picture palace is not empty, but what fills it is a narrative excess, an unreality, that also provides a language for critical reflection. Taking cinema as a point of intersection between modernist studies and Cultural Studies allows us to see how it captures not only "modernity" as a cultural field tangled up with economics, technology, aesthetics, and politics but also experience of, and reflection on, the self, culture, and the world.

2

Portrait of the Young Man as an Artist

Modernism and Adolescence

Youth, when properly understood, will seem to be not only the revealer of the past but of the future, for it is dimly prophetic of that best part of history which is not yet written because it has not yet transpired, of the best literature the only criterion of which is that it helps to an ever more complete maturity, and of better social organizations, which, like everything else, are those that best serve youth.

G. Stanley Hall, *Adolescence: Its Psychology and Its Relations to Physiology, Anthropology, Sociology, Sex, Crime, Religion, and Education*

This chapter focuses on the intersection of two objects—James Joyce and adolescence—to show how the significance of their conjunction is best understood through a model of modernism that exceeds Modernism and encompasses the emergence of Cultural Studies. The first of my objects is central to the Modernist canon—Joyce studies effectively constitutes its own field within modernist studies. The second is a crucial and too often ignored aspect of modernity that is central to the Cultural Studies canon—youth studies effectively constitutes its own field within Cultural Studies. Offering a new perspective on the importance of adolescence to Joyce's fiction, a new context for Cultural Studies' ongoing obsession with youth, and a new argument for the importance of youth to modernity's investment in the contemporary, intersecting Joyce and adolescence also provides another perspective on not only the modernism of Cultural Studies but also how Cultural Studies might understand modernism. First, however, I begin with a proposition that draws these threads together: namely, that adolescence is a modernist invention.

The Modernism of Adolescence

In the "Tradition and the Individual Talent" essay I discussed in the last chapter, T. S. Eliot distinguishes the truly individual artist from, on the one hand, those too wrapped up in their own generation to engage in creative dialogue with the poets of the past and, on the other, those who, overly vulnerable to influence, resemble "the impressionable period of adolescence" rather than "the period of full maturity" ([1919] 2005: 152). That an aesthetic theory of cultural tradition required such a direct, and indirect, reference to "youth" marks the importance of a certain understanding of adolescence that had only recently come to prominence. This understanding can be summarized in some senses by G. Stanley Hall's 1904 two-volume study *Adolescence*, from which my epigraph is drawn and whose subtitle is enough to map out the import with which he sought to invest adolescence.

Adolescence certainly has a history that predates modernism. Directly applying any classical understanding of adolescence to modernity, however, is fundamentally misleading. As I have previously argued in *Girls* (Driscoll 2002a), in the Classical world, adolescence specifies no chronological age. Whereas the Latin *adulescentia* was "the age of *adulescens*, the time between the age of the *puer* and *juvenis*, *i.e.* from the 15th to the 30th year, the time of youth," *adolescens* referred more generally to a process of growth (*Cassell's Latin Dictionary*). While the categories of "childhood" and "youth" are generally perceived as having expanded during modernity with the extension of education and economic dependence, adolescence itself became more specialized and condensed. Michael Rutter discusses this specialization of adolescence as a necessary consequence of modernity: "Adolescence is recognized and treated as a distinct stage of development because the coincidence of extended education and early sexual maturation have meant a prolonged phase of physical maturity associated with economic dependence; because many of the widely held psychological theories specify that adolescence *should* be different; because commercial interests demanded a youth culture; and because schools and colleges have ensured that large numbers of young people are kept together in an age-segregated group" (Rutter 7). I want to think about adolescence here as a new style of reflection on the modern "subject." Across the fields Rutter lists, adolescence began to emerge as a specialized categorization of life.

While any mapping of dominant literary styles onto human development will be too schematic, modernism's renovations of aesthetic style have long been linked by modernist studies to changing models of subjectivity. As Patricia Meyer Spacks notes, in the mid- to late Victorian period, adolescence began to constitute "a version of the self" in literary texts (195). Spacks attributes the "invention" of the "myth of adolescence" to Stanley Hall (228). As Spacks points out, the dangers of youth and its passions had been stressed for centuries, but this tendency does not indicate a modernist concept of adolescence. The dissemination of adolescence as a popular, public, and scientific category mapping both physiological change and psychological development is closely aligned with changes in aesthetic practices that foregrounded the idea of "realistic" character and scene. Spacks also links the origins of adolescence with the origins of modernity, locating the beginnings of the adolescent's "difficulty" in both the dramas of displacement and alienation in Gothic novels (140) and the frustrations of protagonists in "realist" novels (132). She defines adolescence as "the time of life when the individual has developed full sexual capacity but has not yet assumed a full adult role in society" (7).

This definition is obviously teleological, not only presuming the "full adult role" as the natural end of adolescence, but also anticipating modernity's discovery of the definitively sexualized adolescence it invented. In the nineteenth and twentieth centuries, adolescence gradually came to connote both a specific age range with diverse and often conflicting boundaries and a set of practices. This adolescence begins sometimes with puberty, sometimes with a social marker like high school, and sometimes with a specific age, and its end point shifts between legal markers of majority and vaguer boundaries like social stability and independence.[1] The boundaries of this adolescence contract in some contexts to specify the teenage years and expand in others to encompass an ongoing development or spirit of self-invention. At the heart of this adolescence are three interwoven concepts—sex, independence, and individuality—that can be summed up in a single concept—maturity—which they nevertheless contingently interpret.

The modernism of this development can be elaborated by reference to Sigmund Freud, one of the key figures in the invention of a model of adolescence still recognizable to us today. It is less Freud's theoretical impact on psychology than his impact on a range of other popular and public fields that makes him crucial here. The most influential elements of his work in this regard are his model of (sexual) development and his model of the split subject.[2] Freud's theory of "infantile sexuality" was and is notorious (see, for example, Freud [1905] 1953c). It is also premised on adolescence's capacity to explain the psychological equivalent of puberty's activation of the genitals (Freud [1917] 1989b: 158–59). While the equally notorious "Oedipus complex" is premised on infantile sexuality as the means of adjusting children, before puberty, to the sexual objects expected of them, it just as clearly explains the event of puberty as being part of an "adolescent" process of cultural adjustment (see Freud [1924] 1953a). This template should not be mistaken for a teleological (or "grand") narrative, although it very often is.

Freud did make structurally universal claims about his model of development, but the sheer complexity of Freud's model undermines any linear understanding of it. Freud's "A Fragment of an Analysis of a Case of Hysteria" (1904; also referred to as "Dora") exemplifies the impossibility of setting out any linear version of normal Freudian development. As Stephen Marcus notes, Freud is himself "utterly uncertain about where Dora is, or was, developmentally. At one moment in the passage he calls her a "girl," at another a "child"—but in point of fact he treats her throughout as if this fourteen-, sixteen-, and eighteen-year-old adolescent had [adult] capacities for sexual response both physically and emotionally" (Marcus 78). Rather than being an early element of a germinal theory, the difficulty of Dora's case is an apt precursor to the difficulty of the models of adolescence developed in its wake.

Joyce scholars remain undecided about Freud's influence on the writer. As Daniel Ferrer states, "Despite several serious essays and myriad sweeping statements on the question, the precise extent of Joyce's acquaintance with Freud and psychoanalysis remains unknown" (367). Discussing Joyce's reference to "Little Hans" and "The Wolf Man," Ferrer writes that it would be strange if Joyce had not read the other case studies, and indeed such an omission would be remarkable. Ferrer's only suggested reference to Dora in Joyce is "doraphobian" (Joyce [1939] 1989: 478), but references to Dora (or the analysand's real name, Ida Bauer) recur throughout *Finnegans Wake* (e.g., 28, 60, 211). And in this text psychoanalysis itself is much more than just another reference to current debates. It doesn't just appear in allusions like "the eatupus complex" (128) but as its own narrative technique that allows dialogue to work as a kind of mutual reading against the grain. On trial for a shifting set of possible crimes, the father character HCE is a resistant analysand as this exchange with his interrogator makes clear:

—. . . Can you not distinguish the sense, prain, from the sound, bray? You have homosexual catheis of empathy between narcissism of the expert and steatopygic invertedness. Get yourself psychoanolised!
—O, begor, I want no expert nursis symaphy from yours broons quadroons and I can psoakoonaloose myself any time I want (the fog fol-

low you all!) without your intereferences or any other pigeonstealer.
(522)

In subverting linearity (see chapter 6), modernism also disrupts the model of the subject that makes teleological sense of both character and narrative. If there is no exclusively natural linear development in the Freudian model, characterized as it is by disruptions, hesitations, blocks, and fantasy recursions and escapes, there is also little stability to the adolescence central to Freud and other Modernists. Even the apparently linear constitution of adolescence as a rite of passage deemed "naturally" characteristic of premodern societies (see, for example, Mead [1928] 1943) articulates adolescence as a period of both suspension and transformation. Within the Freudian model and in modernism more generally, adolescence is both retrospective and intensely of the present. It compresses and extends time, development, and experience and is largely dissociated from chronological aging. It is the site of childhood and of many potentials, including maturity; it is the site of multiply present performances of self.

Freud's analytic model, equally reliant on his model of multiply divided subjectivity, both influences and draws on the aesthetic and critical practices of modernism. Freud did not invent, though he did redeploy, the modern hermeneutic tradition aptly summarized by Nietzsche: "When we are confronted with any manifestation which someone has permitted us to see, we may ask: what is it meant to conceal? what is it meant to draw our attention from? what prejudice does it seek to raise? and again, how far does the subtlety of the dissimulation go? and in what respect is the man mistaken?" (quoted in Bordwell 72). Among the key interpreters of this tradition for a modern audience, while Karl Marx is undoubtedly as influential as Freud, Freud is the most important figure in terms of placing the subject as both the object and agent of hermeneutics. As David Bordwell notes following this quote from Nietzsche, what Freud and his followers contributed to the hermeneutic tradition was "the dynamic conception of the unconscious, whereby deeper meanings were systematically concealed by a process of resourceful repression" (Bordwell 72).

One reason Joyce's *Finnegans Wake* has often been associated with "postmodernism" rather than Modernism is its refutation of this particular hermeneutic. But where this claim relies on a hard-line taxonomy—the book's style simply doesn't conform to the central conventions of Modernism neatly enough—it exaggerates the coherence of many other texts collected together in the Modernist canon. And the success with which this refutation was elaborated in 1939, decades before the term postmodern emerged to describe something apparently new, seems a much better reason for skepticism about the category postmodern than many critics have allowed. Joyce's language games in *Finnegans Wake* were also games with already important public and popular ideas about the self. Freud's model of language's relation to the unconscious assumes that desire is repressed in the interests of social order (symbolized, not just in literature but for every subject, as ordered language). As the above quotes from *Finnegans Wake* suggest, Joyce's multiplications of meaning spectacularly overturn this normative order. Reading *Finnegans Wake* involves neither the search for meaning behind the text nor the denial of meaning altogether, for the series of meanings always occur at once. As Gilles Deleuze insists, "the great letter of *Finnegans Wake* . . . is not just any chaos: it is the power of affirmation, the power to affirm all the heterogeneous series" ([1969] 1990: 260). But rather than being opposed to a hermeneutic model, *Finnegans Wake* exaggerates it, demanding the search for meaning in every word rather than in the text as a whole.

Joyce's characters as units of "semperidentity" (Joyce [1939] 1989: 582) occupy a scene wherein "every person, place and thing in the chaosmos of alle anyway connected with the gobblydumped turkery was moving and changing every part of the time" (28).[3] With no past or future certain for any character, as Derek Attridge notes, "The *Wake* signals to us each time we (attempt to) read it the strength of our own ideologically-generated but inescapable desire for the stability, coherence, and recognizability of character" (156). In *Finnegans Wake*, every name is in fact a group of more or less associated names. This complexity emphasizes a parallel between the disruption of character and the difficulty of adolescence. An overview of the references assembled in the character of the daughter Issy, for example, would foreground Lewis Carroll's "Alice," Freud's "Dora," and "Christine" from the files of influential American psychologist Morton Prince, each of which provides her with a strikingly different age and different narrative of problematic development. And the difficulty of character in *Finnegans Wake* extends explicitly to the uncertainty surrounding the characters' ages and developmental placement. While some critics presume the younger generation is prepubescent, others suggest they shift between different ages but appear most often as "teenagers" (Eckley 215). In fact, these "children" change ages in the way adolescents do, shifting between different constructions of their maturity.

Adolescence, Progress, and Modernity

We cannot pin the difficulty of modern adolescence or its "discovery" on Freud. Freud's ideas are a means of focusing an array of cultural shifts rather than a discovery that changed the world. Modernity more broadly produces this new model of the subject, defined by Louis Sass as "the Western conception of the person as a bounded, unique, more or less integrated motivational and cognitive universe, a dynamic center . . . organized into a distinctive whole and set constructively both against other such wholes and against its social and natural background" (1). Thus the questions about changes to aesthetics and perception raised around cinema have a corollary here. Modernist aesthetic perspectivism is historically and philosophically coincident with the dissemination of adolescence. They are related categories for explaining the difficulty of modern identity, and adolescence and modernism are thus entwined as modes of critical self-reflection that interrogate both modernity and modern subjectivity.

When Stephen Daedalus, the adolescent protagonist of Joyce's *Stephen Hero* (an early draft of *A Portrait of the Artist as a Young Man* published posthumously in 1957), claims that "The modern spirit is vivisective" (Joyce [1957] 1966: 190), he gestures to a dimension of modernity's quest for "Enlightenment" that is given contemporary critical weight by scholars like Michel Foucault. Like modernity itself, adolescence is an operation of and on knowledge—including some practices and objects while excluding others—and the gradual changes that occur in both modernity and adolescence do not dispute or undermine the power of modernity and adolescence to fix things in place. Adolescence segments and categorizes human life, delineating those who are "not yet" subjects as well as what is proper to the subject. It is a separation of behaviors, lifestyles, and interests from the subject's properly "mature" sphere of action. But if modernist adolescence develops into this comprehensive classification of life, then how adolescence originates in modernity needs to be considered further. Several key texts can stand in for a more exhaustive discussion of the importance to modernity of reconceptualizing youth and maturity: Jean-Jacques Rousseau's 1762 polemic on education, *Émile*; Immanuel Kant's essay, "An Answer to the Question: 'What is Enlightenment?,'" published in a monthly journal to a public audience in 1784; and Foucault's lecture, also called "What is Enlightenment?" that I quoted in the introduction.

For Rousseau, adolescence and puberty are distinct if entwined developments: adolescence is the crucial social training for which the proper management of puberty is an important but not determinant factor. But Rousseau concedes there is a phase where both social training and puberty overlap and the student, physically and mentally, is "neither a child nor a man" (Rousseau 172). Across Rousseau's political and social theory he stresses the importance of creating or training (for Rousseau, they amount to the same thing) citizens who will have the right character for and attitude to civil democratic society. His influence can be seen to be on trial in Gustave Flaubert's *Madame Bovary*, in which more than one boy is unsuccessfully framed by the premises laid out in *Émile* (Flaubert 12, 309). For Kant too, an educational agenda centers the importance and the possibility of "Enlightenment." Kant understands immaturity as man's "inability to make use of his understanding without direction from another" (53), but stresses that immaturity can be self-imposed in a failure of "resolution and courage." If Enlightenment is how men escape "from their self-incurred tutelage" (Kant 58), such immaturity is positioned as a natural state that must be left behind by social progress. Failing to progress to adulthood means becoming comfortable with immaturity, a state of affairs Kant sees as structurally encouraged by poor guardianship and education. This argument proceeds with reference to modernity's newly emphatic compartmentalization of life (unfolding by discrete reference to society, knowledge, morality, and health) and its management (in law, books, religion, and medicine). Against aspiring subject-citizens are also arrayed the largely docile "great masses" that can only slowly, with difficulty and guidance, become an enlightened or mature "public."

It is from Kant's essay as much as from Charles Baudelaire that Foucault draws his definition of modernity as an attitude to the present. We can also use Foucault to clarify Kant's state of "tutelage" or immaturity as something more than childishly incomplete understanding. In Kant's argument, a person who has (as yet) no place as a cog in a social machine can not experience the distinction between public and private forms of reason by which one undertakes and commits to Enlightenment. With this in mind, the education that comprises adolescence must then involve learning both free expression and conformity (Enlightenment and function). This differently inflects, perhaps, both what Foucault sees as the "attitudes of 'countermodernity'" produced as part of modernity and what Kant otherwise sees as the impediments to Enlightenment. Modernity for Foucault is "not simply a form of relationship to the present; it is also a mode of relationship that has to be established with oneself" (Foucault [1978] 1984b: 41). Modernity, Foucault says, compels the subject "to face the task of producing himself"

(42). Enlightenment thinkers not only offered a developmental model of the subject-citizen, but their "Enlightenment" depended on establishing the new pedagogical and critical process of modern adolescence. Foucault adds, "I do not know whether we will ever reach mature adulthood. Many things in our experience convince us that the historical event of the Enlightenment did not make us mature adults, and we have not reached that stage yet." (49) That is, maturity is a goal we still culturally reproduce as the task of our ongoing self-criticism. Moreover, to crucially distinguish this from classical pedagogy, modern adolescence demands that maturity be guided and tested by accredited experts.

The model of adolescence as training for citizenship produced by Rousseau was further modified by nineteenth-century scientific understandings of puberty and, in related ways, by the psychological theories eventually dominated by Freud. Rousseau's child is literally at once a tabula rasa and a primitive animal, a contradiction elaborated in Victorian discourses on the child from Matthew Arnold's call for a cultured education and Carroll's Alice texts to journalism and sociology like that of Henry Mayhew—all of which respond to the Kantian vision of Enlightenment.[4] While this new adolescence proceeded through education before anything else, its rigid demarcation of childhood relied on and produced an account of biological maturation that was both more traumatic and more pivotal. If the modernist adolescent is not yet a subject, the modernist subject is defined by the ends of adolescence: individuality, independence, adult (genital) sexuality, maturity.

At the time Joyce's *Portrait* was being published in 1916, puberty was already considered to correspond, as Mary Moxcey demonstrates in her guidance manual of the same year, *Girlhood and Character*, "with the high-school age, or with legal entering into 'gainful occupations'" (198): "The recognition of adolescence as a period of human life separate from childhood and from maturity has been a slow achievement of civilization. Its beginnings are seen in the puberty rites with which primitive peoples marked the passage of the individual from one status to the other. The most recent development of society's valuation of the 'lengthened infancy' (that is, the longer teachableness) of the individual is the extension of recognized adolescence into the late teens and beyond them" (275). While the word "teen" was used in the nineteenth century, the developing categorization of "teen-age" attributes and behaviors belongs to the 1920s and 30s. The "teenager" foregrounds questions of conformity and frames adolescence as a dialectical relation between dependence and independence. Or, rather, this would be the case except that the "teenager" requires no experience of development or process. They may cease to be a teenager at a certain chronological point, but this alone does not reflect experience or make them an "adult."

Stanley Hall's young men are artists who "conserve their youth" via "the plasticity and spontaneity of adolescence" (547). Joyce's portraits of artists as young men further divine the force of the new in the culture at large as well as in themselves. The adolescence of Stephen Daedalus/Dedalus threads in this way through *Stephen Hero*, *A Portrait of the Artist as a Young Man*, and *Ulysses* (1922), simultaneously critiquing and reinforcing the image of the modern individual that had gradually come to center politics and aesthetics since the Enlightenment. And yet modernism at the same time crucially foregrounds what Andreas Huyssen describes as a "decline in paternal authority" defining Modernist subjectivity: "a change in personality type based on conformity to external standards rather than, as in the liberal age, on the internalization of authority. Internalization of authority, however, is held to be a necessary prerequisite for the later (mature) rejection of authority by a strong ego" (22). Not only did the ideal modernist subject-citizen have an ambivalent relation to the tutelage he had left behind, but this ambivalence also extended to his relation to these masses. Huyssen thus emphasizes the significance to Modernism of the rise of mass culture as "one of the major factors preventing such 'healthy' internalization and replacing it by those external standards of behaviour which inevitably lead to conformism" (22).

If adolescence is indeed crucial to the models modernity has used to explain the subject, this is predicated on the idea that adolescence involves an inherent spiritual component. The contemplation of one's adolescence is a spiritual process, as Stephen makes explicit in *Portrait*. But as Kant's essay already suggests, education always ties this spiritual progress to conformity and thus to the undistinguished masses. Adolescence is, at the same time, being endlessly re-established as the turbulent self-definition that both Joyce and Stanley Hall see as its great regenerative value because a self is actively produced there. Both Joyce's and Hall's adolescents take up a place in a narrative about dependence and independence that has personal, social, and aesthetic forms. What Huyssen sees as an "increasingly consuming and engulfing" (vii) feminized mass culture was in *Portrait* caught in a conflict with the "boy's own" independence of the avant-garde. This important discursive frame for understanding social change in the Modernist period didn't always idealize youth. José Ortega y Gasset, for example, concludes his *Revolt of the Masses* (1932) by arguing that Western civilization's fixation on "youth" undermines its moral order. Ortega y Gasset's "mass-man" defines himself by the receptive and unoriginal consumption that unites mass culture (see chapter 4). For Modernism in general, the dialogue between avant-gardism and mass culture deployed both these senses of "adolescent"—regenerative and degenerative.

Make It New

Modernism is often summarized by its manifestoes, which is a worthwhile shorthand given that the manifesto genre itself says something important about modernism. Manifestoes are always, if not in F. T. Marinetti's precise phrasing, declaring "first intentions to all the *living* men of the earth" (Marinetti 118, emphasis in original). In 1929, "The Revolution of the Word" manifesto published in *transition* (signatories to which were also supporters of Joyce's *Finnegans Wake*, published in the same magazine under the title "Work in Progress") principally refused any obligation for art to communicate. The final four declarations of this manifesto are as follows:

9. WE ARE NOT CONCERNED WITH THE PROPAGATION OF SOCIOLOGICAL IDEAS, EXCEPT TO EMANCIPATE THE CREATIVE ELEMENTS FROM THE PRESENT IDEOLOGY.
10. TIME IS A TYRANNY TO BE ABOLISHED.
11. THE WRITER EXPRESSES. HE DOES NOT COMMUNICATE.
12. THE PLAIN READER BE DAMNED. (Qtd. in Rainey 1011)

These are signal themes in Modernist aesthetics. André Breton's more famous surrealist manifestoes also place surrealism "as far as possible from the desire to make sense" (Breton [1925] 1972: 162). But this is only one, albeit pivotal, aspect of what characterizes the Modernist manifestoes in general—their refusal of obligations and traditions linked to an ostensibly prior generation.[5]

My subtitle, "Make It New," is drawn from a 1934 collection of essays by Ezra Pound more famous for its title than its contents (in true manifesto style). In his early career, as George Bornstein puts it, Pound moved from one innovative project to the next (one having been "Joyce"): "'The artist is always beginning,' he wrote in 'How I Began' (1913). 'Any work of art which is not a beginning, an invention, a discovery is of little worth.' Indeed, the slogan 'make it new' . . . demanded continual renewal rather than ossification yet gestured also toward an 'it' to be remade" (Bornstein 23). This attitude is more or less compatible with Pound's collaborator T. S. Eliot's more cautious claims for the novelty of modern art. While Eliot accepted that repetition was undesirable, he still wanted the new to fit into a pre-existing order of art: "we do not quite say that the new is more valuable because it fits in; but its fitting in is a test of its value" ([1919] 2005: 153). Similarly, Virginia Woolf claimed that "if we can imagine the art of fiction come alive and standing in our midst, she would undoubtedly bid us break her and bully her, as well as honour and love her, for so her youth is renewed and her sovereignty assured" ([1925] 1984: 154).

Woolf elsewhere argues that not only this independence but also a "mature" mind ([1928] 1973: 104) are necessary to art, and indeed it is their immaturity that women writers must overcome once they have escaped dependence. While this is a direct response to the problem of intersecting modernity and maturity for women rather than men—for both Kant and Rousseau women cannot mature or be enlightened just as they cannot be citizens (see Driscoll 2002a)—Woolf's claim has a further dimension in this context. Whether as creative destruction or educational process, modernist modernity is a question of style, giving rise to one of Fredric Jameson's defining characteristics of Modernism: "The great modernisms were . . . predicated on the invention of a personal, private style, as unmistakable as your fingerprint, as incomparable as your own body. But this means that the modernist esthetic is in some way organically linked to the conception of a unique self and private identity, a unique personality and individuality" (Jameson 1983: 114).

What Jameson calls personal style is what Woolf both seeks for women's writing and dislikes in "modern" men's writing as the shadow of the certain individual: "a straight dark bar, a shadow something like the letter 'I'" ([1928] 1973: 98). The modernist dialectic of change and continuity draws together all these examples as a relation between individuality and what we might call the *status quo* or, perhaps, *habitus* (see chapter 5). They thus also reference the challenge of modernist adolescence manifest since Rousseau and Kant—the challenge to both conform and distinguish. And in this way too the language of *Finnegans Wake* can be characterized, in Deleuze and Felix Guattari's sense, as a "minor" language: as an extraction from or variation on a major language that is neither an aspect of the dominant language system nor an impossibly "original" language (Deleuze and Guattari 103). The "minor language" is adolescent in that it embeds its revolutionary difference in citation of existing conventions.

I might argue that modernism involves the "becoming-adolescent" (aka "becoming-new") of the artist, after the style of Deleuze and Guattari's becoming-woman of the modern novelist.[6] The increasing prominence of adolescence as an image of creativity is evident in Joyce's schema for reading his collection of short stories, *Dubliners*, published in 1914. The book is divided into a sequence of stories representing Dublin "under four of its aspects: childhood, adolescence, maturity and public life" (in Ellmann 83). That a city and its life can have such a developmental schema is telling, however pragmatic Joyce's reasons for representing it as ordered at all were. Reading *Dubliners* it is clear that each story does center on a struggle to both make things new and to fit in. In the stories of "childhood," young adolescent boys look back with derision on childhood and forward to a sometimes incomprehensible and apparently disappointing adulthood. Equally, the "mature" characters display a heightened emotionality and social awkwardness that is characteristically associated with adolescence. Each story focuses on the processes of psychosocial placement and subjectification (however thwarted or incomplete), despite Joyce's claim that *Dubliners* represented the paralysis of life in modern Dublin (in Ellmann 83). *Dubliners* presents frustrated adults looking for the promise of an adolescence never seen in the confusion and thwarted passions of the younger characters. The paralysis of *Dubliners*, then, is that of an ideal adolescence that promises what it cannot offer—to make things new. While most criticism of *Dubliners* has qualified or abandoned this structural schema, Joyce's fiction as a whole continues to be read as a portrait of development that invests the young man with a central heroism, thereby endorsing the very developmental models it claims to have superseded.

Joyce's fiction foregrounds adolescence most obviously in the character of Stephen, whose story is exemplary of a modern bildungsroman (and paradigmatically of a *kunstleroman*). Stephen, in his impassioned negotiation of social norms, regimes of knowledge, and the signs of his own and others' style, is an adolescent after Stanley Hall. The young man's becoming an artist is a vocation, a declaration of his place outside social fixities and responsibilities and thus of his cultural mobility. For young women in Joyce's fiction, as in the Ireland Joyce knew, vocations other than marriage were rare and the most visible occupation was domestic service. Like the priests several of Joyce's artistic young men refuse to become, wives and domestic servants are declarations of dependence. The adolescent artist, testing his wings, declares "Non Serviam." In a pattern just as visible in other Modernist texts—such as D. H. Lawrence's *Women in Love* (1920) and Freud's case studies—such servitude is opposed to the identity and self-determination necessary for maturity. However, despite the opposition of servant and artist (an opposition also foregrounded in the first section of *Ulysses*), both are equated with possible immorality and neither with the subject-citizen. In fact, the modern artist, like the priest, the wife, and the domestic servant, is also framed as an adolescent who refuses to grow up and settle down, but this refusal is recast as a kind of heroism.

If the title of *Portrait* is as ironic as that of *Stephen Hero*, "portrait" is nevertheless appropriate to the way in which Stephen becomes the sole object of this narrative in the process of becoming its sole subject. It is telling that Stanley Hall's massive text on adolescence was published the year in which *Ulysses* is retrospectively set. *Ulysses* uses retrospectivity to stress the modernity of both Stephen and Leopold Bloom precisely because a representation of the general populace as typically not as modernist as they were would have seemed unconvincing by the time *Ulysses* was published. Indeed Joyce's canonical status rests largely on *Ulysses* being positioned, as Jacques Derrida puts it, as a work "with something like the necessity of an epoch" (quoted in Jones 181). The avant-gardism of *Finnegans Wake* is generally deployed in turn to place it in the shadow of *Ulysses*—as an exhausted Modernist sophistication. But as Joyce's fiction moves away from narrative perspective and stylistic expressionism it develops more complex reference points for characterization, and its image of the young man as an artist becomes more closely entangled with mass culture and draws closer to the figure of the bricoleur, which is central to much Cultural Studies' discourse on youth.

The portrait of the artist as a young man, however, is not the only narrative of adolescence in Joyce's fiction. Both the avant-garde (differentiating) and the massified (conforming) elements of adolescence are key to *Ulysses* and *Finnegans Wake*. In the latter, philosophical and artistic reference points do not overwhelm the "Feenichts Playhouse," where the stories are part pantomime theatre and part Sennet comedy all adapted from a tabloid romance, and where indeed the adolescent girl is positioned as expert and artist. Issy is both the star—"IZOD (Miss Butys Pott, ask the attendantess for a leaflet), a bewitching blonde who dimples delightfully and is approached in loveliness only by her grateful sister reflection in a mirror, the cloud of the opal" (Joyce [1939] 1989: 220)—and the fan—one of "those crylove fables fans who are 'keen' on the prettypretty commonface sort of thing you meet by hopeharrods" (159). *Finnegans Wake* is an *assemblage* in which what attaches to a character or narrative can and will also detach from it. I will take this term "assemblage" from Deleuze and Guattari, returning to it in subsequent chapters to mark an alternative mode of modernism that it would be a mistake to relegate (or elevate) as either a "counter-modernity" or "post-modern." In this context, I propose that modernist adolescent identity is an assemblage in the Deleuzo-Guattarian sense—a cluster of identifications productive, at its edge, of momentary subjectivities. This assemblage also resembles the way that Cultural Studies represents the deployment of group identifications to construct the identities of "youth."

This resemblance is in a significant way linked to Claude Lévi-Strauss' ground-breaking use of the term "bricolage" to discuss cultural production, a term redeployed by the Birmingham School writers to talk about youth subcultures. John Clarke explains: "In describing the processes of stylistic generation, we have made partial and somewhat eclectic use of Levi-Strauss' concept of bricolage—the re-ordering and re-contextualisation of objects to communicate fresh meanings, within a total system of significances, which already includes prior and sedimented meanings attached to the objects used" (Clarke 177). Dick Hebdige further aligns bricolage with "irrational" surrealist collage, aligning too the "optimism" of bricolage youth culture with surrealism's assault on everyday life (105–6). Punk style was one of Hebdige's key examples of this cultural assemblage but his insights are not confined to the contemporary youth culture of the 1970s.

For Deleuze and Guattari, an assemblage, "in its multiplicity, necessarily acts on semiotic flows, material flows, and social flows simultaneously" (22–23). Reading modernist adolescence in this light means seeing how its most singular events are folded into the rest of the world. This can extend to punk but also to a style of literature as assemblage "with the outside" as opposed to the "book as image of the world"—a style Deleuze and Guattari call "rhizomatic" (23). It is along these lines that the subject-in-process of adolescence becomes a revealing critical paradigm for Modernism and for Cultural Studies, which would also set everything out "on a single page, the same sheet: lived events, historical determinations, concepts, individuals, groups, social formations" (Deleuze and Guattari 31–32). This figure in fact resembles the Cultural Studies definition of "culture" to which I will return in part 3.

Cultural Studies, Adolescence, Joyce

A long history of Joyce scholarship has stressed the critical relation between Joyce's fiction and Modernist theory. The relevance of psychoanalysis, feminism, Marxism, and "formalist" literary and linguistic theories for understanding Joyce has been conscientiously elaborated. The interdisciplinarity of Cultural Studies inevitably seeks out the intersections and contestations between such discourses, and it thus contributes to changing perspectives on the way Joyce's fiction works. It can foreground the way Joyce draws on shifts in the way youth, development, and subjectivity were being reconceived in the early twentieth century. It matters that adolescence is not just a theme in Joyce's work but foregrounds relationships between characterization, style, and cultural context that link so many theoretical and popular modernist reconfigurations of culture and identity.

The pervasive dissemination of modernist adolescence in popular discourses like literature, psychology, cinema, fashion, advertising, and social theory demonstrates its significance and its inevitable engagement with changing aesthetic practices. To say that youth's centrality to modernity drives its centrality to Modernist literature is simply not strong enough. This begs more questions than it answers given that the model of immaturity and education at the heart of Enlightenment theories of progress were radically affected by the later emergence of new modes of expertise and new public discourse designed to both emphasize and manage adolescence. Such developments include universal suffrage, child labor laws, age of consent legislation, and, particularly, the links between these and normative literacy and compulsory schooling, with its concomitant generationalizing of culture. The youthful object of many Enlightenment ideals became the adolescence that was spectacularly central to the postwar teenager via the expansion of expert elaboration on this adolescence in the nineteenth century. The importance of expertise to modernism is a theme to which I will return in more detail, but it is worth stressing here that acknowledging changes to the meaning and experience of adolescence in the nineteenth century is not an alternate version of the argument that modernism emerged then. Kant and Rousseau were clearly already positioning themselves as such experts. Instead, the expanding expert management of the adolescent is an example of the gradual emergence of new and more widely visible versions of what the cultural expert is for. In the development of psychoanalysis, in the emergence of critical theory, and in proliferating media speculation on the modern world, youth is a privileged example of what is construed as positive about life framed by mass culture, urbanization, and globalization; but of course also of what has been lost.

We can also use the figure of the modern adolescent youth (and its supplement, the modern girl) to reconsider debates around the cultural specificity of modernism. While Joyce's work clearly leaves us with a very stably located image of the young man, modernist adolescence is certainly not confined to Joyce's Irish European of the early twentieth century. Stanley Hall's chief contribution to the transformation of adolescence is his role in psychologizing both the social and biological aspects of adolescence, also evident in his having brought Freud and Carl Jung to lecture in America. But he further contributed to a mainstreaming of both sociological and anthropological analysis of youth and thus to all the debates that followed from his characterization of adolescence as *sturm und drang* ("storm and stress") ([1904] 1911: xiii) and his claim that "Modern life is hard, in many respects increasingly so, on youth" (74). Adolescence as trauma, drama, and conflict has retained social currency in "the West," but the modernist obsession with how the self is both differentiated from and placed in the world extends to debating this Western-ness as well. The sturm und drang theory propagated by Hall was most influentially critiqued by Margaret Mead's studies of Pacific Island cultures. Mead's *Coming of Age in Samoa* (1928) famously presents adolescence as no kind of crisis at all without cultural influences that encourage such stress. Mead's work is also explicitly framed as studying Samoan culture to ultimately address the problems of contemporary adolescence in America.[7]

Such debates tied adolescence to industrialized, post-Enlightenment individualism framed by modern democratic concepts of majority, education, labor, and the emergence of mass culture. It might be useful to consider this in terms of Jameson's arguments in *A Singular Modernity*. Can the cross-cultural communication of the modern idea of "adolescence" via various powerful discursive definitions such as age of consent laws, educational models, and theories of puberty be seen as a component of "modernity" that might arrive at different times and in different ways for different cultures but fundamentally describes the same thing? In China, pivotal Modernists like Lu Xun were reconsidering China's modernization through the intersected fields of medicine, linguistics, and literature in tellingly titled New Culture journals like *New Youth* (Xin Qingnian) and *Sprouts* (Meng Ya), but always in relation to transnational popular and artistic conversations (see also Lee).[8] In Japan, the relations between avant-garde and popular arts in the Taishô period (1912–26) not only resembled those thought characteristic of European Modernism, but also deployed what is now widely described as Modernist "Orientalism" as a sign of cultural uniqueness. At the same time, "the massive escalation of technology, urbanization and modern disciplinary and governmental structures (Taishô democracy) as well as a rapid modernization of everyday life in Japan" incorporated new pedagogical, psychological, and governmental narratives on adolescence (Driscoll

2002a: 287–92). But all of these are, at least, unique translations of "Western" modernist adolescence.

If expert modernist commentaries on youth provide a necessary foundation for the shape that youth studies came to have, the emergence of a technologized, urbanized, commodified, transnationalized youth culture is nevertheless pivotal. An ongoing association of youth and youth culture with the question of style permeated the new markets for popular culture emerging after World War I and directly impacted studies of contemporary culture. While earlier psychoanalysis or sociology had linked youth with both rebellion and conformity and with both individualism and the difficulty of individualization, post-war discourses on modern life concretized this association. The changes between the two "Middletown Studies," in 1929 and 1937 respectively, trace both the increasing centrality of institutionalized discourses on adolescence to the study of human society and the expanding dissemination of youth culture.

The adolescent had already become a standard reference for the broadest field of social analysis, including diverse elements of public policy and the public sphere and as an iconic component of popular culture and its perceived audience. "Teenager" became a name for more than one market that engaged expert advice with popular culture, and amidst the public reconstitution of ideologies about gender, nation, the family, and individual freedom after World War II this conjunction of expertise and popular culture constituted the mythical 1950s "teenager." Thus the array of popular "guidance manuals" directed at adolescents and their parents and teachers also took on new forms at this time. It would be less accurate to claim this was propelled by the simultaneous rise to prominence of new variations on developmental psychology than to say that the new public centrality of the teenager and the new power attributed to adolescent psychology mutually reinforced one other. Erik Erikson has been a particularly influential example, still cited for his discussion of adolescence as a crisis that establishes and negotiates identity, and the state-sponsored institutionalization of this model in policy directed toward education, health, and leisure shares important historical space with the state-sponsored institutionalization of Modernism.

It would be difficult to underestimate the impact of the institutionalization of compulsory education on both adolescence and youth studies. If the emergence of normative literacy and "universal" education reshaped adolescence, by the interwar period this adolescence had been integral to at least one generation's perception of childhood and maturity and thus public sphere and popular cultural images of normal adolescence. Schooling and other age-based compartmentalizations of citizenship (such as licenses, age limits, and other regulations) forced adolescents into a separate and distinct relation to a "culture" in which they were not yet participants but on which they were literate commentators and for which they were key consumers. The teenager became a new focus for what Thorstein Veblen had called, with reference to late-nineteenth-century middle-class wives, "conspicuous consumption" (39ff). The teenager, now resident in the family home for much longer as a sign of commitment to training subject-citizens, also took up a cultural place that foregrounded training and experimentation in consumption and style. It is in this context that images of "youth" counter-cultures in the 1960s and 70s drew once more anew on the now well-established ambivalence of adolescence.

The association of youth with counterculture emerges with modernism, and is just as manifest in "the jazz age" and the Chinese New Culture movement contemporary with it as in post-WWII countercultures. By the 1980s, when conversations about "postmodernism" took on real impetus, it seemed that "slackers" and other exhausted images of youthful promise were proper to this moment. But such disappointment with countercultural effort was itself already manifest in the "lost generation" that complemented the jazz age. As Joyce's texts suggest, disappointment and difficulty are as integral to modernist adolescence as vital promise. What was different in the context of debates about postmodernism was that both "Modernism" and its most famous images of adolescence no longer named anything for and of youth (or change), having been reframed as "parent culture" and thus itself as education for citizenship.

The institutionalization of Modernism that made modernism, including its narrative about adolescence, into something only available as history or nostalgia, is the context in which the Centre for Contemporary Cultural Studies at the University of Birmingham rose to prominence with its analyses of youth culture in collections like *Resistance Through Rituals* (Clarke et al. 1975). Encouraged by Cultural Studies' emphasis on both the everyday and "social problems," a range of studies began to focus on public displays of youth culture and, though less centrally, on the domestic or "bedroom" culture more often associated with girls. These relations between bodies, identities, and visibility and this emphasis on the everyday meant that youth cultural forms and practices could be conceived as modes of "being-in-the-world," to take a phenomenological turn, or as manifesting different kinds of "habitus," to take a sociological one. It is crucial, though, that the perspec-

Figure 5. Clara Bow, 1927. Photograph from the Kobal Collection.

tives drawn into these analyses of youth from Marxism, feminism, psycho-analysis, semiotics, sociology, anthropology, and phenomenology were all modernist products.

Youth "style" always articulates a relation between the individual and the masses that is also a means of personal distinction, and this is as true of Joyce's Stephen or Issy as of the Birmingham School's real-life respondents. Issy's characterization is of her time, less Jonathan Swift's "little language" to which critics often compare it than Moxcey's effusive teenage girl style. The recognizability in the field of contemporary girl culture of figure 5—a publicity photograph of the actress Clara Bow to which I will return in the next chapter—is matched by equally recognizable praise and condemnation of adolescent girls in the early twentieth century. "It is as difficult for a girl in the heart of her teens," Moxcey writes, "to use language without italics, superlatives, and exclamation points, as it is for her body to resist the rhythm of music. In a world of prosaic and staid adults, the young girl supplies the charm of the unexpected, the inconstant, the incalculable" (171–72).[9] The increased media visibility of youth and the proliferation of venues for its cultural analysis between 1916 and 1975 is striking, but the continuities between what youth was presumed to mean and how it was presumed to be practiced are still striking. If the gangs and other subcultures of the Birmingham School seem incongruous in terms of reading Joyce, it is less because these are themes yet to gain their later media prominence than because these are not styles of adolescence with which Joyce is concerned. Youth culture styles more broadly form around the conjunction of adolescence, group identifications, and commodity types, and this is as true of the "flapper" of the 1920s as it is of the "punk" of the 1970s.

The adolescence of Joyce's characters refract diverse cultural fields, disseminating a range of ideas about adolescence as the central drama of the self. Joyce's artist as a young man articulates a recognizably irresolvable struggle for a self-owning modern identity. A purely literary approach to this is inadequate. Thinking about modernism through adolescence requires attention to adolescence's constitution, regulation, and performance in a range of cultural fields and social frameworks, from educational models and philosophical and theoretical debates through legislative changes and new social norms, to emerging and changing fields of popular culture and such comparatively new everyday activities as motoring and high school. Each of these fields is assembled in Joyce's fiction in ways that neither depend entirely on nor ignore the formally avant-garde style of his work. Indeed I have tried to show that this avant-gardism itself has "adolescent" connotations. The questions and debates produced around modernist adolescence are made spectacularly visible by their representation in Modernist avant-gardism, and they also belong to a larger context that brings Cultural Studies into view at the same time.

3

Modern Love

Sex Education, Popular Culture, and the Public Sphere

*[I]n Breton's description of [the Théâtre Moderne's] bar on the upper floor—
"it is quite dark, with arbours like impenetrable tunnels—a drawing room on
the bottom of a lake"—there is something that brings back to my memory that
most uncomprehended room in the old Princess Café. It was the back room on
the first floor, with couples in the blue light. We called it the 'anatomy school';
it was the last restaurant designed for love.*

Walter Benjamin, "Surrealism: The Last Snapshot of the European Intelligentsia"

There's an elegiac tone to Walter Benjamin's memory of the Princess Café
that marks the loss, by 1929, of some older way of learning about love as a
mystery. I focus this chapter not on how, in the years before and around surrealism, love became something less impenetrable, or less shaded in blue,
but on tracing a discourse on "modern love" in which this difference from
the past is marked again and again. I also suggest some significance for Benjamin's link between restaurants designed for love, radical Modernist art,
and the European intelligentsia. Love is rarely considered as a dimension of
Modernist revolution; and in focusing on love in this chapter I also want to
displace the now established associations between avant-garde Modernism
and sexuality rather than love.

Michel Foucault sets out in *The History of Sexuality, An Introduction*
(1976) to challenge an image of sexual liberation in which speaking about
sex was both illicit and an inevitable sign of social progress. He positions
sex as something the modern subject is invited to speak about *as* repressed
in ways that reinforce the importance of sex to modern subjectivity. I propose that we tactically reframe Foucault's recognition and overlay his story

about "sex" with one about "love." This step back from the specificity of the discourses Foucault engages in the *Introduction* might allow practitioners of modernist studies to see how their usual subject matter fits into another sort of periodization. It might also re-enliven for Cultural Studies Foucault's very well-used argument. This chapter, like the last, looks at how the modernist mode of situating the subject in the world extends well beyond the great works of Modernism, whether artistic, philosophical, or political. And it provides a new context for thinking about how the always impossible subject of self-knowledge, described in the last chapter as an adolescent, was widely available through a discourse on "modern love" propagated in popular culture, education, and the media and other elements of the public sphere. This subject was also constituted in new "lifestyles" that claimed to capture the style of the times in new relations to love. Modernism is the context in which subjects come to have "styles" of "life" that are always defined in relation to both public and popular culture.

This chapter examines the intersection of the relation between art and the popular raised in chapter 1 with the relation between subjectivity and expertise raised in chapter 2, and finds in that intersection what has come to be called "the public sphere"—an idea as concretely modernist as any in that sequence. Henry Jenkins, Tara McPherson, and Jane Shattuc note that distinguishing between popular culture and high culture leads to an "inevitable focus on the hundred and fifty years when mass production led to the vast proliferation of popular culture" and the wave of critical analysis that followed it (27). This conception of the "popular" on which industrialization could have such an impact is a product of modernity requiring the same idea of "the people" that underpins the equally modern "public sphere." One place where the modernity of popular culture and the public sphere intersect is in the proliferation of fields of representation in which the self as sexual (rather than merely sexed) appeared in dialogue with changed ideas about love.

The Public Art of Sex

I want to begin with two concepts from Foucault's *Introduction* that could stand to be elaborated together more often: bio-power and the injunction to speak of sex. Foucault coins "bio-power" as a term for the modern emergence (since the Enlightenment) of an "anatomo-politics," which seeks to explain and mould the body efficiently, and a "biopolitics" that regulates populations ([1976] 1984a: 139). Sexuality is only one component of the "technologies of power" produced when these poles meet in the new social sciences of the nineteenth century, but it is a crucial one. Nikolas Rose and Paul Rabinow set out the following parameters for recognizing bio-power: "One or more truth discourses about the 'vital' character of living human beings, and an array of authorities considered competent to speak that truth. . . . Strategies for intervention upon collective existence in the name of life and health." And, furthermore, modes "of subjectification, in which individuals can be brought to work on themselves, under certain forms of authority, in relation to truth discourses, by means of practices of the self, in the name of individual or collective life or health" (Rose and Rabinow 2003).

Bio-power names the relationship between what Foucault elsewhere calls "technologies of the self" and broader fields in which "power over life" is exercised. While religion has historically used knowledge of one's self "to alter behaviour, to train or correct individuals" (Foucault [1975] 1977: 203), Foucault notes in "Technologies of the Self" that since the eighteenth century "the techniques of verbalisation have been reinserted in a different context by the so called human sciences in order to use them without renunciation of the self but to constitute, positively, a new self" (1988b: 49). The modern proliferation of ways to speak about sex is key to this new self. They manifest a technology for producing and managing the self given special force by its representation as a secret, not just in psychoanalysis—Foucault's largely undeclared target in the *Introduction*—but also in popular discourses on "new morality" and "sex education." All declare that "sex" is repressed and reinforce the presumption that speaking about sex is transgressive by establishing boundaries within which it is both permitted, if not required, and carefully managed. While psychoanalysis undoubtedly impacted both "the new morality" and "sex education," I want to position it here as part of an ongoing engagement between popular and public representations of the sexual self that are inextricable from a just as pervasive modernist discourse on love.

As Linnell Secomb points out in *Philosophy and Love* (2007), classical discourse on love always referred to "erotic, embodied love" (11), in which even philosophic love is "not the overcoming of the body" but is "itself erotically incarnate" (23). Moreover, classical love is, "like philosophy, the quest for knowledge" (12). Plato's exemplary dialogic form in *The Symposium* suggests that love is a matter for debate and a site of struggle. With this in mind it seems easy to overstate what distinguishes *modern* love. The three volumes of Foucault's *History of Sexuality* mark a path for that distinction—

for Foucault, sex and love in the classical context are clearly distinguishable and in no way equivalent to or determinate of identity—but I will take up instead Secomb's transition from classical love to modern love through the examples of Mary Shelley's *Frankenstein, Or the Modern Prometheus* (1818) and the philosophy of Friedrich Nietzsche.

Shelley's novel unfolds the entwined horrors of modern experience, modern science, and, as Secomb draws out, modern love. Introducing Shelley, Secomb draws attention to *Frankenstein*'s many popular adaptations over almost two centuries, stressing its long relevance as a story about "the spectre of unrequited love" as much as "living-dead horror" (Secomb 24). The monster and science narratives become signs of the extremity to which the human need for love can be pushed. Secomb would argue that love was also Shelley's central theme, but I would add that adaptations of the *Frankenstein* story have refined the type of love involved to, first of all, a sexual relation.[1] Secomb argues that the paradox of love in *Frankenstein* is the way the idyllic ("conventionally romantic") and the monstrous are articulated together. It is the "paradoxes inherent in the love relation" that thus link Shelley and Nietzsche on "the dangers of love: the illusory enchantments of the romance of love and the paradoxical chiasmic intersections between mundane love and uncanny, miraculous and monstrous love" (Secomb 24). With my different emphasis here, what seems to comprise the modernity of love in *Frankenstein* and Nietzsche is the entwinement of experience, knowledge, and regulation. In *Frankenstein*, both love and knowledge must either be under some regulation or risk monstrosity, and in Nietzsche it is just such regulation of knowledge and love that is rejected as the homogenizing weight of the modern world. In both, a *modernist* discourse on love dwells on the experience of love, including of how love can be known. I would thus rephrase Secomb's paradox of love as the entwinement of banality and the limit experience to which "modern love" gives a new structure.

In *The Transformation of Intimacy* (1992), Anthony Giddens argues that "the rise of romantic love more or less coincided with the emergence of the novel: the connection was one of newly discovered narrative form" (40). This positions romantic love as an invention of modernity. This narrative form addressed not only interpersonal relationships but also those between the subject and metaphysical truth (God, Nature, the Sublime) and between the subject and the new formations of the state and its regulatory powers: "The complex of ideas associated with romantic love for the first time associated love with freedom, both being seen as normatively desirable states. Passionate love has always been liberating, but only in the sense of generating a break with routine and duty. It was precisely this quality of *amour passion* that set it apart from existing institutions. Ideals of romantic love, by contrast, inserted themselves directly into the emergent ties between free-dom and self-realisation" (Giddens 1992: 40). Giddens' argument in this book is also a response to the popularity, among contemporary cultural crit-ics, of Foucault's history of sexuality. Although it overstates things to say, as Giddens does, that Foucault is entirely "silent" on the relationship between sexual and romantic love, he certainly does not focus on love in modernity. The heart of Giddens' problem with Foucault, however, suggests a way past it. While Giddens questions Foucault's claim that sexuality was an open se-cret by arguing that the proliferating representations of sex Foucault refers to were "accessible only to very few" (Giddens 1992: 26), he neglects how the expanding discourse of romantic love he has already acknowledged trans-lated this presumption—that sexual desire constituted the hidden kernel of selfhood—into popular culture. That is, romantic love in precisely this narrative form became a means of disseminating, and a crucial corollary to, the open secret of sex.

The sometimes shocking challenges posed by Modernist avant-gardism cannot be extricated from the changing relationships among embodied selves, lived culture, and the physical and human sciences that were brought to bear on understanding them. For example, we cannot detach James Joyce's *Ulysses* from public debates over sex that in turn helped constitute debates over the novel's censorship and subsequent release. As Lauren Berlant and Michael Warner have demonstrated, sex is "mediated by publics," mean-ing not only sex acts but the idea and function of sex including "more tacit scenes of sexuality like official national culture, which depends on a notion of privacy to cloak its sexualization of national membership" (Berlant and Warner 547). And just as mediation by publics forms part of the modernity of sex, the same is intrinsically true of modern love.

Joyce can again serve as illustration. Long before the U.S. trial of *Ulysses*, the difference of its style and content was being discussed as a new form of realism. Early commentary was often interested in Homeric parallels, but that focus also meant discussing how "today" was different from "then" and invited such discussions about love, particularly with reference to the mar-riage of Molly and Leopold Bloom. For many such commentaries, the (new) modern woman was sexually (psychoanalytically) informed, and recogni-tion of this fact functioned as a virtue for those who would praise *Ulysses* and as proof of its degradation of love for critics. *Ulysses* was banned halfway through its serialization in the U.S. magazine *The Little Review*. Although

Molly is a frequent reference point in discussions of the case against *Ulysses*, it was the conclusion of "Nausicaa," in which the lame seaside girl Gerty leans back to expose herself to Leopold, that inspired its suppression.

The statute involved in this case, Ezra Pound discovered to his horror, also dealt with the distribution of "contraceptives and abortion." While Pound quipped about his own works being "classed in the law's eye with the inventions of the late Dr. Condom" (Parkes 66), this is a telling conflation. Adam Parkes is thus led to juxtapose modernist literary censorship with litigation around popular publications such as those of Dr. Marie Stopes. Stopes, the author of *Married Love* (1918) and *Contraception* (1923), also faced transnational libel suits and obscenity trials; indeed, Judge John Woolsey's dismissal of the obscenity charges against Stopes provided one clear reason for delaying the trial of *Ulysses* until he could hear it. Woolsey described *Married Love* as a "considered attempt to explain to married people how their mutual sex life may be made happier" (quoted in Pagnattaro 223). Marisa Pagnattaro argues that this case, rather than the trial of *Ulysses*, is what sets the new legal standard for obscenity as a historically defined category of offence and immorality (224). She notes too that the brief presented to Woolsey in the case of *Ulysses* made this definition clear. It begins: "I. The test of obscenity is a living standard, and *Ulysses* must be judged by the mores of the day" (quoted in Pagnattaro 228).

As Foucault implies, what is now meant by "sexuality" can be largely attributed to the influence of psychoanalysis, or at least to interpretations of it, and always dealt with the self as a whole, rather than with only the explicitly sexual elements of it. This is the context that made Woolsey's judgments about the modern sensibility tenable. The publication of *Ulysses* in the United States was legalized in 1933, the same year as the publication of Sigmund Freud's "Femininity," in which he left the explanation of feminine sexuality, which Joyce was seen to so contentiously invoke, in the hands of the poets (Freud [1933] 1953a). Woolsey's judgment, stressing *Ulysses*' "observation and description," includes the following caveat on obscenity that gave rise to a "reasonable man" (or "person with average sex instincts") test in such cases:

> The meaning of the word "obscene" as legally defined by the courts is: "Tending to stir the sex impulses or to lead to sexually impure and lustful thoughts". . . . After I had made my decision in regard to the aspect of *Ulysses* now under consideration I checked my impressions with two friends. . . . I was interested to find that they both agreed with

my opinion: that reading *Ulysses* in its entirety . . . did not tend to ex-
cite sexual impulses or lustful thoughts but that its net effect on them
was only that of a somewhat tragic and very powerful commentary on
the inner lives of men and women. ("U.S. v. Ulysses")

In the court of appeals the pedagogical tenor of this judgment was given
further support, comparing *Ulysses* to: "works of physiology, medicine, science, and sex instruction [that] are not within the statute, though to some
extent and among some persons they may tend to promote lustful thoughts"
(quoted in Pagnattaro 229).

The certainty about what rational and normal men would understand
from reading *Ulysses* finds its footing in a sense of responsibility for the
public management of not just sex but knowledge of sex, and an equally
public sense of responsibility to the love relationships that justified that
management as a public good. As Woolsey phrases it: "I hold that *Ulysses*
is a sincere and honest book." Freud's hesitancy about naming sex in his
analytic sessions with "Dora" provides a useful footnote. Freud knows he
must distinguish between, on the one hand, information the patient needs
and, on the other, the risk of arousal, ultimately resolving that her innocence will protect her against corrupting knowledge. The same reflection is
evident at the level of the case study itself: using the public good of better
understanding the human psyche as justification for such excursions into
it. And yet within decades of Dora, and hot on the heels of *Ulysses*, George
Bernard Shaw could declare that D. H. Lawrence's "obscene" novel, *Lady
Chatterley's Lover* (1928), "should be on the shelves of every college for bud-
ding girls." Importantly, Shaw added, such girls should not become engaged
until they had read it. Shaw was a "radical," but even as a limit case he indicates that the terrain of sex had changed. I found this quotation in Rachel
Bowlby's *Shopping With Freud* (1993), where her citation for it is intriguingly
long, comparing several sources' interpretations of this "eccentric" claim
and stressing that Shaw had not in fact read the text. Regardless, his claim
is a telling expression of the frequency with which representations of sex,
love, and marriage were being debated. What any girl was supposed to gain
from this text remains unclear. At his most explicit Shaw says, "Lawrence
had delicacy enough to tell her the best, and brutality enough to rub in the
worst" (quoted in Bowlby 1993: 44–45, 125).

Bowlby quotes this passage in a discussion of the trial of *Lady Chatterley*
in which she suggests that "the recommended values of literature" function
"only so far as they can be defined as the obverse of the vilified values of

obscenity" (1993: 26). Bowlby cites the first English legislation on obscenity, proposed in 1857, comparing it to Matthew Arnold's "The Function of Criticism at the Present Time" (1864)—a foundational text for literary criticism that Bowlby reads as similarly anxious over the coarseness of contemporary English life. The trial of *Lady Chatterley* did not take place until 1960, motivated by the introduction of a new "Obscene Publications Act" (1959), in which the obscene text's "tendency to deprave and corrupt" could now more routinely be "overridden by the consideration of 'public good'" (Bowlby 1993: 29). The witnesses at this trial did not include Lawrence's most famous defender in the field of Literature, F. R. Leavis, but it did feature key figures in the emerging field of Cultural Studies, including Richard Hoggart and Raymond Williams. The Cultural Studies attitude to literature manifest in this defense again focused on the importance of Lawrence's commitment to sexual realism.

The suppression of Lawrence's *The Rainbow* in 1915, a direct precursor to the later suppression of *Lady Chatterley*, was deemed at the time "necessary for the protection of public morals and public decency in literary productions" (Parkes 21). Parkes describes Lawrence's construction of this novel as a commitment to "the pursuit of self-realization and consummate marriage" (23). He thus understands Lawrence as working against both established morality and what he saw as the failings of "modern love"—what Lawrence labeled in 1916 "the strange, terrible sex-war" (in Parkes 23). Despite the obvious impact of including artistic merit as a potential qualifier of obscenity in the 1959 legislation under which *Lady Chatterley* was judged, the trial of *Ulysses* indicates an earlier turning point in which changes to the normative perception of love and sex, and the role of art in documenting these, equally worked as a defense. In the 1928 trial of Radclyffe Hall's *The Well of Loneliness*, by contrast, attempts to use both artistic merit and realistic portrayal of struggles with knowledge about sex and love as a defense against obscenity failed. But this work was framed during the trial as a personal declaration, or private symptom, rather than a public good. Radclyffe Hall was a patient of sexologist Havelock Ellis, who himself refused to testify at the trial on the grounds that "since his book *Sexual Inversion* had been convicted for obscenity he was not a valid witness" (Tamagne 321). The novel was published in Paris and then in the United States with a commentary written by Ellis in support of both its realism and its style as the context in which healthy claims about love could be made—Ellis here understood Hall's identity, and that of her central character Stephen Gordon, through his own categorization of sexual types (see Radclyffe Hall 1929).

These examples of literary censorship help us reconsider how bio-power works as a means, to quote Nikolas Rose, of "maximizing the health and welfare of the population" (188). What was at stake in these trials was not first of all a distinction between obscenity and artistic merit, although that was an important part of the proceedings. Neither experimental style nor controversial content were the central object in relation to which these judgments were formed and understood. Rather, it was modern love as "the sex relation"; life, sex, marriage, romance and public good entwined. This is bio-power in action. Bio-power is usually considered alongside sovereignty and discipline as a macrosocial shift in the field of governmentality.[2] But, as Rose and Rabinow frame the concept, "the right of a ruler to seize things, time, bodies, ultimately the life of subjects," reducing them to "merely one element in a range of mechanisms working to generate, incite, reinforce, control, monitor, optimize and organize the forces under it," can also encompass these censorship debates. "Sovereign power is at one and the same time an element in this moral economy and an attempt to master it" (Rose and Rabinow). These trials were in fact debates about the style and content of modern love. Both public and popular, each trial was both a *cause célèbre* and a scandal.

The New Morality

Modernity is punctuated by a series of claims about a "new" morality: claims made by groups or individuals, claims retrospective or utopian, and claims made about different fields for different audiences. Such claims are generally distributed across both popular and public culture—addressed, that is, to consensus on the difference of today's presumed worldview. Talking about consensus in this way does not mean relegating popular culture to a reflection of what has already been negotiated in more apparently serious forums. Figure 6 is the cover of a pulp romance magazine from 1933—one of many such series proliferating in the new interwar publishing world. Magazines like *Thrilling Love* generally presume the sacrosanct importance of marriage, as well as of virginity as a component of bridal promise, but they also put passion on display for consumption by a mostly female readership. They present not only love but also sexual passion framed by the ideal of love as necessary to a satisfying life for men, women, and girls.

Thus a shift in normative sexual and romantic assumptions is not only evident in landmark trials; indeed, without a wider sense of changed morality, cases like those that found in favor of *Ulysses* or *Lady Chatterley* would

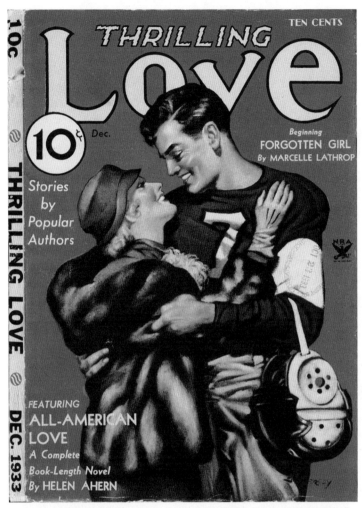

Figure 6. *Thrilling Love*, December 1933 (Cover KM), New York: Standard Magazines. From the Library of Congress, Serial and Government Publications Division (reproduction # LC-DIG-ppmsca-02922 DLC).

not have done so. The procession of claims to locate a "modern" (always new) morality is another reiteration of the modernist "break," but one not in the least confined to aesthetics. One of the advantages of "new morality" as a perspective on bio-power is that it demands no more emphasis on actions and desires that are exceptional than on those that are not, and it requires equal emphasis on the relations between the state and interlocking forms of expertise: legal, scientific, aesthetic, moral, and more amorphously cultural. "New morality" also often appears as a dismissive label for the loss of traditional ideals under the influence of mass culture. *Lady Chatterley's* disparaging reference to an "ugly ugly" cinema showing an equally ugly film—*A Woman's Love* (possibly a 1910 short film featuring Maurice Costello)—should be cross-referenced here with Dziga Vertov's *Man With a Movie Camera*, which lays claims to serious realism by contrasting its own image of a waking woman with a poster for a melodramatic German film, *The Awakening of a Woman* (directed by Fred Sauer, 1927).

The new morality is "modern love" and modern love is sexual love—in and out of marriage. Such a break is still being reiterated today in relation to, for example, television series like *Sex and the City* (1998–2004) or *Gossip Girl* (2007–). But another striking characteristic of "new morality" that continues in contemporary examples is its particular reference to women. This also has a history as long as modernity itself. The scandalized public response to the early romance novels discussed by Giddens was also tied to the expansion of women's new literacy (Jagodzinski 1999). For the suffragettes, modern love displaced the dominant equation between women's success and marriage with an equation between her success and a representation of sexual and romantic competence. And in the Modernist period, whether individual commentators approved of it or not, sex was seen to have transformed love with particularly dramatic effects on women. A *Good Housekeeping* article in 1938 could assert:

> Freud, whether right or wrong, did succeed in convincing [women] that they had sex desires and that these desires were not wicked; that to repress them was as difficult and dangerous to women as to men, and they need no longer pretend that all they wanted was at most motherhood, when it was quite as natural for them to want loverhood. This has been an astounding change. . . . Instead of the terrifying repression of the old maid, we have the complete repudiation of any kind of self-control as a danger to her sanity, or at least to the normal and full development of her age. (Qtd. in White 107–8)

While the article misreads Freud, it exemplifies the critical reflection on modern love familiar to modernist popular culture. In the nineteenth century there were many popular nonfiction guidance manuals for a modern ethics of love. These manuals often appeared either from within or aggressively against what we would now call feminism, and the genre expanded in the twentieth century with texts like Ellen Key's *Love and Marriage* (1911), which claimed that "A woman's essential ego must be brought out by love before she can do anything great for others or for herself" (182), and Stopes' *Married Love*, which explicated this fulfillment.

Images of modern love as fulfillment for women were often understood to be risking self-indulgence as much as self-abnegation. In 1926–27, *The Nation* published a series of autobiographical feminist essays—later collected as *These Modern Women* (Showalter 1978)—that offered a map of modern love conceived as both a sex relation and a matter for expert management. In this collection, sociologist Phyllis Blanchard writes that "Insistence upon one goal—the attainment of distinction by my own efforts without the need to love, honor, or obey any man—became the guiding fiction to which I tried to shape my life. The result was continual rebellion against things as they were" (in Showalter 107). Mary Hopkins, however, describes the typical pattern of young women's love lives as ordinarily bypassing any real experience of love: "After marriage they discarded romantic fancies and stagnated in mild discontent. But I had only one foot firmly planted on solid respectability; the other was sliding round on romance. You recognize this situation as what we now name 'a conflict of desires'" (in Showalter 42–43). And as Beatrice Hinkle claims of the essays as a whole at the time, "behind their stridency and revolt lies the great meaning of woman's struggle with convention and inertia" (in Showalter 141). The struggle with love as a struggle for self-realization is certainly represented here as having been newly sexualized, but one of the key conventions of modern love is this claim to be both new and controversial because of the way it understands the relation between sex and love.

Another return to Freud will be salutary at this point. Freud remonstrates with Dora over her insistence that she did not love or want the man he says she did: "It is true that two years ago you were very young. But you told me yourself that your mother was engaged at seventeen and then waited two years for her husband. A daughter usually takes her mother's love-story as her model. So you too wanted to wait for him, and you took it that he was only waiting till you were grown up enough to be his wife. I imagine that was a perfectly serious plan for the future in your eyes" ([1904] 1953b: 149). The explicit (if unconscious) sexual component of Dora's story and its management by someone more expert than she combine to make it exemplarily modernist. Whether Dora imagines the kisses offered to her remains unclear, but her analysis equates sex, fantasy, and love. Freud even fantasizes Dora's desire for him under the label of transference: "I came to the conclusion that the idea had probably occurred to her one day during a session that she would like to have a kiss from me" (110). His footnotes finally claim the "cure" of neurosis to be precisely this incitement and redirection of love: "Transference, which seems ordained to be the greatest obstacle to psychoanalysis, becomes its most powerful ally, if its presence can be detected each time and explained to the patient" (159).

Although in Freud's discussion of perversion, most notably his paper on homosexuality in women, it is possible to see the impact of ideas about modern women and modern love, in general Freud's later writing on feminine sexuality—including "Female Sexuality" (1931) and "Femininity" (1933)—does not address the changes in "normal" women's behavior over these decades, except indirectly in the mention of women in his audience. This is nevertheless still a discourse on modern love as a site of expert management and its claim to be new is invested there. In this I would argue that the endlessly-under-debate idea of "modern love" is not only a product of modernism but another name for modernist discourse on love. From this distinction between "modern" and "modernist" we can take a useful distinction into part 2 of this book: while all elements of modernity are "modern," only those constituting a critical attitude to modernity are "modernist."

Freud's appeal across public and popular culture rests largely on a new expectation that modern subjects will analyze themselves and their place in the world. It matters, then, that we can see direct and indirect references to Freud in *Good Housekeeping*, in popular fiction and films, and in debates around public policy. I have not yet discussed sex education as it is usually understood—the institutionalized policy-driven dissemination of information about sexual reproduction, health, and (often) sexual practices to adolescents—but those women in Freud's audience are part of the same discursive terrain. While the modernity of sex education is evident in its dependence on modern adolescence and a modern image of sex as a matter for public management, such new moral education extended beyond specific pedagogical claims insofar as the times demanded more "complete" (meaning the most contemporary) knowledge about sex and love, not only for the young but for those wanting to be up to date. Up-to-date ideas about love became a characteristic used to decry the state of the world but also to bemoan its inevitability or to fervently try to inhabit or glorify it.

With reference to Modernism, the phrase "new morality" especially conjures another, "the jazz age," and both phrases are linked to the celebrity author F. Scott Fitzgerald. In his first novel, *This Side of Paradise* (1920), Fitzgerald was seen as providing a template for the new morality. His protagonist, privileged Princeton student Amory Blaine, is a "romantic egotist" typifying a generation with no gods, no causes, and no direction except, as Amory's name suggests, love. Love is the one aim Amory deems worth having, but that love cannot function or be understood as it has in the past. Amory's "attempts to find new words for love" (Fitzgerald 59) end in Fitzgerald's typical reflection on "what now?"—a question tellingly posed as Amory's dialogue with himself about his own and the world's morality (194ff).[3] Across Fitzgerald's fiction, the newness of this morality is consistently tied to the transience of modern life. But this "age" was not merely characterized by a *carpe diem* attitude with more cars; it was also a narrative about changing social structures, including new economies and mobilities that shifted the currency and value of sex and love.

One of the most valuable figures in the economy of modern love is the ingénue, whose development and negotiation of knowledge about sex and love is represented between the lines of Amory's self-interrogation as an exchange of innocent warmth for sophisticated coldness (Fitzgerald 195). The ingénue's conjunction of naiveté and knowledge, of innocence and experience, can be traced through such modernist iterations as Gustave Flaubert's Emma Bovary, and Lewis Carroll's Alice; the trials of *Ulysses*, *Lady Chatterley*, and *Lolita* (1955); and in ongoing publications like *Playboy* (1953–). In figure 5, the movie star Clara Bow represents the ideal type of the ingénue. On film, the ingénue became a particularly refined convention, developing a counterpart in the vamp-come–femme fatale for whom naiveté had been entirely displaced by experience. Figure 5 shows Bow at the height of her brief career: in 1927, the year she made both *Wings*, directed by William Wellman and awarded Best Picture, and the film that signally defined her, Clarence Badger's *It*. From 1922 to 1929, Bow ascended to what we would even now recognize as superstardom as the queen of the "flapper" movie. Many conventions of this genre circulate in similar ways through the later "teen film" genre, routinely hailed and condemned as a sign of the times and yet sometimes positioned as pedagogically necessary. In a 1927 article in *Photoplay* describing the meeting of Senior Judge Ben Lindsay and fellow flapper-star Colleen Moore, Lindsay comments: "if it is opening the subject to all women, [the flapper movie] may look wrong now, but it is to prove an eventual advantage" by introducing women to "the Art of Love" and "the sex question."

The front-page spectacles of movie stars like Bow and sex-centric popular fiction—marketed toward young women then by writers like Elinor Glyn, who coined the term "It" as a euphemism for sex appeal and wrote the novel on which the film was based, and now by writers like Candace Bushnell—

repeatedly represent as new or changing both normative and transgressive ideas about love. While the plot of *It*, which turns on rumors that the heroine has a bastard child, does indicate tensions surrounding new codes for the behavior of young women, "It" nevertheless signified potential for love. This potential for love could, of course, be expressed by the proper performance of "sexuality" and the romance and sex narratives of *It* regulate one another: pure sex would be no more satisfyingly "modern" than pure love. It is not ironic that the same is true of *Lady Chatterley*; rather, both texts belong to the same sexual narrative about modern love. Body, self, sex, and romance are drawn together under the single sign of modern love.[4] Miriam Hansen's claim that Glyn's novels rendered "the erotic a matter of social etiquette to be rehearsed by the aspiring female subject" (Hansen 1991b: 275) tellingly makes Bow's sexy rebelliousness another imitation of a standardized behavioral commodity. This is how "It" becomes less a challenge to prevailing morality than the sign of an already extant "new" morality. *It*'s discourse on morality's popular frontier is less transgressive than it claims to be because while modern love offers an escape, it is from something it construes as already passing.

In this narrative about modern love, Bow was a star and a scandal, setting boundaries for the mass-cultural depiction of both. Despite the sophistication central to the figure of the ingénue, Bow was distinguished, according to critics and supporters, by "vivacity" and other "natural" qualities, rather than talent. Modernist poet and critic Bryher wrote, in 1928: "Clara Bow is excellent, when allowed to be herself. Unhappily she is usually spoiled half way through the film by having to pretend to be what she emphatically isn't. Dorothy Arzner should direct her. A film that brought out only her 'tough' amoral liveliness and cut out the beaded dresses and the sentiment would be a joy to watch" (Bryher 45). The next year Arzner did direct Bow, but more "amoral liveliness" was not what her celebrity persona needed. Troubled by images of her weight and behavior, Bow's public image in 1929 and 1930 exemplifies a now more pervasive game of celebrity limits. In her offscreen image as much as her onscreen roles, Bow plays out the imperatives of popular genre, both succeeding and failing by the tightness of generic convention. As flapper ingénue, Bow exemplified a self-regarding love that was sometimes applauded, often decried, and endlessly repeated around and after her. With little alteration, figure 5 could appear in a contemporary girls' magazine because her image of self-regarding love as a difficult form of self-management, as much as the ambiguities she invoked around age, gender, and sexual activity, are still central to girl culture. And the same disposition is still decried as narcissistic as often as it is praised for producing girls as ideal objects for themselves or others.

A range of earlier texts prefigure this self-regarding dimension of modern love, always hinting at its banal uniformity. Catherine Morland in Jane Austen's *Northanger Abbey* (1818) also has a modernist attitude to love because her fascination with it is gripped, empowered, and constrained by both the "mass" fantasies of circulating Gothic novels and disapproval of them. Such ambivalently commodified love fitted neatly into discourses on women's education and women's self-regard at the time. A century later, drenched in the advice and sentiment of women's magazines and popular fiction, Gerty in *Ulysses* offers a starkly different take on the same empowering standardization, again accompanied by its dismissal. Gerty "would try to understand" her man "because men are so different" (668–69), but the popular guidance manuals around and after her represent this rehearsal of modern love as both a form and a problem of self-development.

Modern love understood in this way is easily dismissed as a mass-disseminated reiteration as opposed to a real feeling (as critics as different as Nietzsche and Simone de Beauvoir would suggest). Mary Moxcey complains, in 1916, that "Current magazine fiction is responsible for the selfish and sordid view of love which is held by so many girls" (208) and the Lynds' first *Middletown* study also dismisses the thrills of sex and love disseminated by mass culture: "[F]our leading motion picture houses were featuring synchronously four sex adventure films, *Telling Tales* on the Middletown newsstands was featuring on its cover four stories, 'Indolent Kiss,' 'Primitive Love,' 'Watch Your Step-Ins. . .,' and 'Innocents Astray.' The way Middletown absorbs this culture about (to quote the advertisement of a local film) 'things you've always wanted to do and never DARED' was suggested by the coverless, thumb-marked condition of the January 1925 *Motion Picture Magazine* in the Public Library a fortnight after its arrival" (Lynd and Lynd 242). However, more high-minded discourses on modern love were also available.

Men in Love (Or, Sex Education)

Modern love remained tied not only to the centrality of emotion in Romanticism—alongside which it emerged and for and against which modernists rallied—but also to the disciplined management of relationships in political,

philosophical, and psychological terms. Interested authorities such as Theodor Adorno and D. H. Lawrence argue that, while works of "art" are ascetic
and unashamed, the "culture industry" is pornographic and prudish, down-
grading love not to sex but to romance because "The mass production of
the sexual automatically achieves its repression" (Adorno and Horkheimer
139–40). Such dismissal of romance is as old as its mass distribution, but so
is its defense, usually in terms of realism, as I have already suggested, or as
a form of moral education.

If the simultaneous abandonment and intensification of self among
"women in love" pervades accounts of modern love, the same seems true
for men within a starkly differentiated public frame. This can be seen in, for
example, both Nietzsche and Lawrence. Seeing the value of egoistic love, Nietzsche refuses its construal as "romance." But Lawrence's novels and essays
go further, and the most modernist element of the dilemma he repeatedly
represents is its reference to a conflicting set of educational agendas around
love. *Lady Chatterley* describes modernist love as inseparably promiscu-
ous and intellectualizing: "Love's another of those half-witted performances
today. Fellows with swaying waists fucking little jazz girls with small boy
buttocks. . . . Or the joint-property, make-a-success-of-it, my-husband-my-
wife sort of love" ([1928] 1960: 42). *Lady Chatterley* perhaps paradigmatically emphasizes the way modernist discourse on modern love was always
accompanied by equally modernist opposition to it. But Dorothy Sayers
provides a more popular articulation of the same sentiment, again voiced
by someone opposed to such "progress" in love: "In my day," the Duchess of
Medway tells Lord Peter Wimsey in the story "The Entertaining Episode of
the Article in Question," "one had to have either brains or beauty to get on—
preferably both. Nowadays nothing seems to be required but an absence of
figure" (Sayers 30).[5]

The texts, events, and debates I've discussed in this chapter all betray an
investment in the education and management of love lives, no matter how
they frame the relation between romantic fulfillment and sexual comple-
mentariness. In comparison to the Darwinist and eugenicist movements
shaping some modernist theories of love, psychoanalysis approached love
as a form of radical individualism. Even Gilles Deleuze and Felix Guattari, dedicated opponents of the psychoanalytic model of the subject that is
predicated on a lack that desire must try to fill, acknowledge, "psychoanalysis demonstrated that desire is not subordinated to procreation, or even
to genitality. That was its modernism" (Deleuze and Guattari 154–55). For

psychoanalysis, desire is an everyday presence. At the same time, a conflict-ridden relation with social norms allows the categories of love and desire to remain entangled in Freud and be no more clearly distinguished in Jacques Lacan and his followers.

For psychoanalysis, girls' sexual, romantic, and identity development was both very difficult and inherently tied to narcissism (Freud [1914] 1953d). The "more fortunate" boy does not escape the difficult negotiation between self-love and object-love, but he "has only to continue at the time of his sexual maturity the activity that he has previously carried out at the period of the early efflorescence of his sexuality" (Freud [1933] 1953a: 138). The same body retains the same masturbation, the same sexual object, and a continuous if continually divided subjectivity. While the sexual development of boys was thus construed as more natural, it was nevertheless the object of surveillance and education. Foucault traces the eighteenth-century emergence of the schoolboy as a public problem about sex: "Around the schoolboy and his sex there proliferated a whole literature of precepts, opinions, observations, medical advice, clinical cases, outlines for reform, and plans for ideal institutions" ([1976] 1984a: 28). Foucault sees this as not merely observing the sex of boys, but bringing into being as a definite object, complete with boys' own active participation as agents of this discourse through studious and serious comprehension of it (29). The "social hygiene" movements of the nineteenth century equally exemplify the interplay of disciplinary expertise and bio-power traced by Foucault. The more "unruly" characteristics associated with masculine sexuality, such as "uncontrollable" erections, are still often pressed into the category of "physiological" characteristics, drawing on this same language of social hygiene to define concessions for more diverse sexual practices among boys but, at the same time, strictures on the public responsibility of their sexual activity. This does not, in fact, mean that "love" is not an issue for boys within the field of modernist sex education. In the range of movements that make up this field, the institutionalization of psychiatry was intersected with and impelled by biology, economics, and politics to attempt to direct the problem of sex as equally manifest in body, mind, and soul. And in the interests of all three the doctrine of social hygiene, just as clearly as that of romantic love, distinguished sex from love and yet represented these concepts as inseparable.

Carl Jung provides an influential example of the "universal sex-relation" and the "eternal complementarity" of the heterosexual couple trained, on either side of a stark gender divide, to both distinguish and equate sex and love for their own and the public good. In "The Love Problem of a Student" (1928), Jung outlines a crisis in modern heterosexual relationships, which sex education is meant to address. For many adult men, he writes,

> the period of psychological puberty is not yet over. Puberty is a period of illusion and only partial responsibility. . . . Into this childishness sexuality often breaks with brutal force, while, despite the onset of puberty, it often goes on slumbering in a girl until the passion of love awakens it. . . . That is the reason why very many women have no understanding at all of masculine sexuality—they are completely unconscious of their own. With man it is different. Sexuality bursts on them like a tempest, filling them with brute desires and needs, and there is scarcely one of them who escapes the painful problems of masturbation. (Jung 32)

Modernism refines the expected difference between what men and women mean by love so that the model of complementarity proposed by writers as different as Jean-Jacques Rousseau and Nietzsche also addresses a question of regulation. Modern love presumes the necessity of love to the health of all subjects, the institution of healthy love as a matter of public concern, the conversion of attitudes to and styles of love into ways of being, and finally the routinization of love as both leisure and as mental and physical exercise. Such discourse persistently continues in genres like the "self help" guidance manual. And it is as a precursor to this discipline that Rousseau's training for Émile not only included the right attitudes to and practices of sex, but also love. In such Enlightenment narratives we can see the emergence of modernist expertise addressed to an equally modernist consciousness of the "love problem."

Modernist discourse on love is a site of contestation—even Rousseau saw his model for Émile's education in love as controversial. I turn again to Lawrence's fiction for a further example of such contestation over men in love. While Pound found in Lawrence a "loaded ornate style, heavy with sex, fruity with a certain sort of emotion" (in Bowlby 1993: 31), Lawrence understood his style, and his model of love, as stark and real. He represented his ideal love as a "manly love," aligned with Walt Whitman and stressing the "real implicit reliance of one man on another" (Lawrence [1920] 1989: 105). Lawrence's men are endlessly absorbed in being troubled about love, from Paul Morel's indecisive dissatisfaction in Sons and Lovers (1913) to Oliver Mellors' determined commitment to an image of love in which men could again dance in red stockings for their women. In between, there is the sequence of *The Rainbow* and *Women in Love* (1920), which are both, more than anything else, novels about what men do and do not want from love.

The philosophical, theoretical, aesthetic, and political perspectives on love debated by Rupert Birkin and Gerald Crich in these two novels range from the semi-mystical "phallic cult," through aesthetic and personal endorsements of absolute sensuality, to tentative abstractions about spiritual love between men and its apparently logical consequence, naked wrestling by firelight. Across these discussions, while popular culture is a powerful distraction from real thought about love, the public sphere is a crucial site for it. Rupert and Gerald want to know what kind of love is the right love for Man, not just for them. They debate a newspaper columnist's vision of the "rise of a new man who will give new values to things, give us new truths, a new attitude to life" (Lawrence [1920] 1989: 439–40). Although it isn't clear that this public sphere reflects the needs of men any more clearly than the popular, it is understood to raise the questions in the right terms—in terms of the self-regarding sex relation and for the good of mankind. Rupert insists that nature allows and indeed requires the love of men for men, sometimes clearly in addition to and sometimes instead of marriage. Gerald is far less certain. Across it all, Lawrence's narrative style is both contemplatively romantic and didactic at once, and for modernist discourse on love this is no contradiction.

The proliferation of popular culture during the Modernist period is now often discussed in modernist studies, even if it often appears as not much more than background color for studies of canonical texts. But the significance of the expanding public sphere at this time has been less discussed, partly because the term itself did not have wide currency for the field until the 1989 English translation of Jürgen Habermas' *The Structural Transformation of the Public Sphere* (1962), and partly because Habermas generally positions Modernism as having failed rather than extended the public sphere. A range of scholars have taken on the challenge of considering how a public sphere equated with the Enlightenment might survive the challenges posed by changing modes of governmentality, media, and communication. But if modernity provided the necessary conditions for the emergence of the public sphere—the public use of reason in matters of public concern—the idea itself is a critically reflexive modernist one. It seems paradoxical, then, that Modernism is used to represent a point at which the public sphere began to seem unattainable if not obsolete. Habermas sees this aspect of Modernism as the negative consequence of specialization, in ways I will discuss further in chapter 8. Both experts and the public are seen to have failed the public sphere in this way: "The sounding board of an educated stratum tutored in the public use of reason has been shattered; the public is split apart into minorities of specialists who put their reason to use nonpublicly and the great mass of consumers whose receptiveness is public but uncritical" (Habermas [1962] 1989: 175). In fact, "the public sphere," like many other modernist utopias, is a narrative about loss as much as revolutionary promise—an as yet unfulfilled potential, a threatened ideal, and a thing of the past.

The kinds of contention I have been tracing around "modern love" in this chapter do map "a domain of our social life where such a thing as public opinion can be formed"—precisely what Habermas wants from the public sphere. But at the same time, as the censorship trials clearly demonstrate but perhaps the decline of Clara Bow does as well, this is not a domain where opinion forms "without being subject to coercion" (Habermas [1962] 1989: 231). There are clear limits on various capacities to express and publicize one's views formed by industrial systems, like the studios, or by forms of "capital" (see Bourdieu [1979] 1986), like the idea of Literature, as much as by legal statutes. By the Modernist period, what resembles the public sphere is clearly too fragmented and multiple to conform to the Habermasian ideal. Nancy Fraser's critique of Habermas (1992) suggests that a model of the public sphere that encompasses such multiplicity is possible, but the modernist public sphere differs from Fraser's model too in being internally differentiated not only by interests and thus voices, but also by genre, audience, and popularity. In short, it is too hard to untangle from popular culture. While "public sphere" is not a key concept for modernist studies as a self-identified discipline, it is so for many versions of Cultural Studies. One of the things Cultural Studies can contribute to thinking about modernism is critical thought about popular culture, the public sphere, and more generally attention to the ways in which discourses and cultural forms are produced and disseminated. Both modernism and Modernism emerge from a particular conjunction of the public and the popular in which the venues and forms for addressing public good continue to diversify. This cannot be restricted to Modernist icons of intelligent dialogue, like "little magazines" and artistic salons, but is equally manifest in transformed relations between the state and everyday life, of which education on sex and love is exemplary.

In closing this chapter I want to return this question of the modernist "public" to the example of censorship with which I began. The British specification of obscenity in 1857 targeted "works written for the single purpose of corrupting the morals of youth, and of a nature calculated to shock the common feelings of decency in any well-regulated mind"; it was amended in 1868 to address questions of access and to stress the danger of any tendency to "corrupt those whose minds are open to such immoral influences and into whose hands a publication of this sort may fall" (in Bowlby 1993: 31). This reflects the modernist diversification of cultural markets, as is made clearer by the 1959 legislation, which acknowledged the diversity of cultural forms that might be obscene and of cultural consumers who might be corrupted. Now shaped by the institutionalization of Modernism, which allowed a place for art as responsible observer of obscenity, the public and popular efficacies of literature included the expert comprehension of modern love. While in the context of Shaw's extolling the virtue of *Lady Chatterley* it was a radical text on love and sex, in the context of the 1960 trial it was an artistic ideal: "a potential antidote" to the prevailing "shallow and corrupting values with regard to sex and the relationship between the sexes" (Bowlby 1993: 33).

The very idea of "progressive" sexual images or movements is intrinsically modernist: from William Blake's "madness," through the pro- and anti-feminist "free love" movements of the nineteenth century, to the more widely debated sexual freedoms of the jazz age and the later "sexual revolution." The structures by which adjudications such as "progressive" take place simultaneously in popular and public fields expand with modernity. The modernist negotiation of modern love demonstrates the complexity, the multivalency, of such processes. "Free love" is a case in point. It was both radical and assiduously romantic, bound into modernism's endless renegotiation of what individualism, self-consciousness, and freedom mean. Shaw, on the one hand, claimed "free love" undermined and trivialized socialism and did not serve the interests of women (Griffith 170), while some feminists argued "free love" aimed to "abolish marriage, establish free union in which each sex would have an equal voice, and make love the only law regulating the relationship of the sexes" (Dennehy 100). While Wilhelm Reich, for example, believed that "Sexually awakened women, affirmed and recognized as such, would mean the complete collapse of the authoritarian ideology" ([1942] 1978: 138), popular guidance manuals might insist to a very different audience that "Many young girls of the 'flapper' type, in particular, are victims of these conditions of unrestrained sex education" (Stanton 40). Such debates over how the management of sex and love work to discipline and produce selves and practices with an appropriate measure of freedom are explicit in the trial with which I will conclude—that of Vladimir Nabokov's *Lolita*.

The censorship debates around *Lolita* demonstrate the extension of modernist discourse on love as a form of bio-power into the present (with controversial film adaptations in 1962 and 1997). While its U.S. publication was cautiously arranged, *Lolita* was never found obscene despite its controversial content. The book appeared in a context in which no obscenity charge could have done more to deploy the idea of modern love as a mode of self-management than the book did itself. The prologue tells us that "'Lolita' should make all of us—parents, social workers, educators—apply ourselves with still greater vigilance and vision to the task of bringing up a better generation in a safer world" (Nabokov 7). In the context of institutionalized adolescence, the sexual dimensions of modern identity as the grounds for any possible love were no longer a matter of debate. The simultaneously normal and transgressive realm of sex and love belonged to the sphere of knowledge of all "reasonable men," including pedophiles, as long as they were properly managed.

Humbert Humbert's narration, as well as a range of agencies and institutions, manage and categorize his love for Lolita amid various mechanisms for training selves in relation to love. Humbert's account of his own sex life, crafted to seduce Lolita's mother Charlotte, is comprised of the "soap-operas, psycho-analysis and cheap novelettes" (85) that will let his story match hers. Bowlby's reading of *Lolita* aligns this tactic with the triumph of adolescence discussed in chapter 2 as well as the triumph of commodity culture to be discussed in the next chapter. Clearing his car of signs of Lolita, Humbert throws out her magazines: "You know the sort. Stone age at heart; up to date, or at least Mycenaean, as to hygiene. A handsome, very ripe actress with huge eyelashes and a pulpy red underlip, endorsing a shampoo. Ads and fads. . . . Invite Romance by wearing the exciting New Tummy Flattener. Trims tums, nips hips. Tristram in Movielove. Yessir! The Joe-Roe marital enigma is making yaps flap" (367–68; see also Bowlby 1993). This popular culture embraces a regime for the management of sex as love and, however different it might seem, is thus continuous with public-sphere narratives refracted through schools and courts and diagnoses. We can also see here the effects of that institutionalization of Modernism that was in process in the other trials. *Lolita* was prepared for the popular and public spheres by rallying behind it not merely famous authors and cultural critics, but also the certainty that art had a crucial role to play in explicating both modern love and its various misuses.

2

REFASHIONING MODERNISM

4

The Life of a Shopgirl

Art and the Everyday

*As one reads the captions beneath the style photos, the columns of beauty
advice and the articles on the co-ordination of wardrobes and furnishings, one
senses that those who bought these things were not varied as to age, marital
status, ethnicity or any other characteristics. Out there, working as a clerk in a
store and living in an apartment with a friend, was one girl—single, nineteen
years old, Anglo-Saxon, somewhat favouring Janet Gaynor. The thousands of
Hollywood-associated designers, publicity men, sales heads, beauty consultants
and merchandisers had internalised her so long ago that her psychic life had
become their psychic life. They empathised with her shyness, her social awkwardness, her fear of offending. They understood her slight weight problem and
her chagrin at being a trifle too tall. They could tell you what sort of man she
hoped to marry and how she spent her leisure time.*

Charles Eckert, "The Carole Lombard in Macy's Window"

Consuming Every Day

The shopgirl is one of those "types" that Walter Benjamin describes as the
only way people can appear in the marketplace (Benjamin [1927–40] 2002:
14). She appears amid the new and proliferating significance to modernity
of mass consumption and increasing urbanization. In the context of her
urbanity several other key characteristics of the shopgirl demand attention
here—she is both a worker and a consumer; she is emphatically ordinary;
and she is a girl. In *The Gender of Modernity* (1995), Rita Felski discusses a
set of types by which modernism has explored the importance of gender to
modernity—focusing on the hysteric (including the hysterical suffragette),

the "voracious consumer," the prostitute, the feminized aesthete, and the sexual pervert. She aims in this text "to establish points of connection between the texts of the past and the feminist politics of the present" (Felski 1995: 33), and the shopgirl is a particularly telling figure for such a discussion. This chapter will position the shopgirl at an intersection of all the types Felski identifies as representing the complex relation between women and modernity, but it does so with the aim of highlighting another concept that underpins them.

In "The Invention of Everyday Life," Felski notes that gender has also traditionally assumed an important role in conceptualizing the everyday. Indeed, many social theorists, including Henri Lefebvre, have regarded women as both the "quintessential representatives and victims of the quotidian" (Felski 2000: 17). Lefebvre claims women "are the subject of everyday life and its victims or objects and substitutes (beauty, femininity, fashion, etc). . . . Likewise they are both buyers and consumers of commodities and symbols of commodities (in advertising, as nudes and smiles)" ([1971] 2005: 73). This association depends in turn on the association between women and the domestic sphere to negatively define "women" and "femininity" by opposition to the public, the citizen-subject, the producer, and the artist. The shopgirl provides a new instance of nonspecialized labor that is both not domestic and yet not opposed to the domestic.

As Felski also notes, the everyday "is one of the most self-evident, yet most puzzling of ideas" (2000: 15); it is something in which everyone actively participates, and yet it evades precise definition. Philip Wander, introducing Lefebvre's *Everyday Life in the Modern World* (1971), determines that everyday life refers to "dull routine," "the trudge of daily existence" and what we "know simply as the grey reality enveloping all we do" (in Lefebvre [1971] 2005: vii-viii). As Lefebvre himself acknowledges, "there is a certain obscurity in the very concept of everyday life": "Where is it to be found? In work or in leisure? In family life and in moments 'lived' outside of culture?" ([1961] 1991: 31). The now established emphases of Cultural Studies would insist that the everyday is firmly *within* culture, but this insistence also depends on a changed conception of culture that modernism itself produced (see chapter 8). While an interest in the mundane activities of life did not suddenly materialize in modernity, Lefebvre links the concept of everydayness to the way capitalism and industrialization transformed the perception and experience of life in the nineteenth century. As more and more people were amassed together in big cities, the repetitive elements of life became more noticeable and the diversity of visibly specialized activities increased.

We can see this emphasis on the everyday in nineteenth-century sociology, such as Thorstein Veblen's *Theory of the Leisure Class* (1899). Veblen is concerned with the whole of modern life, including the everyday, insofar as it is ordered by economic relations. Although routine activities such as sleeping, eating, dressing, cleaning, and so on are easily classified as everyday, the multiplicity of locations for such activities, and the difficulty of clearly distinguishing between them and activities required by work or other specialized roles, blur the boundaries by which we define the everyday. Veblen acknowledges that the everyday has always connoted something inferior, but argues that, whatever its tenacity in people's perceptions, social hierarchies based on "occupation" were made redundant by the "modern industrial community." Veblen also links this change to new models of "leisure," which made leisure less a measure of "a worthy or beautiful, or even a blameless, human life" (Veblen 22) because it was now more finely differentiated along a scale of "pecuniary" worth. How one articulates pecuniary worth in everyday life became a crucial social factor. And thus Veblen stresses that the everyday is not what is necessary, such as the mere facts of eating or food. Instead it is striated by statements about and measures of social position.

Cultural Studies' presumption that it approaches culture through the "ordinary" elements of contemporary life has been integral to its differentiation from other disciplines. Practitioners of Cultural Studies generally agree on both the importance of the everyday as a category and what it should comprise. Remembering earlier precursors for such attention matters not only for historicizing the discipline and its relation to other disciplines like sociology. It matters also for understanding what is meant by "everyday" in contemporary cultural analysis. Veblen attends to the social meanings of such everyday activities as maintaining lawns (Veblen 74) and fighting between children (139ff). But Veblen's key contribution to understanding the everyday is his simultaneously philosophical and economic account of everyday life as a field of consumption.

Histories of consumption frequently focus on either its origins in Victorian "consumer society" or its transformation and new dominance after World War II. While both shifts are vital to an understanding of modern commodity culture, a longer modernist frame that brings these shifts together emphasizes that the emergence of the commodity is necessarily accompanied by a theorization of industrial, capital, and consumer practices. Despite Michel Foucault's recognition that Marx was a "fish" of the nineteenth century (Foucault [1966] 1973: 262), the appropriation of Marx's ideas and their broad application to not only social but also individual development in work such as Veblen's, George Simmel's, or Walter Benjamin's brought Marx to the forefront of cultural analysis. Capitalism requires the circulation of products among consuming subjects, and consumption is valorized in modernity through construction of these consuming bodies as "individuals." The alienation of subjects from their labor, which Marx claims commodities enabled (Marx [1867] 1990: 163–280), was explored in diverse ways by social theorists interested in the transformation of workers into "hands." These hands—consuming as much as working—were ready to be subject to the assembly line of Henry Ford, the "scientific management" of efficiency expert Frederick Taylor (founder of "Taylorism"), or the marketing science of Eckert's Hollywood associates.

Just as the mass production of goods required a regulated labor force, it also required both an additional transformation of the daily practices of the general populace and, according to Stuart Ewen, the "nullification" of the "customs of ages" to "break down the barriers of individual habits" (19). Ewen suggests that social changes including shorter working days and higher wages accompanied the rise of commodity capitalism in acknowledgment of the fact that, as the Modernist macroeconomic theory of Milton Keynes also insisted, "time out for mass consumption [was] as much a necessity as time in for production" (Ewen 30). At the same time, consumers, like the commodities themselves, were represented as being de-individualized by their association with commodities. This is also how women become connected to commodities, being well placed by the new clarity of the "domestic sphere" to represent the alienation and objectification of the subject associated with commodities after Marx. The "conspicuous consumption" Veblen describes as a determining factor of modern social life was perfected in the nineteenth-century bourgeois wife's "vicarious consumption" (43ff) on behalf of her husband's labor and status. And yet the commodity culture to which Veblen's analysis points positions the consumer as a crucial social actor and indeed as producing "self" rather than "status" in a manner that is not at all vicarious.

Despite its apparent opposition to any specialized activities, the everyday became synonymous with commodities and thus with the inauthentic and alienated, a product not only of the processes of the labor market but of the homogenization of everyday lives. In 1933, F. R. Leavis and Denys Thompson argued that "mass-production has turned out to involve standardization and leveling-down outside the realm of mere material goods" (3), suggesting a concomitant devaluation of the subject that clearly overlaps with Theodor Adorno and Max Horkheimer's work some years later.[1] Leavis and Thompson oppose contemporary alienation to a nostalgic vision of England as "organic community" (87ff), which they believe can be reinvigorated through certain forms of avant-gardism. D. H. Lawrence is one of their examples, and they cite Connie's horror at the ugliness of consumer culture and other signs of the decay of England in *Lady Chatterley's Lover*. This new England, Connie feels, blots out the old, "And the continuity is not organic, but mechanical" (Lawrence 1960b: 158; Leavis and Thompson 94–95).

Now solidly located in the canon of Cultural Studies, the concept of the everyday is usually discussed using more recent reference points. But the well-known accounts of everyday life by Michel de Certeau and Lefebvre draw on this existing international field of modernist theory. For Certeau, the everyday is the "cultural activity of the non-producers of culture, an activity that is unsigned, unreadable and unsymbolized" ([1984] 1998: xviii) and thus opposed above anything else to *cultural analysis* as "the place from which one deals with culture" (1997: 123). Lefebvre defines everyday life as life lived in constant negotiation between "repression and evasion; compulsion and adaptation" ([1971] 2005: 146). This puts forward a paradox crucial to the modernist conception of, and struggle with, the everyday. Talking about or reflecting on the everyday is, it seems, not everyday. Marcel Duchamp's "readymades," separated from most of their everyday uses once they are nailed to the floor or suspended from the ceiling or placed on a plinth, exemplify the definition and containment of the everyday through critical examination. Precisely this critical process demands that the *idea* of everydayness transcend the ordinary that it denotes and therefore cease to be everyday. But some modernists, such as Friedrich Nietzsche, attacked what they regarded as everyday life's nonintellectual relationship with the world while others, like Charles Baudelaire, speculated that a critical attitude permeated the everyday of late modernity, if not in the same way for everybody. And this continues to be a crucial point of contention in Cultural Studies (see Morris 1990; chapter 9).

In his essay on Enlightenment to which I have been returning, Foucault identifies in Baudelaire "the will to 'heroize' the present" ([1978] 1984b: 40). Foucault cites Baudelaire's insistence that "The attitude of modernity does not treat the passing moment as sacred in order to try to maintain" or exoticize it. That, rather, is the posture of the flâneur, Baudelaire's "idle, strolling spectator . . . satisfied to keep his eyes open, to pay attention and to build up a storehouse of memories." Instead, the "man of modernity," "gifted with an active imagination, ceaselessly journeying across the great human desert—has an aim loftier than that of a mere flâneur, an aim more general, something other than the fugitive pleasure of circumstance. He is looking for that quality which you must allow me to call 'modernity'" (Baudelaire quoted in Foucault [1978] 1984b: 40). Baudelaire's flâneur has generally been held up as an icon of the everyday because of this evasion of specialization. The section (or convolute) on the flâneur in Benjamin's *The Arcades Project* (1927–40) presents an assemblage of ideas about and associations with the flâneur, from Baudelaire to Benjamin's contemporaries.[2] According to Benjamin, while the flâneur maintains individuality ([1927–40] 2002: 429) he is nevertheless led by accident: an "idle passerby" rather than the *promeneur* who is represented as "meandering capriciously" (Baudelaire quoted in Benjamin [1927–40] 2002: 442). In both Baudelaire and Benjamin, the flâneur is compared to Edgar Allen Poe's "Man of the Crowd," the subject of a general observation that can lead to impassioned (fatal) curiosity. In "The Painter of Modern Life," Baudelaire moreover suggests that the flâneur might be likened "to a mirror as vast as the crowd itself; or to a kaleidoscope endowed with consciousness, which, with each of its movements, represents the multiplicity of life and the flickering grace of all the elements of life" (Baudelaire 9–10; also quoted in Benjamin [1927–40] 2002: 443).

Found Objects

In "Work Avoidance: The Everyday Life of Marcel Duchamp's Readymades," Helen Molesworth argues that Duchamp's art was a direct challenge to the primacy of ideas about work that had materialized in the early stages of the twentieth century with the implementation of Taylorism. The rapid expansion of Taylorism and other forms of modern labor management, including new economic theories, made a range of mundane activities more visible and also reinterpreted their significance. Molesworth argues that Duchamp responded to an increasingly fragmented and regimented labor market by representing and reflecting on labor's identified counterpart, the realm of the everyday (Molesworth 61). She stresses that it is the blurring of temporal and spatial boundaries that constitutes the idea of the everyday in Duchamp's "readymades" (sometimes called "assemblages"), considering not only their physical sourcing in "everyday" objects but also their everyday life in his home and studio and the staging of the everyday in his strategies for exhibition. One example she focuses on is the installation *Sixteen Miles of String* (see figure 7), in which lines of string were stretched across and

Figure 7. Marcel Duchamp's *Sixteen Miles of String*, 1942, photograph by John D. Schiff. Photograph from Arensberg Archive, Duchamp, Marcel/photographed by Schiff, John D., "Installation of the exhibition F," Philadelphia Museum of Art: Marcel Duchamp Archives, Gift of Jacqueline, Peter, and Paul Matisse in memory of their mother, Alexina Duchamp, 1998.

around the expanse of a gallery. This installation both comments on spatial and temporal perspective and human movement and gestures toward the ordinariness of string among and as art. The vocabulary of Modernism was often fervently antidomestic, construing the home as "a space of familiarity, dullness and stasis," opposed in particular to the life of the city, a place of "unexpected events and a site of random encounters" (Felski 2000: 23). Despite the banality of string, Duchamp's installation is no exception, catching art gallery viewers in awareness of their own movements and gazes within what is explicitly gallery space.

Molesworth claims the readymades refuse distinctions between the everyday activities of work, home, and leisure. While this does not seem to me to recognize the ways works like *Sixteen Miles* are distinguished from all of these activities by virtue of being "art," her argument raises an interesting network of connections. Citing early twentieth-century home economist Christine Frederick's arguments for making domestic labor "modern, routinized and efficient," Molesworth compares the "factorization" processes recommended to better manage housework to the Taylorist approach to labor. She sees both, alongside the readymades, as "tapping into the modernist sensibilities of the time" and looking toward an ideal life "unhampered by traditions of the past" (Molesworth 54; see also Harvey 23). Many of Duchamp's everyday objects were everyday but not, in fact, domestic. *Bicycle Wheel* (1913) and *Fountain* (1917), for example, foreground public relations to or functions of the everyday and other works have more commercial than private associations. The everydayness of Duchamp's objects also represents modernity as never entirely private, even in its most banal manifestations.

In Friedrich Engels we can find an influential Marxist approach to the nexus of commodification, labor, urbanity, and banality that gives context to the readymades as surely as any history of surrealism: "however much one may be aware that this isolation of the individual, this narrow self-seeking, is the fundamental principle of our society everywhere, it is nowhere so shamelessly barefaced, so self-conscious, as just here in the crowding of the great city" (Engels 48; also quoted in Benjamin [1927–40] 2002: 428). By contrast, however, Simmel provides a more ambivalent account of urbanization than the analysis of massified hands brought together for the convenience of industry. Simmel echoes Baudelaire's discussion of the city as alienating but also invigorating—demanding active negotiation of relations between the individual and the masses. But if modernism is especially characterized by urbanization it matters that we have hardly stopped becoming urbanized and these discussions of what increasing urbanization means, and how the city is experienced every day, remain relevant to us.

One of the most cited accounts of everydayness in Cultural Studies is Certeau's essay on "Walking in the City," which focuses on the experience of the city for its ordinary practitioners, who "live 'down below,' below the thresholds at which visibility begins" ([1984] 1998: 93). Walking through the city weaves spaces together, he argues; it is a form of enunciation that can never be finally predicted or captured by strategic use of power: "If it is true that *forests of gestures* are manifest in the streets, their movement cannot be captured in a picture, nor can the meaning of their movements be circumscribed to a text. Their rhetorical transplantation carries away and displaces the analytical, coherent proper meanings of urbanism; it constitutes a 'wandering of the semantic' produced by masses that make some parts of the city disappear and exaggerate others, distorting it, fragmenting it, and diverting it from its immobile order" (102).

For Certeau, the practice of everyday life includes being tactically able to manipulate spatial "organisations, no matter how panoptic they may be:

it is neither foreign to them (it can take place only within them) nor in conformity with them (it does not receive its identity from them). It creates shadows and ambiguities within them. It inserts its multitudinous references and citations into them" (Certeau [1984] 1998: 101). Walking as "pedestrian" activity is thus something more than transit from one event or action to another. It is intentional and creative: the self's tactical orientation in a known system. The colloquial imagery of *Les Fleurs du Mal* and Baudelaire's focus on the artist's grasp of the city in "The Painter of Modern Life" are often cited as influencing Certeau, and for Certeau stressing a literary model for thinking everyday urban life has a special significance. But his thoughts about the "long poetry" of walking in the city are indebted not only to Baudelaire but also to Benjamin, who suggests a wider range of examples of modernist discourse on urban everydayness, from histories to journalism and advertising as well as works by Poe and Honoré de Balzac.

For Benjamin, the city offers up stories and signals, and "inconceivable analogies and connections between events are the order of the day" ([1929] 1996c: 74). And this poetry also resembles the filmic "symphonies" that pay homage to the city in the 1920s—films like Dziga Vertov's *Man With a Movie Camera*, Mikhail Kaufman's *Moscow* (1927), Walter Ruttman's *Berlin, Symphony of a Great City* (1927) and, differently, Jean Vigo's *A Propos de Nice* (1930). These films attempt to capture not only the everyday but also the meanings to be made from it in the context of the city. The genre's commitment to realism centers on the way the everyday, synonymous with habit and routine, is the background against which everything happens. If, as Lefebvre notes, the modern "stands for what is novel, brilliant, paradoxical," while "the quotidian is what is humble and solid, what is taken for granted . . . undated and apparently insignificant" ([1971] 2005: 45), these are, despite their opposition, mutually defining categories.

The relation between art and the everyday is generally discussed in terms of mimetic representation: the everyday proves that something materially real is being invoked. In both the emerging generic conventions of "realist" fiction and in Benjamin's history of the reproducibility of art as the reproducibility of life—where lithography displaces drawing and is then displaced by photography and later film—more meticulous and complete representation continues the progress narrative of the Enlightenment into modernist art. But the heightened sensitivity to ordinary detail characterizing modernist literature from the new realist novels of Émile Zola and George Eliot to the experiments of *The Waste Land* (1922) and *Mrs Dalloway* (1925) also pointedly transcends the ordinary, inattentive experience of most people's lives. Even where new psychological or phenomenological theories inspired a realism that was more self-consciously subjective, the everyday verified the reality of a representation rather than merely providing a more complete *mise-en-scène*.[3]

More complete representation does not seem to be the aim of surrealism and dada, which constitute the explicit context in which Duchamp's readymades appeared. The readymades defy the mise-en-scène version of realism by demanding a different perspective on one component of it. Thus they do not make everyday sense, as Breton insisted surrealism should not, but detach the object from its common meaning. It is consistent with this reflection, then, that the readymades are the most "reproducible" of Duchamp's work. It is impossible to entirely own *Fountain*, however good the provenance of the version you possess. And it is this confounding of what Benjamin called the "aura" of the work of art (see chapter 1), rather than the newspaper physically embedded in Picasso's *Guernica* (1937), that returns surrealist art most forcefully to the everyday. Benjamin's argument that "that which withers in the age of mechanical reproduction is the aura of the work of art" (1969: 221) positions the work of art as absolutely singular; not only rooted in a time and place but also definitively not everyday.

I want to pursue this connection in the work of two very different artists, chosen both for the feminist perspective Felski suggests is needed on the everyday and for the multi- or trans-generic perspective that Benjamin foregrounds as best capturing the everyday: Virginia Woolf and Rebecca West. Beyond substantial differences in style, taste, and reception, West and Woolf agree on some important conclusions regarding modernity and art. Their most famous critical works, West's "The Strange Necessity" and Woolf's *A Room of One's Own* (both 1928), are not only written at the same time by women from cultural positions more similar than they are distinct, but both are also essays on art in relation to everyday life. I quote them here as a way of approaching the confluence of modernist ideas on art and the everyday they reference. I am not looking to find a homogenous project that unites West and Woolf but to foreground a shared field of inquiry in their journalism, diaries, criticism, histories, theory, and fiction.

To begin with, West and Woolf share a number of key motifs, including the walking artist. In these essays West and Woolf might be seen to exemplify that elusive *flâneuse* that appears in the margins of Baudelaire's texts. Woolf scholars have discussed at length the role of walking in *A Room*, where walking is a means by which the narrator takes an idea and makes it "work in and out of daily life" (Woolf [1928] 1973: 1). This circumlocutionary style—rambling in the text and the narrative—is also identified in Woolf's novel *Mrs Dalloway*. There, as Rachel Bowlby suggests, walking is a means of producing both narrative and character. Bowlby focuses on one character's fantasies about a woman whom he follows. Her notes on this gendered story about the city are suggestive. While the character Peter Walsh's fantasy self is carefully distinguished from the "accoutrements of masculinity on display" in shop windows, the fantasy woman is "an extension of the fetishistically feminine bits and pieces visible as they pass" (Bowlby 1992: 34). While clearly not all walking is urban or for shopping, this entirely modern way of walking—through the corridors of commodification—recurs as a powerful theme from Baudelaire to Certeau to the present. In Australia, as I write this, an upmarket retail chain is running a series of ads in which a former Miss Universe walks the streets appreciating her own and other girls' wardrobes as "statements," with each look framed on screen by quotation marks. But even this image stresses the extent to which the ordinary is only "everyday" from a certain point of view.

Both West and Woolf use the walking woman's association with both commodity culture and everydayness to open a discourse on art and life. "The Strange Necessity" opens as follows: "I shut the bookshop door behind me and walked slowly down the street that leads from the Odeon to the Boulevard Saint-Germain in the best of all cities, reading in the little volume which had there been sold to me, not exactly pretentiously, indeed with a matter-of-fact briskness, yet with a sense of there being something on hand different from ordinary commercial transactions: as they sell pious whatnots in a cathedral porch" (1). While West soon abandons the narrator proceeding through his or her daily life for a more declarative mode, this opening section is crucial to the essay's argument about the way art is abstracted from the experience of the everyday, and a surprisingly similar argument can be found in Woolf. In her essay on Woolf and the everyday, Liesl Olsen stresses Woolf's distinction between "moments of being" and "moments of non-being," differentiating between what is reflective and what is everyday. Woolf claims that although we typically remember consciously important or unusual moments, it is moments not lived consciously and therefore not remembered that constitute the majority of our lives. These moments of "non-being," she suggests, play an important role in revealing character. Furthermore, moments of revelation ("moments of being") can occur during performance of the habitual, the mundane, or everyday tasks (Olsen 45) that in fact form the ground from which reflection proceeds.

While as the narrator in *A Room* walks she is met by obstacles, misdirection, confusion, and ellipses, West's narrator commands all she surveys. But what walking means in these essays can be better understood through other shared tropes, such as the shopgirl and the tree. The tree in both essays is a figure for art and the artist. Woolf compares the overwhelming "I" in modern novels to the shadow of a tree falling over the text "as hard as a nut, and polished for centuries by good teaching and good feeding." While this is an "I" she respects and admires, "in the shadow of the letter 'I' all is shapeless as mist" (100). The tree in "The Strange Necessity," however, is a model for how art should synthesize its components and is used to explain why James Joyce fails as an artist. Instead of synthesizing some position in *Ulysses*, West's narrator argues, Joyce is distracted by sentiment and reassured by his own radical inventiveness: "the sentimental artist is becoming nothing, he has ears, he has eyes, he is being intelligent, he is playing a game, he is moving certain objects according to certain rules in front of spectators. Those objects one may take as the isolated units of his material which he has passed through his imagination by an unfortunately discontinuous process" (West 1928: 6). In unsentimental art, West argues, there should be instead "no part which rebels against the whole" and just one tree-like theme that is "the logic of the book's being" (6).

In their chapter titled "Rhizomes," in *A Thousand Plateaus*, Gilles Deleuze and Felix Guattari use similar metaphors to discuss modern literary style, grouping some books as "trees," others as "fascicular" (bundles), and still others as "rhizomes." Contra West, they would cite both "becoming nothing" and "playing a game" as reasons for praising rhizomatic texts that begin in many places, move in many directions, and are not organized by a single order—a style I suggested in chapter 2 might characterize Joyce's *Finnegans Wake*. In agreement with West, however, they would use characteristics like having eyes and ears and being intelligent, and other kinds of unassailable organization and claims to authority, as reasons to criticize Joyce. They categorize his *Ulysses*, in particular, as fascicular in terms that suggest they might even agree that Joyce's process of binding fragmented things together in an orderly way is a kind of sentimentality. "Fascicular" texts, they argue, are not as revolutionary as they claim to be. Woolf, who is applauded as truly revolutionary by Deleuze and Guattari, also derides what West calls Joyce's "use of obscene words" (West 1928: 10) as only falsely radical. Woolf describes *Ulysses* as narrow and confined despite its genius, and her private notes further deride it as "diffuse," "brackish," "pretentious," and "underbred, not only in the obvious sense, but in the literary sense"—ill educated and immature, like a "queasy undergraduate scratching his pimples" (Woolf [1978] 1981: 188–89; see also Driscoll 2002b).

Comparing West and Woolf to Deleuze and Guattari via Joyce helps to make visible the ways in which both women writers want to draw out everyday observation from art, and yet see representing everydayness as a difficult trap. Both suspect Joyce of a false everydayness; a posturing banality. They disagree, however, on what would better represent life: for West it is a polished idealism (the tree), which Woolf less dogmatically thinks she may be rather tired of. West sees Joyce as failing to transcend the ordinary world, to lift his subject away from "the human burden of discrimination and calculation, that load of pricking needles" (1928: 4). In another essay in the same volume, West describes the true artist as "having the power not to lose his way among the phenomena of life" (254). But this transcendence, however often she returned to it in criticism, does not quite describe West's own style of writing. Despite her explicit argument, the tree West identifies as the model of ideal art is not concealed in the more common lot of life. The tree is there in the leaves falling around the restaurant in which West's narrator has lunch and around the undergraduate directing his little boat through Woolf's narration. And in both West and Woolf the woman walking is the object of art, the subject as artist, and a critical perspective on art all at once.

"The problem of art," West claims, "is to communicate to the beholder an emotion caused in the artist by a certain object." The artist will "catch sight of" that object "in the world of physical fact, in the work of naïve realism" and then remove it from that world in order to treat it as art (22). This approach seems to resonate with that of Woolf's narrator, whose search for art leads to all the "infinitely obscure lives" on the street that "remain to be recorded" ([1928] 1973: 89). These lives are not perceived as possessing beauty but a crucial everydayness. Woolf, in fact, is far more consistent in this approach. The personal, the accidental, and the everyday disappear from "The Strange Necessity" but not from A Room. Abandoning the well-informed collection in the British Museum, Woolf's narrator asks herself, "If truth is not to be found on the shelves of the British Museum, where, I asked myself, picking up a notebook and a pencil, is truth?" ([1928] 1973: 26). The pencil and notebook she carries away signifies the persistence of the same questions in the artist's everyday life.

Moving to another pair of texts, we find further engagement with these themes in Woolf's novel Between the Acts and West's travel history Black

Lamb Grey Falcon (both 1941). The connections between these texts lie not in their style or central content—which are very different despite both being retrospective accounts of England awaiting World War II—but in their use of the everyday as an aesthetic field through which history can be understood. One of the overarching themes of *Between the Acts* is the struggle to capture a moment. I return to the historical sense of this novel in chapter 6, but here I want to consider its depiction of the struggle to represent which continually juxtaposes art and the everyday. Early in the novel, the elderly Captain Oliver is brought to a halt in his walking by a spot "where the country . . . looked like a picture" (12). His little grandson George, at the same time, finds a luminous flower while "grubbing" in the dirt. Neither of these relations between life and art constitutes that higher analysis or synthesis West extols. George does capture a moment that transforms the world for him, but he cannot possibly analyze this or communicate it on the order of art. The Captain finds beauty only where it repeats what he conservatively accepts has been defined as art. While West might say that Woolf draws George and the Captain out of the world of her experience as things that can only be expressed by art, any synthesis manifest in Woolf's novel itself is momentary, fleeting, and dispersed. Woolf tellingly described *Between the Acts* as "more quintessential" than all her other novels (Woolf [1941] 1992: xvi) and yet "random and tentative" (xvi)—a precise evocation of the everyday.

While the Captain and George are encountering one another in the garden, George's mother Isa provides another alternative, contemplating love through the clutter of luxuries on her mirrored dressing table and, quite consciously, by "slipping into the cliché provided by fiction" (13). Her abstractions about love become a recollection of poetry that in turn becomes worry about the fish for lunch. At the same time, on a contiguous line, Isa defines beauty through both Sappho and "one of the young men whose photographs adorned the weekly paper" (14). Amongst these reflections Isa observes herself and her peers looking "at what they knew, to see if it might perhaps be different today. Most days it was the same" (48). And yet every material moment of Isa's life tracks change, from the slow transformation of the Poyntz Hall library by "shilling shockers," through the airplane that cuts through their English country house traditions, to the silver hairbrushes that still impress the residual ladies' maids. Leaving the historical perspective being assembled here for later discussion, let me redirect Isa, the maids, and these impressive brushes to another figure where they all meet up—the shopgirl.

The Life of a Shopgirl

In "The Strange Necessity," the figure of the shopgirl is a marginal one, but similar figures appear in West's other work, always on the edge of the artist's life as clearly as the maids are ordinary things known by Isa. The shopgirl is, however, vitally important to *A Room*. She is an intersection of art and the everyday that also serves as a counterpoint to the woman as modernist novelist. Modernist debates over cultural consumption consistently employed girls as figures of modernity and, perhaps most centrally, as images of the potentials and failings of mass culture (Driscoll 2002a: 203–34). The girl as icon of commodity capitalism appears in a wide range of writings, including the Frankfurt School's influential representation of girls as enthusiastic audiences and equally enthusiastic commodities. But such enthusiasm is also continually associated with dissatisfaction. Eliot's "little typist" in *The Waste Land*, appearing with a break in the text marked by the words "Unreal City," lays out her "food in tins" and washes her purchased glamour. She is bored, tired, and indifferent, anything but awaiting her seduction by a "carbunculor clerk." The unspoken aspirations laid out in her underwear are met more satisfyingly by her gramophone (Eliot [1922] 1998: 42–44).[4] Between enthusiasm and dissatisfaction such working girls become a sign of mass culture itself. Connecting "Americanization," modernity, capital, and popular girls' dancing troupes, Siegfried Kracauer exemplarily writes, in "Girls and Crisis":

> the Girls were artificially manufactured in the USA and exported to Europe by the dozens. Not only were they American products; at the same time they demonstrated the greatness of American production. . . . When they formed an undulating snake, they radiantly illustrated the virtues of the conveyor belt; when they tapped their feet in fast tempo, it sounded like business, business . . . one had the vision of an unbroken chain of automobiles gliding out of the factory into the world and the feeling that there was no end to prosperity. ([1931] 1994: 365–66)

But when they appear as "little shopgirls" at the movies ([1927] 1995), girls also suggest to Kracauer the ordinary viewer's capacity to place movie narratives in more than one line of meaning (see chapter 1). This exemplary role is aided by the fact that, on screen, working girls were portrayed in a set of stories about personal transformation and escape from the banal difficulty of modern life. The ordinary working girl made extraordinary, wanting to be made extraordinary, or thrown into extraordinary circumstances, was a staple of musicals, comedies, dramas, and suspense.

Both West and Woolf directly situate the working girl at an intersection of art and the everyday. The narrator of *A Room of One's Own* finds her like this:

> in imagination I had gone into a shop; it was laid with black and white paving; it was hung, astonishingly beautifully, with coloured ribbons. Mary Carmichael might well have a look at that in passing, I thought, for it is a sight that would lend itself to the pen as fittingly as any snowy peak or rocky gorge in the Andes. And there is the girl behind the counter too—I would as soon have her true history as the hundred and fiftieth life of Napoleon or seventieth study of Keats and his use of Miltonic inversion.[5] (90)

The shopgirl is everyday modernism. I have no canonical, institutional, or historical access to her of the kind that would allow me to write the thousandth book chapter on Joyce or Woolf, except between the lines of some other text—she is someone a commentary passes by.

David Joselit argues that Duchamp conceived of his piece *The Bride Stripped Bare by Her Bachelors, Even (The Large Glass)* (1915–23) as a shop window that captured the impact of commodification and reproduction on eroticism (Joselit 137–38), but somewhere in that window, either reflected or behind it, there was a girl. There was a girl, moreover, specifically placed to not walk on and with a clear economic relationship to precisely the moment Duchamp aimed to capture. West's narrator navigates the streets, shops, and scenes of Paris, just as deep in thought as Woolf's as she passes among the shopgirls:

> I had been to my dressmaker and had bought a black lace dress under Pruna panels in which there plunged through blue-green waters nudes so enchanted by the marine moment that they had suffered a slight seachange from humanity. . . . I had been to a milliner's shop which the head vendeuse of a famous house had just started as her own venture and had ordered three hats, and had sat playing with the models, two on my lap, one on my head, changing them about, little dove-like things that laid wings of felt softly against the face. . . . I had lunched in a divine house that is at the end of the Ile St. Louis like the prow of a ship, in rooms with walls golden as the last leaves that fluttered down from the trees on the quay. . . . I had called at a bank

for letters from people whom I really like, I had had half an hour with a lawyer discussing an investment. And all the time my mind had pounded away at this matter of *Ulysses*. (West 1928: 44–45)

The black dress, Pruna panels, hats, letters, and lunch (perhaps even the bank) will each have brought the narrator into contact with some version of the shopgirl, although we see only shadows and hints of her. For West, moments spent contemplating Joyce are distinguished from those that could not claim her attention as fully, and this determination erases the shopgirls almost entirely.

A useful point of comparison here is Jean Rhys' novel *Good Morning Midnight* (1939), which also reflects on *Ulysses*, albeit very differently. *Good Morning Midnight* chronicles the life of a shopgirl that West would not and Woolf does not write: the story of Sasha, an aging ex-shopgirl "visiting" Paris in 1937. Sasha is not in Paris by her own choice, although, not being an artist, she cannot claim anything as glamorous as exile. Her every step, directed to pleasure or to survival, is dominated by economic and cultural flows to which she is insignificant. Lacking the economic and cultural power to be an exception, if ever she chooses to move against these currents she is quickly brought under regulation by the expectations of others. Above all it is other people—other girls and men in cafés and bars; the hairdressers, attendants, and shopgirls—who form the landscape Sasha must negotiate, and her chief daily task is managing other people's opinions of her (Rhys 49–52). Sasha shows us that flâneur or flâneuse is not a particularly good description of the purposeful wandering of Woolf's narrator in *A Room*, however much that narrator's landscape is crafted by the imagination. Sasha suggests that the shopgirl's equal relation to the crowd may make her more like the flâneur, with the caveat that, as Sasha also shows us, such girls are not citizens of every public space and are in fact impelled by the politics of places (and memories) to move between these spaces in particular ways. There is at least a form of empathy that passes between the shopgirl and the flâneur (who perhaps belongs to a very distinct moment in the relation between the city and commodities that cannot now be replicated): "Empathy with the commodity is fundamentally empathy with exchange value itself. The flâneur is the virtuoso of this empathy. He takes the concept of marketability itself for a stroll. Just as his final ambit is the department store, his last incarnation is the sandwich-man" (Benjamin [1927–40] 2002: 448).

Sasha provides a counternarrative to the liberatory story about aesthetically-minded foreigners on the Left Bank in Paris. She has no power to record her own perception of the world, although she thinks often enough about how it might be done: "What about that monograph on lavabos—toilets—ladies? . . . A London lavabo in black and white marble, fifteen women in a queue, each clutching her penny, not one bold spirit daring to dash out of her turn past the stern-faced attendant. That's what I call discipline" (11). Having been employed as an amanuensis, a tour guide, a shopgirl, and a mannequin, Sasha is now reliant on an inheritance far more modest than Woolf's aspiration for women artists of 500 pounds a year—and a direct reference to Woolf may well be intended. Sasha has no alternative to the cultural scripts everyone uses to describe her, and even the rooms and the streets she passes through define her: "this is my plane. . . . Quatrième à gauche, and mind you don't trip over the hole in the carpet. That's me" (12). Sasha is a tiny node in the everyday life of Paris at this time; completely singular and yet recognizable to everyone.

For Woolf, the shopgirl stands at a nexus—between the city and its commodities and between everyday forms of beauty and aspiration—that might offer something more than Sasha's present alienation. Woolf's narrator exhorts her new woman novelist to consider not only the details of commodities sold by the shopgirl but the practices that surround her and connect her to the artist: "above all," she says, "you must illumine your own soul with its profundities and its shallows, and its vanities and its generosities, and say what your beauty means to you or your plainness, and what is your relation to the everchanging and turning world of gloves and shoes and stuffs" ([1928] 1973: 90). Of this passage, Bowlby comments that "What looks to the eye of the reader like a predictable call for indiscriminate documentary detail is actually a passage which creates all sorts of complications about the claims of documentary writing and the claims or place of the documentary observer" (1992: 37). The shopgirl is never reducible to a list of common products or preferences, but rather helps circulate and give meaning to them.

If consumers give life to the modern fetishization of the new that envelopes products like cars and cigarettes but also politics and art, the pursuit of self through consumption is aligned with new modes of shopping. As modernity unfolded, mass-distribution produced and took place in new sites: specialty and chain stores, department stores, stylish "boutiques," cinemas and mass-circulation magazines. The now canonical reference for this history is Benjamin's immense draft of *The Arcades Project*, unpublished when he died but elaborating the shopping precinct as the great modernist space and form. The shopping arcade, mall, or center has come to signify commodity capitalism in ways that sometimes forget that it is a product of the nineteenth century. Kevin Hetherington represents the eighteenth-century complex of gardens, arcades and shops known as the Palais Royal as a precursor to this new shopping space. As a social meeting place for the bourgeoisie, a place of public leisure for the poorer classes—containing venues for sedition, resistance, and marginal social practices—the Palais Royal does seem to resemble "the shopping malls of today" (Hetherington 4), lacking only management of site-appropriate content. In the creation of a space that claims to be open to all for both commerce and leisure, and thus in providing a public venue for the performance of social identities mediated by commodity culture, there is something very contemporary about the Palais Royal and about modernist *shopping*, as distinct from just buying things.

More familiarly still, Benjamin's arcades are "a world in miniature," a description he takes from an *Illustrated Guide to Paris* (Benjamin [1927–40] 2002: 3); they are miniatures, too, of what Foucault would later call the "network of analogies" that cohere in an episteme. Benjamin uses the phrase "a world of secret affinities" (874) to talk about the way different elements of the arcades speak together of their shared "conditions of emergence." I use this phrase, now more often associated with Foucault, to point out the extent to which Benjamin is a precursor to this element of Foucault's approach. It is also the phrase, in translation, that Howard Eiland and Kevin McLaughlin use to foreground Benjamin's attention to the economic and technological shifts that made the arcades possible: "the boom in the textile trade," "the beginning of iron construction," and utopianism (see Benjamin [1927–40] 2002: 3–5). The passage that contains the "world of secret affinities" speaks also to Woolf's figuration of the shopgirl as a kind of muse: "On the walls of these caverns, their immemorial flora, the commodity, luxuriates and enters, like cancerous tissue, into the most irregular combinations. A world of secret affinities: palm tree and feather duster, hair dryer and Venus de Milo, prosthesis and letter-writing manual come together here as after a long separation. The odalisque lies in wait next to the inkwell, priestesses raise aloft ashtrays like patens. These items on display are a rebus" (Benjamin [1927–40] 2002: 874).

Such poetic images of modernist shopping need to be kept, as Woolf and Benjamin would both remind us, close to the economic. In the 1920s and 1930s, the new science of market analysis began to define shopping in terms of what Eckert calls "the sovereignty of the consumer" (39). As Bowlby also notes, "There is an intimate connection, institutionally and intellectually, between psychology and marketing during the first forty years of this century and beyond. As psychology became separated off from philosophy on the one hand and neurology on the other as an independent discipline, the primary questions with which it was concerned were often identical to those that preoccupied advertisers, who wanted to know how people acted and thought in order to know what would get them to buy" (1993: 96). In the epigraph to this chapter, Eckert discusses the importance to the film industry of marketing directed at the shopgirl as ideal consuming prototype. And what experts "could tell" this girl wanted was largely a product of the new art of market research also writing the life of the shopgirl.

The final essay in West's collection *The Strange Necessity* is titled "Tribute to Some Minor Artists." On the surface, West means something dismissive by the term, but this is an essay about art in ordinary life and ordinariness as art. The minor artists are an architect, a-no-longer-very-successful playwright, his wives and servants, and a cook with a tragic past. But it is also the "I" of the narrator: Rebecca West, artist in residence in the south of France. The essay opens, "This summer I am living on the French Riviera, which does not mean what you might think it must" (West 1928: 361). This is no glamorous social whirl out of F. Scott Fitzgerald or celebrity magazines but a private life embedded contemplatively in "the little village," which "has the disorder of a studio" and in which the villagers slouch about like "artists at work," "practising an art in merely living, for they . . . design their days like pictures, balancing as in a skilful composition the human need for leisure against the human power and necessity to pay for leisure by work" (West 1928: 361).

The sympathetic but critical description of this life is languorous and detailed. The horrors of the kitschy bad furnishings downstairs are described in a way that also echoes Benjamin's description of the arcades. But West appreciates their meanings and effects in a patronizing tone, which adds to her analysis of this everyday scene the tastes and *habitus* of the narrator herself:

There is a chaise-lounge with a back shaped like a couch, painted with aluminium paint; there are chintzes on which crawl the many-coloured fruits of marriage between flowers and centipedes, and statuettes everywhere, of terra-cotta ladies wriggling bare shoulders and saying they cannot do a thing with their hair the day after they have washed it, of Joan of Arc sitting listening with that exasperated air of a young French woman in charge of an office, as if she did wish the voices wouldn't shout, and would speak at more regular hours. (376)

Though she is not a modern working girl, the cook is an equally generic sentimental tragic heroine. Face to face, the narrator cannot help but be engaged: the cook's melodrama and misery are compared to J. M. W. Turner's paintings and her attention to her tasks seen as artistically sincere. Confronted by tragedy, the cook can only respond by going on with her ordinary life, practicing her banal arts. The artist does not escape a similar response. In West's prologue to *Black Lamb*, the destruction of some Yugoslavian dresses inspires the narrator's return journey to that country. In these dresses, West sees not only what she values about the Balkans (its "culture," see chapter 7) but also testimony to the everyday relevance of global events. While the prologue narrates the long lead up to European war through its personal resonance to the narrator and her nurse, this lead up is juxtaposed with a close reading of a newsreel of the Yugoslav king's assassination, reducing great history to the scale of the ephemeral and smoothly commodified ([1941] 1994: 15ff).

The everyday never belongs entirely to either the ordinary existence of things or their use, but always to both. It is proper to no specific space but orders spaces, as Certeau suggests. It is precisely located and yet nothing particular; it is defined by transience and duration at the same time. Roland Barthes argues that the camera has a particular relation to the everyday in these senses because cameras were initially related to precision measuring instruments (Barthes [1980] 1982: 15). And this is the version of cinematography that fascinated Vertov in moving from newsreels to the selective cataloguing of the everyday in films like *Movie Camera*. As I discussed in chapter 1, while Vertov was committed to avoiding character and narrative, *Movie Camera* does convey characterization. However, some characters communicate the everyday more effectively than others. In the early scenes of *Movie Camera*, a sleeping girl wakes with the city and dresses to go out for the day as the city's activities commence. This sequence is juxtaposed with mannequins in windows—at sewing machines, on bicycles, and modeling hairstyles—all of which also take up meaning as the city's day unfolds. The girl's ordinariness is emphasized by details like her torn underwear as much as by the way the camera watches her without needing to know who she is, let alone frame her as important and in this ordinariness she signifies the film itself as clearly as the city: her blinking eyes cut to shutters on windows and then to the shutter on a camera.

The use of the everyday in the surrealists' readymades is quite different from this sequence. For Duchamp, the gesture of art is what produces art, but in making a urinal into *Fountain* he maintains a clear distinction between the "art" and the urinal, a distinction that provides the art's shock value. The domestic life melded into Man Ray's *Cadeau* (1921)—a flat iron studded with nails—is also transcended by the gesture of art (perhaps most of all in the numerous later copies of the work made for sale). It is not this everyday-thing becoming art that I see in West and Woolf and Vertov. Rather, it is the becoming everyday of art that remains everyday and thus can never be complete or transcendent. The incompleteness with which one perceives anyone else's everyday life, or everydayness in general, provides openings in which varied perspectives must be suggested. Neither West nor Woolf write the life of a shopgirl; neither Duchamp nor Man Ray reproduce everyday life with their readymades. But these are displacements and citations of the everyday with far-reaching effects. Cultural Studies, like Modernism, gener-ally focuses on the everyday that it might be distinguished from it and diag-nose, dissect, and analyze it. The everyday is presumed to be characterized by an inability to perform this necessary critical reflection for itself. Shaped by its reading of Lefebvre and Certeau in particular, Cultural Studies relies on the unknowability of everyday life and "consistently supports the idea that culture, in terms of the way it is understood and lived, contains a funda-mentally unknowable content. . . . 'there precisely as it is recognized, but as it is not known'" (Driscoll 2001: 383–84, quoting Certeau). But it has learned this strategy from Modernist responses to the problem of the everyday as an experience particular to modernity and a concept integral to modernism.

5

Chanel

The Order of Things

She wore a slipover jersey sweater and a tweed skirt and her hair brushed back like a boy's. She started all that.

Ernest Hemingway, *The Sun Also Rises*

Fashion is modern. This might mean no more than that the conditions of modern life, as George Simmel suggested in 1911, exacerbate the starkest tendencies of fashion (191). But the tendency most often foregrounded in discussions of fashion is, as Elizabeth Wilson puts it, the "rapid and continual changing of styles. Fashion in a sense *is* change, and in modern western societies no clothes are outside fashion" (3). The gradual conversion of "fashion" into a field encompassing all clothing practices and thus all modern subjects opens a space in which we might ask about whether *modernist* fashion exists. This chapter focuses on one of the fashion "breaks" of the Modernist period, captured in Hemingway's image of the fashionable woman as an avant-garde artist and revolutionary leader. We could also call this image "Chanel." The position of groundbreaking innovator in the field of women's fashion that is widely assigned to Chanel is one form of the modernist break. It is typical, too, in that such breaks are sustained for cultural history by the institutionalization of great names like "Chanel." In fact, it is in installing a look that is both "classic" and "modern" that Chanel constitutes a rupture: she claims to be a forceful periodization of fashion that delineates what will always be true (in style). It is clear that Chanel is not the single creator of, or even inspiration for, the transformations of fashion in the Modernist period, and still less of modernist attitudes to fashion. But in this I am not simply dismissing Chanel as less radical or innovative than she is sometimes seen to be. Instead, I want to reconsider what we want from the radical innovations of Modernism when we seek to apply them to fashion and what we want, moreover, from the installation of Chanel as a classic.

Fashion participates in that popular (as well as canonical) image of Modernism as, to quote Jennifer Craik's *The Face of Fashion*, "a commitment to new ways of living that explicitly rejected the old" (75). Wilson also prioritizes the "desire for the new" (63) in fashion, but her *Adorned in Dreams: Fashion and Modernity* (2003) adds to this a more complex understanding of the relation between fashion and modernity. "The concept of 'modernity,'" she argues, "is useful in elucidating the rather peculiar role played by fashion in acting as a kind of hinge between the élitist and the popular" (60). In fashion, as Wilson records, we can trace the impact of the industrial revolution and even the emerging modes of thought that transformed morality, art, and science into recognizably modernist forms. The history of fashion, she suggests, is that of modernity itself. In praising Constantin Guys' attention to the everyday, Charles Baudelaire also sees the man of modernity as he who "makes it his business to extract from fashion whatever element it may contain of poetry within history" (12). This man of fashion writes the history of the present and the history of himself in the various dimensions of his performance of fashion and perception of fashion in others. Indeed, Baudelaire stressed the importance of fashion as self-representation, "the asceticism of the dandy who makes of his body, his behavior, his feelings and passions, his very existence, a work of art" (Foucault [1978] 1984b: 41).

While fashion merged with mass consumption through changes to the way clothes were produced, it never lost this potential to re-orient the self in the world. It is in part fashion's capacity to re-order the world that Foucault draws from Baudelaire as the "critical attitude" of modernity. He writes:

> modernity in painting does not consist, for Baudelaire, in introducing black clothing onto the canvas. The modern painter is the one who can show the dark frock-coat as "the necessary costume of our time," the one who knows how to make manifest, in the fashion of the day, the essential, permanent, obsessive relation that our age entertains with death. "The dress-coat and frock-coat not only possess their political beauty, which is an expression of universal equality, but also their poetic beauty, which is an expression of the public soul—an immense cortège of undertaker's mutes (mutes in love, political mutes,

bourgeois mutes . . .). We are each of us celebrating some funeral."
(Foucault [1978] 1984b: 41, quoting Baudelaire)

Phrased in this poignant way, the modernity of fashion cannot be reduced
to a cycle of death and rebirth, redundancy and innovation. And I want to
draw into a discussion of Chanel a wide range of implications from this
quotation.

Despite Baudelaire's attention to fashion, it is generally excluded from
versions of the Modernist canon, deemed too transient and too superficial to count among its central revolutions. However, as Nancy Troy's *Couture Culture* (2003) argues, and the 2005 Chanel exhibition at the Museum
of Modern Art (see Koda and Bolton) attested, the contested borders of
Modernism are now sometimes extended to include high fashion, and the
name most persistently conjured in this way is Gabrielle (Coco) Chanel.
For a Cultural Studies approach to Modernism, there is no question that the
Chanel brand and "Coco Chanel" (her star status during her lifetime and
her iconic status after it) together form a key figure in renovating relations
between art, industry, leisure, consumer culture, and modern identity.

The Chanel Look

Apocryphally, Chanel once met fellow designer Paul Poiret in the street. She
was dressed in her own highly fashionable black and he asked who she was
in mourning for. She reputedly retorted, "For you, dear Monsieur!" It is just
as often quoted that Poiret dismissed the Chanel look as "undernourished
telegraph boys dressed in black jersey." But Chanel's democratic "undertak-
er's mutes," to invoke Baudelaire again, are not the sum of modernist fashion, which names instead the field in which they appear. Even Modernist
fashion is not confined to the simplicity of the Chanel design any more than
to the exotic, romantic, or surreal styles of Poiret, Erté, or Elsa Schiaparelli.
It also incorporates what the new idea of the fashion designer meant and
to whom. If the first thing striking thing about Chanel is how she dressed
her women at the leading edge of changes to dominant fashion and gender
norms, the second is that there could be a "Chanel woman" for whom these
clothes spoke to new ways of living and new possible styles. In fact, for
the purposes of this chapter I am not discussing Chanel, the biographical
woman, or even, more strangely, Chanel, the label, but rather the Modernist
moment in fashion we have come to call "Chanel."

The early twentieth century saw dramatic changes in dominant standards of dress and an expanding field that could be called "fashion." Fashion pages, the expanding genre of fashion magazines—out of a blend of dressmaking and society publications—and the mass-distributed patterns from this time all record a narrowed "silhouette," a reduction of fabric and clothing, and a new everyday place for the dramatic fashion statement: the short dress of the flappers; the "medieval" drapery of Erté in the 1920s; the tailored but feminine exaggeration that moves from Adrian in the 1930s to Dior's "New Look." Describing these changes in this way shows how they also drew on the expansion of haute couture—the avant-garde of fashion, which, like other avant-gardes, has a strong, but not an immutable, impact on dominant styles. As Craik claims, "Everyday fashion (dress codes, a sense of fashionability) does not simply 'trickle down' from the dictates of the self-proclaimed elite. At best, a particular mode may tap into everyday sensibilities and be popularised" (ix). And as Valerie Steele puts it, "Couturiers like Worth, Chanel, and Dior were not so much dictators or radical innovators as they were astute barometers of fashion trends" (Steele 1998: 5).

As Steele elaborates, a range of broad social shifts and a collage of other designs and designers contributed to what has come to be the Chanel look: "most of the literature on Chanel is wildly inaccurate: she is said to have abolished feminine frills, liberated women from the corset, and almost singlehandedly introduced sportswear, the 'poor boy' look, bobbed hair, designer perfume, suntans, and the 'little black dress.' With a little research, however, it is easy to use the facts of fashion history as sniper's ammunition to pick off these inflated claims" (Steele 1998: 247). Such changes in the Modernist period depended upon the expanding mass production of ready-to-wear clothing for almost all modern urbanized subjects, a process furthered by Chanel's blend of haute couture, zeitgeist rhetoric, and revolutionary class-mobile styling.[1]

Chanel emphasized a "total look": the Chanel woman was seen to co-ordinate every element of her attire and lifestyle, from shoes to drinks, for which Chanel was the model as artist and artist as model. Chanel was and is often described as quintessentially modern: "Exercise, diet, bathing in the sea, an uncorseted body . . . the modern woman was born. And she resembled Gabrielle Chanel in every detail" (Baudot 12). In fact, Poiret was the leading figure in shifting fashion away from the corseted image of the female body. But, as Harold Koda puts it, "The disjunction felt in the juxtaposition of a Poiret woman viewing Picasso's *Les Demoiselles d'Avignon* (1907 [see figure 8]) evaporates if she is imagined dressed by Chanel." Koda

Figure 8. Pablo Picasso, *Les Demoiselles d'Avignon*, 1907. Oil on canvas, 8' × 7'8" (243.9 × 233.7 cm). Acquired through the Lillie P. Bliss Bequest, 1939. Digital Image © 2009 The Museum of Modern Art, New York/Scala, Florence. Courtesy of ARS.

thus aligns Chanel with "the advancing aesthetic principles of art and architecture" (Koda 11) and, indirectly, with the institutionalized media status crucial to iconic Modernism. He also attributes to Chanel the capacity to perceive and insist on something more fundamental behind the ornament of conventional appearance, something as groundbreaking as Pablo Picasso's juxtaposition of masks, women, and cubist style in *Les Demoiselles*.

If the modernist transformations of everyday life emerged alongside critical reflection on it, the same is true of modernist fashion. This chapter will sample a range of modernist commentary on fashion—some now well known and some not—but let me begin with Simmel. Simmel saw in fashion a system of differentiation in dialogue with conformity. In "The

Philosophy of Fashion" (1911), Simmel argues that fashionable "individual appearance never clashes with the general style, but always *stands out* from it" (191). He also presents fashion as a signifying system—without using that turn of phrase, but with an understanding of the network of shared meanings taken from fashion that intersects with Roland Barthes' more famous discussion in *The Fashion System* (1967). Simmel argues that urbanization created a greater need for people to demonstrate individual difference, particularly given the transient nature of urban relationships. While in "The Metropolis and Mental Life" (1903), Simmel notes that urban life demands that the subject exaggerate the "personal element in order to remain audible even to himself" (184), in "The Philosophy of Fashion," he figures the main impetus behind the rapid changes of fashion as a desire to belong: "it satisfies the need for distinction, the tendency towards differentiation, change and individual contrast. It accomplishes the latter, on the one hand, by the change in contents—which gives to the fashions of today an individual stamp compared with those of yesterday and of tomorrow—and even more energetically, on the other hand, by the fact that fashions are always class fashions" (Simmel 189). But this argument, consistent in many but not all respects with Thorstein Veblen's representation of fashion as conspicuous consumption, does not work for Chanel, even if she should not be seen as single-handedly having changed this system.

As the various systemic approaches to fashion insist, choosing one or another fashion item involves a complex social positioning. Veblen and Simmel both stress that an economy of style shapes one's relations to strangers along lines that also support Baudelaire's conception of modern style as always performed in transit. But after Chanel, fashion was not predominantly a statement of "pecuniary strength," "written in characters which he who runs may read" (Veblen 49). In fact, the expensiveness of Chanel required a certain skill to divine in others. This consciousness foregrounds from these writers what Pierre Bourdieu would later describe as a system negotiated by taste. Bourdieu writes: "every change in tastes resulting from a transformation of the conditions of existence and of the corresponding dispositions will tend to induce, directly or indirectly, a transformation of the field of production, by favouring the success, within the struggle constituting the field, of the producers best able to produce the needs corresponding to the new dispositions" ([1979] 1986: 231). This idea of dispositions in fact clarifies not only how Chanel impacts on the way fashion indexes social change, or what is generally presumed for any individual—what Bourdieu calls "habitus"—but also how her *style* works among significations of "taste."

Taste, Bourdieu says, is not a sign of something outside it (like access to what is beautiful) but a classifying statement that "classifies the classifier" ([1979] 1986: 6): "taste is the basis of all that one has—people and things—and all that one is for others, whereby one classifies oneself and is classified by others" (56). This denaturalization of taste—replacing beauty with style—is not a "postmodern" product but part of the complexity of modernist discourse on fashion.

Images of fashion within the critical terrain of Modernism generally focus on what style means, which isn't to say there are not substantial disagreements on the subject. Simmel's interest in differentiation from the mainstream via fashion is as typically modernist as the dismissal of fashion by others. He argues that it is impossible to ignore fashion altogether and that even those who claim to disdain fashion in fact make fashion "statements" that situate them in relation to fashion, and Simmel's account of this can not be reduced to a homogenizing "culture industry." Even those Modernists most stridently critical of mass culture acknowledge fashion's creativity. Adorno emphasizes the proximity of avant-garde art and fashion: "The bourgeois religion of art would like to keep art neatly apart from fashion. This is simply impossible. Ever since the aesthetic subject began to take a polemical stand against society and its objective spirit, it has maintained a secret link to that society through the medium of fashion" ([1970] 1984: 436). The fashionable language of renovation will be important to chapter 9, but it matters here that Adorno's aesthetic theory concedes how fashion materializes "incisive individual impulses that are saturated with history. . . . It is no accident that in German and French the terms 'fashion' and 'modernism' are related etymologically" (437).

Yet another Modernist account of fashion can be found among the newly visible psychologies. To take just one example, in 1929, psychologist Elizabeth Hurlock discussed fashion, following Havelock Ellis, as a secondary sexual characteristic. By her account, fashion progresses in line with "civilization," and she understands a twentieth-century decrease in ornamentation as the maturation of modern women (Hurlock 145–64). Hurlock is responding in particular to the success of Chanel, for which "Perfect grooming demands that there be no ornamentation or display of any sort, and even the artificially restricted figure has been replaced by the natural one" (Hurlock 160). Her argument must also be contextualized in relation to the architect Adolf Loos' more famous exhortation to extend the Modernist tendency to abandon ornament in architecture to all decoration of surfaces as a remnant of primitivism: "I have discovered the following truth and present it to the world: *cultural evolution is equivalent to the removal of ornament from articles in daily use*" (Loos 226–27, emphasis in original). Hurlock's psychological approach nevertheless agrees that fashion is at once a system of differentiation and coherence: that fashion and its changes are both social and political. It is the sociological approaches to style that more directly lead to Cultural Studies, only to be displaced by the influential semiotic analysis of Barthes.

Wilson claims that the problem of how fashion changes has particularly baffled the most cited commentators, including Barthes. She dismisses Barthes' theory of fashion as a "signifying system," "based entirely on the idea of irrationality, since for him the sign, like language, is a system of arbitrarily defined differences" (Wilson 57). In fact, no language is ahistorical from the Saussurean perspective on which Barthes bases his analysis in *The Fashion System*, and Wilson thus misses some of what it means to think of fashion as a language. The structure of fashion, according to Barthes, is composed of the separate circulation of "image-clothing," "written clothing," and "real clothing" (Barthes [1967] 1983: 3–5), and a change in any of these registers can affect all the others. There are both precedents and crucial contemporary contexts for the impact of Chanel's sportswear and other lines, but the use of jersey, the shape called "cardigan," or the sign "little black dress" are not meaningful in themselves but only in relation to a system where jersey was not used in women's dresses, cardigans were practical warmth for working men, and black was reserved for mourning.

Ready-to-Wear

As Steele indicates, a range of historical contexts is needed to make sense of how Chanel became "Chanel." She stresses the impact of World War I and indeed the ready-to-wear clothing that enabled so much of Chanel's success—because it was easier to look *like* a Chanel when one could not afford it—had initially been employed for uniforms (see Wilson 74). And by the end of the nineteenth century, as Wilson notes, women's fashions had already begun to adapt the new "sports" styles for women to modern city life, as men's fashions had done the century before (40). The adaptation for women's fashion of locknit and flannel from men's sportswear and underwear, still in the same muted colors (Wilson 40), did not so much invent new pieces as rearrange how those pieces fit into the fashion system. Chanel stands for the prewar experimentation with these conventionally masculine fabrics, later extending to others like corduroy and tweed and this new medium consciously inverted the gender and class distinctions that had been central to fashionable "style." Cardigans and trench coats became fashionable accessories, loose fitting trousers became glamorous rather than a practical necessity, and costume jewelry became a desirable dressed-down look. The renovation in women's clothing we associate with Chanel certainly gave new functions to a range of common materials, but the stronger claim would be that it disrupted the way fashion's signifying practices had run parallel to, had mapped onto, those of gender and class.

Pulling apart her iconic Modernist image as revolutionary style-leader in women's clothing, Steele settles on one key to Chanel's image: "To her supporters, then and now, Chanel represented comfortable, realistic, 'classic' dressing" (Steele 1998: 247). As commentary on modernity from Baudelaire to Fredric Jameson has often suggested, it is precisely the concept of the classical, as that which sits outside of modernity and thus against which modernity is defined, that marks the emergence of modernity—not only or even principally as that which is displaced by modernity but as that endlessly reassembling continuum in relation to which innovation is perceived and set aside. Fashion is a continually self-reflexive attitude and can never settle on one thing as "fashionable." There was not, in fact, one Chanel look, but there were some unwavering Chanel principles. Understatement was one, reinforcing a shift in the important distinction between day and evening wear and the role of particular fabrics in articulating wealth and the conspicuousness of fashion consumption.

After the war, "To appear to pay too much attention to clothes was *démodé*, while to wear one's clothes *avec désinvolture*, in a free and easy manner, was the look of modernity. Because this remains true today, we still admire Chanel" (Steele 1998: 248). As many writers have noted, Chanel's "poor look," of which figure 9 is a classic example, was radical enough to be referred to as an "antifashion posture" (Davis 164), reversing the systemic copying of the upper classes by the lower, which in 1911 Simmel could claim was structurally characteristic of fashion (190). The use of the low and the poor translates the mobility of Chanel into mobility across social contexts, as her use of men's fabrics and reference to men's tailoring translated into some mobility between gender norms. While this was *"poverty de luxe,"* it also echoes themes raised in the last chapter. Chanel's "black dress and the slight suit were the apotheosis of the shopgirl's uniform, or the stenographer's garb" (Wilson 41); "It was the look of the working girl hitherto unknown to fashion" (Hollander 19).[2] Whether or not it was a unique innovation in her collections, Chanel's "little black dress" became the iconic representation of urbanely casual modern femininity: a new fashion grammar enabling new articulations. The phrase, label, or slogan, "the little black dress" is now often cited, but usually in forms long detached from what it was that Chanel's first little black dresses actually looked like (figure 9 is an example circa 1927).

Chanel was neither functionalist nor minimalist. Layers and accessories were both crucial to the Chanel look despite Chanel's refusal of what she deemed excessive ornamentation. We could compare this to the fashion for and style of Imagist poetry. In 1913, soon after the appearance of Simmel's essay and around the same time as Chanel's first successful sportswear lines, Ezra Pound abjured aspiring poets to "Use no superfluous word, no adjective, which does not reveal something" ([1913] 1972: 30). As Loos exemplifies, this avoidance of what was seen as outdated or unnecessary ornamentation also characterized contemporary architectural and interior designs. While, by contrast, the "Camellia Brooches" designed for Chanel by Gripoix (Koda and Bolton 178–79) are without doubt ornamental, the dramatic difference of Chanel's look was that it confined ornament to what we would now recognize as "accessories," thus crafting a more mobile basic style with exchangeable extras. Like Pound, Chanel's principle was to "Use either no ornament or good ornament" (Pound [1913] 1972: 30), within her own parameters, of course, for what counted as "good." Chanel's use of costume jewelry and ropes of fake pearls (see figure 10) suggest that good ornament was a purposeful stylistic statement rather than a display of wealth. While this is not as obviously true of dresses crafted from sequins, exceptional laces, or tiers of tulle—and not only was "real" Chanel prohibitively expensive but she did also design luxury evening wear—such designs add the accessory of "luxury fabric" to what is otherwise a simple design. That is, ornament has the function of indexing a Chanel design to a particular use or moment.

The Chanel look captured in Man Ray's 1935 photograph of the designer (see figure 10) is such a moment of *this* hat and *these* pearls and *this* cigarette and *these* bracelets, which also means it is *this* pose and *this* attitude, all assembled in relation to a proper name. I use this formulation, appropriated again from Deleuze and Guattari's discussion of "assemblage," to point to how the Chanel look explicitly (re)orders identity—or at least the appearance of identity. In this photograph, the proper name can be either "Man Ray" or "Chanel," but each produces this image as a different assemblage. The little black dress on its own (see figure 9), not yet attached to anything else via ornament and other components of *the look as the moment*, is as-

Figure 9. Coco Chanel, "Dress" [day ensemble], c. 1927, (manufacturer: House of Chanel, founded 1913). Silk, wool, metal. Length at center back, 21¾ in. (55.2 cm); length at center back, 40 in. (101.6 cm); length: 40½ in. (102.9 cm). Marking: [label] c) (on buckle) 'Chanel.' Purchase, The New-York Historical Society, by exchange, 1984. Digital Image © 2007 The Metropolitan Museum of Modern Art/Scala, Florence.

Figure 10. Man Ray, "Gabrielle Chanel," 1935. Photograph from Man Ray Trust/ ADAGP Paris 200. Courtesy of ARS.

sembled under "Chanel" in one sense, but it also assembles as a saleable identity all its own. What is often called modernist minimalism is actually an openness to such assemblage rather than an ascetic approach to detail. The famous 1925 Paris *Exhibition des Arts Decoratifs*, after which the design category "Art Deco" was later named, featured Chanel and other fashion designers alongside architecture, furniture, and domestic design. Art Deco does exemplify Modernist art and design's preference for the geometric and the streamlined—the machinic—but always in relation to movement and flow. In Chanel's terms, movement within the fabric required softness that complemented the design's hard lines, and give in the fabric belied her style's geometric edges by undermining the visible structure. Chanel "blurred the boundaries of [sic] the *flou* (dressmaking) and the *tailleur* (tailoring) by applying the dressmaker's draped effects to her suits and coats and the tailor's pattern-driven precision to her dresses" (Koda 11).

All this speaks to the mobility of and in Chanel's designs. "When photographed for the leading fashion journals of the day," Koda points out, "the models in their Chanels run, pull back their jackets, and plunge their hands into their pockets, a clear counterpoint to the static, stylized poses characteristic of the period" (12). Chanel's fashion mobility distinguishes not between degrees of ornamentation or between public roles and personal display but between synchronic styles of womanhood. The Chanel look—for day or evening, work or play, motoring, shopping, or dining—was an active orientation in the world. Chanel was not the only designer associated with this new active woman. The overwhelming champion of women's tennis in the 1920s, Suzanne Lenglen, for example, famous in part for her clothes on and off court, was dressed by Jean Patou rather than Chanel. By the late 1920s, a typical fashion photograph was as likely to capture movement as it was a static pose—not only avoiding corseted and structured styles but also embracing the movement that was crucial to the Chanel woman. Chanel's star status and the timeliness of her designs were simultaneously imported into productions of *timeliness*, whether those were magazine pictorials, fashion parades, or the collaborative art projects for which Chanel designed costumes: for example, for Le Ballet Russe's 1924 *Le Train Bleu*, both new sports and leisure travel were referenced by the costumes Chanel designed to complement Picasso's sets.

Wilson describes Chanel's designs—"Agile and full of movement"—as "the spirit of modernity and futurism" (41). In Chanel's mobile and streamlined designs, like avant-garde art and aesthetics but also popular culture and everyday life at the time (for example, in the rise of radio and car cultures), we see the continued meaningfulness of an iconography of the machine. Indeed, if a house is a "machine for living in," as Le Corbusier (Charles-Édouard Jeanneret) claimed in *L'Esprit Nouveau* (1921, see Corbusier et al. 86), then fashion might also be described that way. While modernist images of the machine cannot be reconciled into a single project,[3] fashion as much as modern architecture and design stresses the conjunction of machine and subject (see also Wigley). The Chanel dress was a city machine and a people machine as clearly as the double-decker buses that inspired F. T. Marinetti (see Marinetti 118). Just as the ideal modernist cities (see Harvey 25–26 and chapter 7) described networks of lives, and networks of cultures intersecting them, so Chanel addressed a conception of the modern woman through fashion as technology. Innovation at this level affects something like Bourdieu's "habitus." I find the account of habitus that is linked back to Gottfried Leibniz most useful here: "an agent's disposition to do something regularly but in a spontaneous way" (Shusterman 4). The changes we summarize as "Chanel" impacted not only what people wore but how often and in what ways people needed to change clothes, and how they could and would deport themselves—even how they might stand or walk. Habitus means more than recognizable expectations, describing influences on practice and identity that exceed rules or reasoned judgment: influences based in a learned disposition.[4]

The Order of Things

Discussing the Exposition culture that appeared in the late nineteenth century and expanded in the early twentieth, Tom Gunning claims that the dominant discourse of modernity "is not only one of innovation, but precisely one of novelty, maximising the dazzling experience of the new" (2004: 43). Most studies of fashion emphasize just such a constitutive process of renovation and novelty. However, Gunning also notes that in these Expositions, "the carefully arranged lay-out of space and the logic of form and color in the architecture, evoke cultural associations and determine the temporal and spatial unfolding of vistas and patterns" (43). While this may contribute to a novelty effect by the combination of particulars, the elements themselves are already known—as the phrase "evoke cultural associations" makes clear. They rely on a pre-existing order of things. I think this provides a new perspective on how the set of changes we give the shorthand "Chanel" reordered the expected forms of fashion to foreground new possibilities. In the relation between modernity and technology, Gunning argues that

Martin Heidegger's "discussion of work in terms of the dynamic of the tool shows that we can suddenly gain a new perspective on technology through an interruption of habitual actions. His conception of the tool as 'the ready to hand' gives us another way to conceive of the 'unconsciousness' of habit in terms of technology" (Gunning 2004: 45). Technologies, that is, are always experienced as exchanges between the everyday and novelty, a recognition that can be used to rethink fashion's relation to both consistency and novelty.[5] As Gunning also notes, Heidegger contends that a tool only demands attention when it does not work in some way. Extending this idea to fashion, "not working" might mean articulations of style that are unrecognized in a current system or, in cases like Chanel, that can form alternative orders for fashion.

If modernism is always a reflection on the present it includes those elements that can be consigned to habitus and, at the same time, those openings in which things as they are might be ordered differently. This is precisely why Chanel should be understood as avant-garde. If, like other modernist avant-gardes, this difference was soon incorporated as a dominant style, trying to recapture the moment when Chanel was disruptive might help us consider the difference between the avant-garde and an epistemic break— a conflation that underpins much discussion of Modernism. Rather than avant-garde, I want to try out another term for Chanel. In *The Order of Things*, Foucault uses the term "heterotopic" to signify an "other" ordering, an apparently disorderly order. Fashion clearly has utopian forms, such as the modernist dress reform movements (see Wilson 208–27), but like all utopias they work only insofar as they do not come into being.

In his lecture "Of Other Spaces," Foucault reuses the concept of heterotopia to distinguish sites where "all the other real sites which can be found within the culture are simultaneously represented, contested, and inverted" (1986: 24). Heterotopic fashion might form a particularly interesting juxtaposition with "the utopia of the mirror" (24): as a place, rather than a non-place, where the self is reflected and suspected at once. This is a concept worth pursuing because, while fashion is not a site in the same sense as the garden, theater, or cemetery, it is "a simultaneously mythic and real contestation of the space in which we live" (24), requiring, on the one hand, certain efforts and "rituals" to enter and installing, on the other, "hidden exclusions" (26). Chanel's reordering of the fashion system is not directed toward any particular transformation but rather brings into question, by reordering, how elements like "women," "dress," "trenchcoat," and "Chanel" are in an everyday way distinguished (or not) in relation to each other. The phrases "she dressed for the evening" and "she put on a work dress" mean something different after Chanel because the possibility of distinguishing a work dress from an evening dress is problematized and, just as significantly, because distinguishing "dressed" from "put on" no longer works in the same way.

Foucault's early examples of heterotopia are revealing here and include the illogicality of Jorge Luis Borges' "Chinese Encyclopedia," and the surrealist aphorism from Comte de Lautréamont via André Breton: "Beautiful as the chance encounter of a sewing machine and an umbrella on a dissecting table" (Foucault [1966] 1973: v-viii). These examples are linked by the impossibility of finding a locus for ordering, and thus knowing, them. The "table where, for an instant, perhaps forever, the umbrella encounters the sewing-machine" makes strange the "table, a tabula, that enables thought to operate upon the entities of our world, to put them in order, to divide them into classes, to group them according to names that designate their similarities and their differences" (xvii). To bring some of these terms together, we might say that while the heteroclite—Foucault's example is the incoherent patterns of an "aphasic" sorting colored skeins—is disorder that seems to have no habitus (no place in which it makes sense), the heterotopic is the presence of disorder within the habitus. Chanel does not have to shock after the fashion of James Joyce's *Finnegans Wake* in order to constitute, at least for a time, a disruptive order.

Foucault foregrounds surrealism here because surrealism surprises by problematizing the meanings classification gives to objects. In saying this I make room for the claim that surrealism comprises a set of games with meaning rather than a movement that is now finished. Even Breton never settled on one manifesto for it. Debating whether it is ahistorical to call artists like Cindy Sherman and Louise Bourgeois surrealist misses the lack of coherence that is fundamental to surrealism. In Whitney Chadwick's collection *Mirror Images* (1998), for example, a number of essays distinguish between Modernism and postmodernism in terms of the latter's abandonment of a "real" which modernism (and surrealism) is presumed to support. Katy Kline sees Claude Cahun as representing "selves" in comparison to Sherman's "roles" (Kline 79)—as if Cahun's self portrait as a man (see figure 11) represents *herself* any more than when she poses, in other photographs, as Buddha. In the same collection, Susan Suleiman distinguishes Sherman's mannequins (a 1993 example is included as figure 12) from Hans Bellmer's mannequins (an example from the most famous 1934 series is included as figure 13) by stressing Sherman's "critical" stance (see Suleiman 1998). A more extended account of the transformation of surrealism in a postmod-

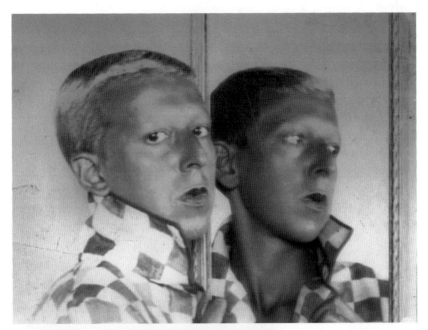

Above: Figure 11. Claude Cahun, self-portrait, 1919. Courtesy of the Jersey Heritage Trust Collections.

Left: Figure 12. Cindy Sherman, *Untitled, #282,* 1993. Photograph, chromogenic print, 231.6 × 155.3 cm (91³⁄₁₆ × 61⅛ in.) Ernest Wadsworth Longfellow Fund, 1993. Photograph © 2009 Museum of Fine Arts, Boston.

Figure 13. Hans Bellmer, "Die Puppe," 1934. From *La Poupée*, edited by Robert Valencay. Paris: GLM, 1936. Courtesy of ARS.

ern context is given by Natalya Lusty, who represents Sherman as returning to Bellmer and surrealism (Lusty 147ff). Certainly Bellmer's doll is a threatening appropriation of the fashion mannequin as a sexual object and an image of abjection, violence, and death to which Sherman's work has a different relationship. But Bellmer's doll, or puppet, is also a critical appropriation of how the human subject as well as the human form—and there are male versions of "Die Puppe"—is objectified in art. The doll or mannequin in this sense was a popular Modernist theme, as I will consider again in chapter 7: from the adult wax dolls of Lotte Pritzel (see Rilke), through Mikhail Fokine and Igor Stravinsky's ballet *Petrouchka* (1911), to the inhuman mannequins in the windows of *Man with a Movie Camera*.

Seeing more continuity than difference between Bellmer and Sherman does risk losing the historically, and to some degree culturally, specific impact of surrealism. In "Looking Back on Surrealism" (1956), Adorno both stresses that surrealism cannot escape being framed by the expectations of art, and argues that "What is deadly about the interpretation of art . . . is that in the process of conceptualization it is forced to express what is strange and surprising in terms of what is already familiar and thereby to explain away the only thing that would need explanation" (Adorno 2005a: 1113). This essay is certainly premised on the idea that surrealism is no longer possible. But the art of Cahun, Bellmer and Sherman works by defamiliarizing or disturbing expected modes of representation: by staging in new media or new aesthetic frames the styles and poses proliferating around them or the foundational components of those styles. Bellmer and Sherman show that the mannequin can be damaged, disassembled, or reassembled in ways that both promise human completion and threaten human fragmentation at the same time. There is a critical continuity between them by which both still say "corpse" as much as "fashion mannequin."[6] While many of Sherman's most famous images, like the "Untitled Film Stills" (1977–80), are striking for their familiarity rather than any shock value, they nevertheless all work by disrupting the order by which images mean something. Rather than a linear historical story in which Sherman disrupts Modernism by reproducing it, I see in Sherman the surrealist defamiliarization of a cultural present, including its residual elements.

The violent edge of surrealism still present in Sherman also moved along other trajectories in the twentieth century. When Dick Hebdige takes up Claude Lévi-Strauss' bricoleur to talk about the way youth culture styles open new symbolic spaces by misrepresentation, he does so by making a direct comparison between punk and surrealism, seeing in the punk style I discuss in chapter 2 something heterological. Hebdige's punks provided "self-conscious commentaries on the notions of modernity and taste" (107). They not only appropriated "commodities by placing them in a symbolic ensemble which served to erase or subvert their original straight meanings" (Hebdige 104), they also disturb by ostentatiously refusing to fit into the world they draw on and, at least for a time, gesture to some other place where they might make sense.

Breton saw the disorderly orders created by surrealism as both intrinsically modern and aligned with fashion. According to Breton, surrealism's laughter at the most disturbing disruptions of order is vital to modernity and thus not confined to a particular period.[7] In his *Anthology of Black Humour* (1966), Breton gives surrealism a history parallel to that of modernism—from Jonathan Swift and the Marquis De Sade through Edgar Allen Poe, Baudelaire, Lewis Carroll, and Friedrich Nietzsche to Breton's contemporaries in an open present tense. Mark Polizzotti's 1997 introduction to this anthology finds "a lot of what today we would call 'attitude' in these pages. This attitude, which takes the form of both a lampooning of social conventions and a profound disrespect for the nobility of literature, is perhaps the one thread that links these otherwise disparate writers" (in Breton [1966] 1997: vi). But such humor is not a literary endeavor. Breton contends that it "has been pointed out in kitchen utensils, it has been known to appear in bad taste, and it has its winter quarters in fashion" (Breton [1966] 1997: xv). As it appears in fashion the disturbance of expected orders, and even of common sense, is crucial to the humor still built into haute couture. But even the illogicality of haute couture depends on opening up fashion's possibilities for representing not the body or identity so much as life. And the interplay of recognition and disruption is more important here than the cycle of death and renewal often used to discuss fashion.

My insistence here on the continuity of surrealism into the present has particular implications for thinking about the modernism of fashion. Many writers claim that, between 1950 and 2000, fashion was transformed utterly, "fragmented into hundreds of competing looks—what Ted Polhemus calls 'style tribes'" (Steele 2000: 7). Steele follows this claim with a discussion of the ways in which Polhemus' focus on youth/street styles can be adapted to find adult "style tribes, epitomized by different fashion labels" (7). This "stylistic proliferation" means that no new encompassing "Look" can now be launched for any fashion season and any such claim would be met by ridicule based in the "antifashion" sentiment now thought to be a characteristic of postmodernity (7–9). This postmodern version of designers as barometers rather than originators—examples include Mary Quant and André Courrèges (Steele 2000: 10)—is distinguished from the great Modernist names by stressing its debt to youth or street style, but whether or not this argument for a "break" could be countered by talking about the relation between Chanel and the flappers, sports stars, and shopgirls around her ends up being irrelevant. Steele closes this essay with an appropriate reprise of the continuity within which the emergence, installation, and critique of Modernism remains modernist: "fashion itself remains alive and well, always new, always changing" (20).

The youthful look of the 1960s in many ways reprised the youthful look of the 1920s and was just as readily displaced by more exotic and then more tailored "work-related" styles in ongoing conversations between society and personal style. But cycle is the wrong way to talk about fashion because of its simultaneous dependence on continuity and disruption. Fashion enables a culture of ongoing consumption in which clothes are not built to be worn for years, however "classic" they claim to be, but rather take part in a system where particular components or motifs are redeployed repeatedly. In Chanel's "classic" fashionable look we find a refusal and an overt framing of the way fashion works to foreground time as passing. "Fashion (as we conceive of it today)," Barthes explains, "rests on a violent sensation of time" ([1967] 2005: 106), but this time can nevertheless be articulated differently.

In an essay on Courrèges, Barthes argued that "From Chanel to Courrèges, the grammar of timescales changes" (107); that time is a style for Chanel, but a fashion for Courrèges (107). Chanel, he contends, merely "varies" the same model from one line to the next like a musical theme (106). Chanel's designs are thus "classic" fashions in an exclusively modernist sense: they both emphasize their timeliness and claim to be timeless. What retains present usefulness or currency from outside *the now* of fashion is a "classic," whether in literature, clothing, or music. One ongoing implication of "the classic," then, is that it will not pass away except in always being past in some sense. And this pastness requires that the classic belong to a (closed) order. Like the Modernist canon more generally, all "classics" are rhetorically positioned as part of an order that cannot now be reordered, despite all evidence to the contrary—the Modernist canon has never been stable in any medium. And this is the form of Chanel's Modernism that brings her into museum culture and becomes part of a sometimes nostalgic sometimes politically and aesthetically fraught narrative about the closure of modernism itself.

Commodity Art

If nineteenth-century trips to the theater or a ball were ways of mapping what was being worn by people whose culture one was presumed to share or to want to emulate, the modernist emergence of movies and magazines and mass-produced fashion apparently reversed this sense of "going to see." Benjamin's argument about mechanical reproduction and art could be reintroduced here and gives us another perspective on why the Modernist Chanel can never be equal to the modernist "Chanel." The nineteenth-century designer Charles Worth perhaps, but certainly Chanel and her peers, attempted to invest clothes with a value that could not be easily reproduced. Both the Chanel brand and Chanel's name function to invest "fashion" with something superficially like an aura (and which we might usefully compare to the moviestars discussed in chapter 1). Importantly, however, this "aura" claims to be almost reproducible if the cost can be met. As Simmel argues, "the objects of fashion, embracing as they do the externalities of life, are particularly accessible to the mere possession of money" (190). Not despite but *because of* Chanel's rejection of some of the most visible elements of conspicuous consumption in dress, only Chanel herself can exactly have— or at least be consumed as having—the precise Chanel style.

Chanel was a modern celebrity in the mode of the stars among whom she moved. Figures like Chanel and Man Ray exemplify an imagined Modernism populated by superstars and shameless self-promoters. In fact, the emergence of "high fashion" is precisely the emergence of the auteur designer, a nineteenth-century history bound up, as traced by Troy, in the increasing role of mass production in the clothing industry. The couturier expressed opposition to mass-produced clothing. Troy quotes Poiret: "I am not commercial. Ladies come to me for a gown as they go to a distinguished painter to get their portraits put on canvas. I am an artist not a dressmaker" (Troy 2003: 47). Nevertheless, in 1916, Poiret traveled to the United States to promote a new clothing collection intended for American women and described as "genuine reproductions" (Troy 2003: 302). Fashion produces a particular dialogue on the relation between art and mass culture in the distinction between haute couture and *prêt-à-porter*. Other fields where Modernists worked across art and mass culture (for example in Bauhaus design or in Corbusier's expansion into furniture) do not make this distinction so clearly. But as Troy argues in *Couture Culture*, modernist fashion intersects with modernist visual art in its approach to product differentiation and to the merchandizing of taste as style.

Renato Poggioli argues that fashion is in fact what enables the avant-garde to be seen and admired and thus also what defeats it by inevitably drawing it into the mainstream. Hebdige makes a similar argument with reference to the co-option of "cutting edge" subcultural style by the popular mainstream and this similarity is directly due to the extent to which Hebdige appropriates his idea of style from Modernist avant-gardism. Poggioli insists that the concept of artistic originality at stake in this dynamic is an entirely modern concept:

> According to Baudelaire's clever paradox, the chief task of genius is precisely to invent a stereotype. . . . The modernity of the stereotype is worth emphasizing. The tacitly enunciated task of classic art was the splendid repetition of the eternal maxims of ancient wisdom; impossible, then, for it to conceive of the commonplace pejoratively. . . . Classical thinking on art admits of only a single negative category: the ugly . . . the classical aesthetic, contrary to the modern, was in no position to admit into the category of the ugly those forms that might be said to have a not-new beauty. (Poggioli 80–81)

As Rosalind Krauss has also argued, the attachment to originality so crucial to defining Modernism requires a solipsistic picture of the relationship between famous works and artists and their historical and social contexts. It also obscures the relation between art and the copy that was so pivotal to the iconic Modernists but appeared in the realm of fashion in very different ways because it had not been preceded there by the same history of art.

Fashion thus has a privileged position when it comes to the art of modernism. The continual replacement and co-option of old avant-garde movements by "the new" defines avant-gardism as driven by fashion: spurning the masses but requiring an audience of like-minded "individuals" and spurning mere novelty while insisting on the new. Troy argues that the work of both Marcel Duchamp and Poiret circulated around an uneasy distinction between the original work of art and the mass-produced copy that comprises one of "the most recalcitrant (and compelling)" problems "of the modern period" (Troy 2003: 292). While the readymades extract art from the everyday, haute couture calls for the everyday to respond to its art. The relation between the unique work of art and the copy is repeatedly given new inflection by the way fashion expresses both similarity and difference, and it is not the popularity of a style that leads to its devaluation so much as its loss of specialization.

Wilson claims, "It was perhaps Chanel who announced the death knell for old-style couture." (89) In her famous *Vogue* interview on re-opening in 1953, Chanel declared: "I am no longer interested in dressing a few hundred women, private clients; I shall dress thousands of women. But . . . a widely repeated fashion, seen everywhere, cheaply produced, must start from luxury." Quoting this interview, Wilson continues: "Soon the Chanel suit was being reproduced everywhere, particularly in the United States, where, Cecil Beaton felt, it had indelibly stamped the American 'working girl' of the fifties; while the bright, sharp Mary Quant style of the 1960s was really a marrying of the style of the Chelsea art student with Chanel" (89). If her particular embrace of commodification shifted in Chanel's "return" it had always linked her interdisciplinary work in fashion, theatre, design, and advertising through her own name.

In general, Modernist avant-gardism is never opposed to branding and selling its products and Jennifer Wicke insists on the broad significance of advertising to modernism, remarking that "if advertising did not literally bring about modern life, it may be its chief emblem, a sign of the sign of the times" (593). Advertising is as modern an art form as the newspaper or the photograph, and was not just well placed to take advantage of modernism's emphasis on speed and ephemerality but centrally helped produce that experience of modernity. Thus advertisers have quickly adopted the changing techniques of modernist art—in fashion as everywhere else—precisely because from the outset they shared a heavily stylized commitment to selling novelty. The groundbreaking New York Armory show of 1913, featuring many famous proponents of surrealism and dada, is reported to have attracted "more than 10,000 visitors a day" (Harvey 28). Dramatically publicized by this show, Duchamp's "readymade" was itself a kind of brand, manifesting a particular mode of consumption—*Bicycle Wheel* and *Cadeau* are not in any literal sense already "made" before they are taken up as art—and a fashionable style of Modernist art. In turn, Chanel's style was both singularly hers and a mass-producible model, an ideal image and a collectable set. She just as often stressed the latter in advertisements, linking her designs to the efficiency of streamlining associated with iconic slogans like "Less is more" (Ludwig Mies van der Rohe quoted in Baudot 2–3). Troy also compares Chanel to Corbusier in terms of their embrace of an "international style" that relied on the commodification of that style (see chapter 7). Certainly both Chanel and Corbusier, well before Andy Warhol, used their names to label a sphere of production that incorporated the work of others.

In 1926, French *Vogue* labeled the little black dress "a Ford signed Chanel." Within the month, American *Vogue* reiterated: "The Chanel 'Ford'—the frock that all the world will wear—is model '817,' of black crêpe de Chine." The Ford image comprised style leadership, technological innovation, reliable repeatability, and the combination of all these images in that of "America." The Europeanness of Chanel makes this an interesting conjunction. On both sides of the Atlantic it worked as advertising: she was Paris for the Americans and Ford for the French. Elizabeth Hawes' *Fashion Is Spinach* (1938) claimed that the United States was "the only country in the world which can produce garments in masses. Any woman in America can buy a Chanel dress for whatever amount she has to spend" (120). But Hawes also understood such fashion as a middleclass copy of *style*: "Nobody ever told [the middle class woman] about style. She's fashionable,—God help her" (127). Chanel's relationship to this conception of authentic style is complex. She claimed, and her designs claim, that "Chanel is a style," but her explication that "A mode becomes demoded. Style never does" (Troy 2005: 21; see also Davis 162) depends on a modernist context in which fashion and style can be both entwined and opposed. Style, as recognizable and authoritative command of a particular historically changing representational schema— whether painting, literature, dress, or ways of living—could only be outmoded by fashion itself becoming redundant. But because her art needed to be fashionable, Chanel also embraced the possibility of being "copied" as a verification of her originality.

To be communicated as style, a "lifestyle" must always refer to fashion and belong to an intensely present-tense set of distinctions. Like all incarnations of "the New Woman," Chanel's version of her "generation" was a lifestyle that combines attachments to commodities and practices (such as bicycles or cars, shirt-waists or cigarettes, cocktails or lipstick). While scholarship and commentary on Chanel understandably stresses the freedom of movement in her loose-fitting uncorseted designs, this "freedom" nevertheless still participated in the imposition of a fashionable body type and associated lifestyles. These not only could be copied but were disseminated with the imperative that they must be copied if one was to be truly modern. Simmel concludes his essay on fashion by claiming that, while the "seeds of its own death" are intrinsic to fashion, "this transitoriness does not degrade it totally but actually adds a new attraction" (192)—fashion's constitutive openness to reinvention. But modernist fashion also openly frames itself as ideological in order to ward off the image of its own ephemerality. Fashion must make a claim at the level of habitus, whether it is a heterotopic one or not.

The body cultures that emerged with modernism always intersected with fashion in this way. In 1925, Rudolf Kayser could speak of the physical appearance of European Americanism as a combination of body styles opposed to the past even while they varied according to taste (395–97). In emerging discourses on health and fitness, in the physical education of the nineteenth century merging with the moral tenor and zeitgeist power of physical culture in the early twentieth, and in the glamorous aesthetics of modern ballet or sport that proposed new ideological subjectivities, modernist body cultures express fashions in the body and clothing as entwined sets of identities and practices. Their coherence comes from their regulatory claims, rather than from the designs themselves.

Craik's caveat that icons of fashionable identity—such as the flapper in the 1920s—cannot simply be translated into assumptions about actual lives (Craik 75–76) is an important one. But it also presumes that the modern "lifestyle" involves wholesale adoption. It is possible, if not unavoidable, to have more than one lifestyle. It is true that few women were "flappers," but few women were untouched by the changes to images of women's everyday lives and expectations that the flapper signified. For example, by 1925–26, the first years of Chanel's iconic "little black dress," it was widely presumed by popular and public culture that the bobbedhair girl was everywhere. Some employers would not hire women with bobbed hair, but while public voices debated whether they were immoral, radical, foolishly derivative, or just the new commonplace, women also bobbed their hair to get a fashionable job or just to be seen in a fashionable style. Bobbed hair signaled not only "flapper" but a recognizable position in relation to the range of ways of living available to women. Bobbed hair belonged to clubs, dancing, motorcars, and cocktails; identified artists, scholars, and professional or businesswomen; and was a recognized declaration of independence in which the avant-garde *bohème* met acceptable style. There was a time when Chanel was similarly disruptive and pervasive at once.

I have left the importance of the fact that Chanel designed for women more or less in the background. But the entwined impact of new lives for women and feminist politics on the stylization of the gendered self is indisputable, and Chanel's peers, if not interlocutors, include the first feminist theorists of gender. Virginia Woolf was a contemporary and, amid Chanel's fame, Joan Riviere was formulating her own Freudian theory of femininity as masquerade (Riviere 1929). The modernity of "gender," which names not only a sense of self but also ways of living is also evident throughout Simone de Beauvoir's classification of modes of womanliness in *The Second Sex* (1949). From Riviere to Judith Butler (see Lusty 18; 43) via Beauvoir, the stylization of gender, like fashion, is a relation to what precedes us—what we recognize as being stylistically available to us and as making sense in a given context.

Sherman's photographs respond first of all to continuity in styles and genres of gendered representations. But for Cahun gender and fashion are just as clearly intersecting languages for identity as for Sherman. Chanel also provides a productive point of comparison. While many of Cahun and Sherman's most famous images are striking for their familiarity against the grain of habit rather than for any shock value, they work by disrupting but remaining within the existing order. While not as confrontational as Cahun (see figure 11), Chanel's cross-gender references contribute to the popular ground on which Sherman works, including those self-portraits in which she posed as a young man. It is in coming after the institutionalization or mainstreaming of such questions (after Chanel, then, as much as after Cahun) that Sherman's disruption of gender performance through conformity to gender expectations seems to require the term "postmodern." She comes after, that is, "the end of style and the death of the subject" (Jameson 2002: 5) presumed to mark the end of Modernism. But, as Jameson points out, "museums and the art galleries can scarcely function" without a modernist sense of the "new" predicated on innovative style (5). Sherman's reproductions are just as clearly reliant on recognizable style, and Chanel has clearly been installed as a Modernist classic in the realm of fashion—still succeeding first of all on the grounds of a recognizable style that is disruptive enough to generate excitement but clearly functioning within the present system.

As Peter Galassi argues, Sherman's approach to popular culture does not take it as "a subject (as it had been for Walker Evans) or raw material (as it had been for Andy Warhol) but a whole artistic vocabulary, ready-made" (Galassi). Sherman thus may not introduce anything new to the grammar of photography, but, as the term ready-made suggests, she also does not merely copy the content of a film still or a fashion shot. Like Chanel, Sherman's film stills and her mannequins intervene in an expected language to produce a narrative that incorporates both the everyday and mythical dimensions of gender and that is equally historically specific and "classical." Between Chanel and Sherman we can construct a conversation about the singular and the copy, the expected and the exceptional, and the mediation of both through style. From Baudelaire to Chanel, from Marinetti to Hebdige, from punk to Calvin Klein, modernist style is the interplay of the personal with the masses—a relationship between singularity and field. And in the apparent irrationality of fashion's intervention in this relation we find its capacity for heterology and for critical reflection on ourselves.

6

Between the Acts

The Time of Modernism

Like quicksilver sliding, filings magnetised, the distracted united. The tune began; the first note meant a second; the second a third. Then down beneath a force was born in opposition; then another. On different levels they diverged. On different levels ourselves went forward; flower gathering some on the surface; others descending to wrestle with the meaning; but all comprehended; all enlisted.

Virginia Woolf, *Between the Acts*

It seems almost not worth remarking that modernity presupposes a relation to history—after all, a historicizing claim is built into the very concept of modernity. The term suggests that what modernism foregrounds in the experience and representation of modernity is a new historicity, a new temporality. Modernity, Michel Foucault notes, "is often characterized in terms of consciousness of the discontinuity of time: a break with tradition, a feeling of novelty, of vertigo in the face of the passing moment" ([1978] 1984b: 39). This chapter sketches a complex array of modernist accounts of history and time rather than reprise well-known critical conversations about the belatedness of modernism and the further belatedness of postmodernism. While the previous two chapters provided examples of what Modernism made available to Cultural Studies, this chapter turns to some of the conceptual foundations of modernism with a view to finding there the conditions for Cultural Studies' particular relations to history and the present. To give focus to such an extensive field, I structure this chapter by unfolding a range of influences on and implications of a single "classic" Modernist text: Woolf's final novel, *Between the Acts*.

Classics

Just as transforming Chanel into a "classic" places her designs, if not the brand, outside of modernity's currents of change, the wider installation of Modernist art among the "classics" constructs this art as a done-with revolution now absorbed into the realm of official culture. The more classically Modernist something is the less relevance it still claims for the present. The institutionalization of Modernism itself was always this sort of reactionary gesture—installed to defend territories and decry critics, imitators, or inferior successors. Early use of the label "Modernism" revolved around positioning Modernism as something already established rather than emergent. Even in 1929, Henry-Russell Hitchcock was impugning the imitative "modernism" of certain buildings; and both Georg Lukács' 1938 attack on "modernism" as antirealist and Clement Greenberg's 1939 defense of it against "academicism" and "commercialism" seek to establish modernism as an already recognized category.

But the temporality of modernism is contradictory.[1] Charles Baudelaire's well-known definition of modernity as "the transient, the fleeting, the contingent" continues as follows, although it is quoted far less often: "it is the one half of art, the other being the eternal and the immutable" ([1863] 1995: 11). In any given slice of modernism as a particular date range or specific generic field we find both of these elements and other historicities as well. We find, for example, a belatedness that looks principally to the past. In his essay on tradition, T. S. Eliot both dismisses "repetition" and insists that "tradition" enables sensitivity to the vital importance "not only of the pastness of the past, but of its presence":

> the historical sense compels a man to write not merely with his own generation in his bones, but with a feeling that the whole of the literature of Europe from Homer and within it the whole of the literature of his own country has a simultaneous existence and composes a simultaneous order. This historical sense, which is a sense of the timeless as well as of the temporal and of the timeless and of the temporal together, is what makes a writer traditional. And it is at the same time what makes a writer most acutely conscious of his place in time, of his contemporaneity. (154)

Literary allusions aside, this accounts for the classicism of Chanel as much as of Eliot himself.

The complexity of modernist historicism can also be found in the paintings and ideas of the Pre-Raphaelite Brotherhood who, from 1848, formulated a manifesto style that "reclaimed" the medieval, the Renaissance, and the Classical all at once in a rejection of what were seen as the dominant styles of the present. The Pre-Raphaelites thus overlap in important ways with the range of modernist histories that foreground the value of particular pasts for the present, including the popular history disseminated through archaeological expeditions and exhibitions and of widely read publications on "myth."[2] Such images of the past's continuity with the present are as crucial to modernism as its break with the past. To take the kind of literary example not usually employed to talk about Modernism, while the abridgement of Christian history from the 1922 edition of James Frazer's *The Golden Bough* pressed it into a more exotic story about the magical past, the 1890 edition had already laid out the significance of a particular completed history for establishing the shape of contemporary religion—"Our Debt to the Savages" overlaid onto the classical past. A survey of modernist historicism must also, to extend this example, include a range of primitivisms: of the Paul Gauguin style; in the essentializing human conflicts of *Heart of Darkness* or D. H. Lawrence's *Kangaroo* (1923); in appropriations exemplified by the "primitive" African masks in Pablo Picasso's *Les Demoiselles d'Avignon* (figure 8) or Man Ray's *Noire et Blanche* (1926); or in the passionate "native" engagements of ethnographers like Bronislaw Malinowski or Margaret Mead.[3]

Primitivism and futurism were in fact often entwined, as in Aldous Huxley's *Brave New World* (1932), where John the Savage provides a scathing commentary on modern life, or in the Futurists' mix of unfettered "drives" and technophilia. Thus we cannot reduce even Modernism, let alone modernism, to one attitude to the past or the contemporary. The same slice of modernism will also provide us with examples of an obsessive focus on the present that eschews whatever is thought to be of the past, whether "classical"—reinvigorating modernity through reference to a particular bounded past—or "primitive"—exploring the shape of modernity through what is perceived as untouched by it. Modernism's repeated claims to "break" with something thus may refer primarily to the past or to the present, but usually to both—usually some history of the present is being rejected. Some such breaks take on greater historiographical significance from time to time and this changing evaluation will be missed if we cannot return Modernism to its modernism. The Modernist complex of discourse on past, present, and future is drawn together in multiple ways by the historically grounded self-reflection of modernism. This chapter thinks about a cluster of modernist breaks that in no way forms a sequence or proposes a teleology ending in something postmodern. I begin with one of the most foundational modernist breaks for Cultural Studies: the intervention of "critical theory," the modernism of which is often forgotten and the historicism of which is sometimes also neglected. Doing so will also give context and content to reconsidering what Woolf meant by her distinction between "moments of being" and "moments of non-being" discussed in chapter 4.

One crucial element of modernism's critical attitude is clarified by the concept of the "dialectic" that stretches from G. W. F. Hegel through Karl Marx, the Frankfurt School, the Russian "formalists," and beyond, each time articulated as an intervention in dominant discourse. Inflected also by Antonio Gramsci and Louis Althusser, dialectical analysis has been overwhelmingly influential on both modernist studies and Cultural Studies. According to Hegel's dialectical model, every proposition or state emerges from contradictions inherent in a preceding one. This has been so influential on theories of modernity and modernism that it seems almost possible to argue that "postmodernity" could only refer to a state in which the contradictions of modernity had been overcome—or at least displaced by entirely new ones. The dialectic accounts for the necessity of reflexivity; of the "critical attitude." But is not the only modernist approach to history Cultural Studies deploys. Both Mikhail Bakhtin and Ferdinand de Saussure, for example, also provide influential critical tools for considering the Cultural Studies emphasis on the way history is built into a present system. Although Bakhtin himself is clear that his project should be distinguished from Saussure's, the modernist invention of "structuralism," where every term belongs to a system of differentiation from other terms, and the equally modernist "dialogics" produced by Bakhtin, whereby a text inevitably incorporates the complexity and conflicts of its historical context, are better understood relative to one another and to the historicisms to which they sometimes seemed opposed. Roland Barthes acknowledges as much in one of his famous arguments for semiology:

Less terrorized by the spectre of "formalism," historical criticism might have been less sterile; it would have understood that the specific study of forms does not in any way contradict the necessary principles of totality and History. On the contrary: the more a system is specifically defined in its forms, the more amenable it is to historical criticism. . . . The important thing is to see that the unity of an explanation can not be based on the amputation of one or other of its approaches, but, as Engels said, on the dialectical co-ordination of the particular sciences it makes use of. ([1957] 1973: 112)

Graeme Turner makes European structuralism's influence on early British Cultural Studies very clear (Turner 10ff). Cultural Studies takes up not only the dialectical approach but also the dialogic approach that developed from it and the semiotic approach that, as in Barthes, post-structuralism came to reconcile with it. Perhaps more than any other derivation, however, the Marxist interpretation of Hegelian dialectics and the model of ideology it produced have become canonical tools for Cultural Studies. Indeed one way of tracing the emergence of Cultural Studies would be to trace the ways in which ideology critique was applied to cultural production, distribution, and consumption. The dialectical method also underpins the practice of many of the theorists and philosophers who have shaped post-Birmingham School approaches to culture within the discipline. In *Subjects of Desire*, Judith Butler argues that even Foucault is a "tenuous dialectician," always reliant on the structure of opposition and overcoming founded in the Hegelian dialectic (Butler 1999: 217–29).[4] The persistence of the dialectic in Foucault is also evident in Hans-Georg Gadamer's *Truth and Method*, where "historically effected consciousness" means not only that people are constituted historically but also that their self-reflection is historically framed: *"To be historically means that knowledge of oneself can never be complete.* All self-knowledge arises from what is historically pregiven" ([1960] 2004: 301). Gadamer is responding here to Martin Heidegger's renovation of phenomenology, which I consider in the next chapter. Although far less often associated with Cultural Studies, phenomenology is broadly concerned with historicized experience: with relations between the subject and the historically conceived world. In *Being and Time*, Heidegger argues that Dasein's (Being's) "own past . . . always means the past of its 'generation,'" having "grown up into and in an inherited interpretation of Dasein" ([1927] 1962: 20). If we hear echoes of this in Pierre Bourdieu's *habitus* also, it is because each of these theorists aims to account for the same modernist experience: the impact of modernity on (the modernist production of) subjectivity.

This historically located consciousness is not always understood in such apparently compatible ways. That is, we cannot tell a single story about the modernist conception of the relation between subject and history, and sometimes, as with Sigmund Freud, a single model will not even do for a single modernist. When Gilles Deleuze and Felix Guattari want to account for what cuts through "territorializing" structure in modernist literature they argue that "Literature is assemblage. It has nothing to do with ideology. There is no ideology and there never has been" (Deleuze and Guattari 5). This critique is a point of departure for their concept of assemblage, which searches for a nonhierarchical, nonteleological model of relations between identities, practices, and contexts (see chapter 4). This "assemblage" formation does not newly appear in the realm of the postmodern but is exemplified for Deleuze and Guattari by artists like Woolf, the painter Paul Klee, and the filmmaker Jean-Luc Godard. This formation is also captured for modernism under labels like bricolage, collage, and, as I suggested in the last chapter, heterotopia. The different modernist traditions of hermeneutics (including ideology and psychoanalysis) and of assemblage are both influential.[5] However, Modernism and Cultural Studies are often discussed in ways that prioritize one over the other: Sergei Eisenstein *or* Dziga Vertov; Marx *or* Friedrich Nietzsche. Cultural Studies' strong institutional relationship with ideology critique has often meant its focus on assemblage is neglected although in fact the discipline clearly embraces both approaches. This prioritization of ideology critique is of course often framed as a political question. But Deleuze and Guattari, extolling Woolf's capacity to critique via assemblage—to write politically engaged fiction in the middle of things rather than teleologically—are not refusing a critical attitude but, instead, contesting what kind of engagement a critical attitude involves.[6]

Time: Tick Tick Tick

Jean-François Lyotard famously defined postmodernism by its "incredulity towards metanarratives" (Lyotard xxiv), an incredulity exemplarily manifest in the post-structuralist critique of history posed by such different methods as Derridean deconstruction and Foucauldian genealogy. I turn now to unpacking the modernist historicity of *Between the Acts*, and thus its critical engagement. I want this reading first of all to suggest that, given the complexity of modernist ideas about history, further complicating matters with the belatedness of "postmodernism" is unnecessary. Modernism is itself already "belated," among other things.

Woolf's novel, positioned in 1941 at the end of what is usually seen as Modernism, is often read as a text tensely positioned between elegy for a more meaningful experience of the world and trepidation at what the present says is coming soon. But discussions of the nostalgia of *Between the Acts* miss some crucial contexts and counternarratives. *Between the Acts* looks to the past embedded not only in England and Poyntz Hall but in people and their relationships—particularly in the local community that stages the fundraising pageant that dominates the novel. The pervasive presence of English history, which the pageant treats, does not obscure the presence of the future, and the story is equally weighed down with anticipation and foreshadowing. Beyond this, *Between the Acts* equally marks the rhythm of unfolding time at the level of cultural history, around the pageant as annual event, in narrative structure and its reception, and in the mechanics of a day that must go forward as days do.

The necessity of change here is not only the necessity of death and loss but also of mundane modernization, like electric lights in the church (Woolf [1941] 1992: 160). In one assemblage of perspectives, the audience reflects on the pageant's presentation of an ideal Victorian home:

> Change had to come, [Mrs. Lynn Jones] said to herself, or there'd have been yards and yards of Papa's beard, of Mama's knitting. Nowadays her son-in-law was clean-shaven. Her daughter had a refrigerator.
> . . .
> "Were they like that?" Isa asked abruptly. She looked at Mrs. Swithin as if she had been a dinosaur or a very diminutive mammoth. Extinct she must be, since she had lived in the reign of Queen Victoria.
> Tick, tick, tick, went the machine in the bushes.
> "The Victorians," Mrs. Swithin mused. "I don't believe" she said with her odd little smile, "that there ever were such people. Only you and me and William dressed differently."
> "You don't believe in history," said William.
> The stage remained empty. The cows moved in the field. The shadows were deeper under the trees. (156–57)

The book focuses on a new visibility for relations between time and space that needs to be unfolded more complexly than as the opposition often deployed in conversations about postmodernism. It is worth stressing here that the pageant—the play within the book—does not have a more complicated relation to the problem of history and the experience of time than does the rest of the narrative.

Between the Acts anticipates coming change from multiple vantage points. The last words of the novel are "Then the curtain rose. They spoke" (197). It is impossible to know if something changes here or not. Most days, Isa knows, are all the same, despite how much and how little everything means. *Between the Acts* is a book about attachment, hope, memory, despair, art, history, change, and life, and these affects and concepts are like waves retreating and advancing in the long movement of the tide—there's a fabric to life that is both within and between the acts. Although reception of this novel has generally been inflected by Woolf's suicide before it was published, *Between the Acts* is no more mournful than hopeful. As with the pageant itself, *Between the Acts* suggests that life holds together and goes on between apparently significant and insignificant acts. If *Between the Acts* seems to close on several final notes—a curtain, a conflict, the coming night—each of these are also situated as repetitions. Isa and Giles have "spoken" before; Miss Latrobe has expected her own frustration with the pageant's reception. The story is not suspended on the edge of a monumental break, and the beginning of the pageant is as evasive as the end of the novel: "Then the play began. Was it, or was it not, the play?" (76).

There has been a tendency to see this pageant as the purpose of the story—as Brechtian theatre, as antifascist pageantry, as a call for a truly public art. The pageant ends with a "shock," when the players turn an array of mirrors and other reflective surfaces on the audience. As Michael Tratner suggests, the pageant implies that the present cannot be assembled in the same way as the historical vignettes that constitute it up until this "shock." But this is not necessarily because something has been lost and the "scraps, orts and fragments" around them are no longer enough to build or rebuild English culture. The images of the past from which the pageant is assembled—along with the responses of the audience and the distractions of machine, author, and environment—are not in fact strictly of the past, and the audience knows this. The many unspecified voices that thread between the named ones in the pageant's audience mirror the narrative unfolding onstage and blend in with the same mix of visibility and anonymity in the pageant's production. The borders between actors, audience, production team, and staging mechanisms are present but unclear and part of the pageant's reflection on history.

Tratner sees in the pageant's "shock" a mirror of Walter Benjamin's claims about film's capacity to reinvigorate art by representing everyday life (Tratner 116–17). Tratner's qualifications of this comparison center on the fact that *Between the Acts* embraces not only its own artfulness but the traditional image of art: "Woolf thinks that art has not been 'auratic' enough, not enough a source of belief" (Tratner 129). In the introduction to *Virginia Woolf in the Age of Mechanical Reproduction* (2000), Pamela Caughie argues that the gramophone, which provides the soundtrack to the pageant, undermines any such claim to the aura of art (xxiii). Certainly the gramophone provides a set of overlapping refrains, ranging from the clichés of popular culture (like "Home Sweet Home") to a combination of sound poetry and radio static. But after these many different contributions by the gramophone, it is "jagged" and "abrupt" contemporary music that accompanies the shocking display of mirrors. This music references a present the audience feels does not include them, increasing their discomfort: "Very up to date, all the same. What is her game?" (Woolf [1941] 1992: 183). If *Between the Acts* unpacks nostalgia as comforting historical fantasy, claims for the power of public art are also qualified by the presence of multiple publics— Mrs. Manresa does her makeup in the mirrors that appall Colonel Oliver, and the jazz or foxtrot so popular with some audiences is shocking to at least the most audible element of this one.

Caughie sees in the audience's "distracted listening or reception" a "working against Fascism's efforts to organize the new masses into one receptive listener" (xxiii). She adds that the pageant's invocation of radio-disseminated popular catchphrases "might be read as an effort to restore the pre-BBC days when producers served particular publics and managed immediate experience" (xxiii). In fact, *Between the Acts* would question whether such a time existed any more materially than the past recaptured by the Pre-Raphaelites. But the claim that Miss Latrobe's pageant serves a particular public for which she effectively manages immediate experience needs to be considered more carefully. Watching from the bushes and corners that constitute the backstage, Miss Latrobe frets that the audience will lose focus: "The audience was on the move. The audience was strolling up and down. They kept their distance from the dressing-room; they respected the conventions. But if they wandered too far, if they began exploring the grounds, going over the house, then . . . Chuff, chuff chuff went the machine. Time was passing. How long would time hold them together? It was a gamble; a risk. . . ." (Woolf [1941] 1992: 151).

Most events punctuating the ongoing stream of daily life in *Between the Acts* are stage-managed, like Mrs. Manresa's sudden appearance at Poyntz Hall and Miss Latrobe's attempt to "douche" her audience "with present-time reality" (179). This attempt goes wrong, she thinks, because reality is "too strong" (161) and the audience instead wants a plot where things move in a more certain direction than they do in real life. But while she waits for the mirrors to have a dramatic effect she knows they cannot, the music in the background has half done her work. The final scene inspires her audience (as a mass, not as particular voices) to ask why: "Ourselves? But that's cruel. To snap us as we are, before we've had time to assume . . . And only, too, in parts. That's what's so distorting upsetting and utterly unfair" (165). The parts the audience plays, as well as those the mirrors literally reflect, are incomplete. While the generalized audience is disconcerted, there are more singular responses. Old Lucy Swithin enjoys the sense of having had (and here, the tense matters) the potential to be Cleopatra as much as her ordinary self with her own little life. Miss Latrobe laughs at the idea of Lucy being Cleopatra and is more satisfied by the grander interpretation that she has revealed to Lucy "her unacted part" (153). But both the story's other artists—Isa and Mrs. Manresa (whose self-creation is also a kind of art)— might suggest that "Cleopatra" is the kind of cliché idealization from which people's historical sense of the world is generally comprised.

It is very hard to align this layering of fantasy and anxiety with the claims of Brechtian theatrical realism. But just that set of modernist debates is raised in the novel, intersecting it with what Renate Holub calls "the realism/modernism debate." The leading figure in this debate was Lukács. As Holub accounts for it, Lukács' attack on expressionism is another critique of the assemblage tradition by the hermeneutic one, rejecting "a vision of the world that finds delight in fragments rather than totality, in gaps rather than relations, in multiplicities of viewpoint rather than objectivity and truth. . . . What matters for Lukács is the totality the text evokes" (Holub 7). While it would be possible to make claims for the realism of *Between the Acts*, and its invocation of a totality in which things are at once changing and staying the same, this would not satisfy Lukács, whose critique of literature has much in common with André Bazin's opposition between the cinema of reality and the cinema of the image, in which some modernists were not "Modernists." Lukács understood his attack to be on "modernism" as avant-gardism, but he used these terms in a very particular way and, from our vantage point, singled out an "expressionist" tendency that did not, for example, include Bertolt Brecht or Thomas Mann as Modernist. In *The Meaning of Contemporary Realism* (1962), one of Lukács' starting points for this critique opposes Mann to Joyce, seeing in the latter no deep analysis of the world but instead what I have called assemblage (and which Deleuze and Guattari accuse Joyce of never really producing): "The perpetually oscillating patterns of sense- and memory-data, their powerfully charged—but aimless and directionless—fields of force, give rise to an epic structure which is *static*, reflecting a belief in the basically static character of events" (Lukács 18). Moreover, Lukács extends this opposition between sensation and development to Modernist philosophy, rejecting in direct parallel Heidegger's ideas about historicity and Heidegger's own opposition to experience as sensation. Lukács claims that what Heidegger calls "thrownness-into-being" (Heidegger quoted in Lukács 20)—and privileges as the modern condition of never having "power over one's ownmost Being from the ground up" (Heidegger [1927] 1962: 330)—is ahistorical. Construed as "thrown-into-being," "the hero is strictly confined within the limits of his own experience" (Lukács 21). What is interesting here is not whether or not Lukács reads Joyce or Heidegger well, but that aesthetics, philosophy, and politics are all organized around the term "Modernism" as reflection on the present.

The Writing of History (Chuff, Chuff, Chuff)

Writing about a surrealist movement less than ten years old, Benjamin claims that "The trick by which this world of things is mastered—it is more proper to speak of a trick than a method—consists in the substitution of a political for a historical view of the past" ([1929] 1996c: 70). In "The Angel of History" Benjamin further presents an image of history as futilely attempting to clarify what can never be fixed. The angel of history has "His face turned toward the past" and the storm of progress "irresistibly propels him into the future to which his back is turned, while the pile of debris before him grows skyward" ([1939] 1969: 257). Set alongside the essay on surrealism, this famous image of the burden of history becomes a vivid thread in the modernist historiographical tapestry. Michel de Certeau's introduction to The Writing of History (1988) also stresses the impact of modernity on what could be conceived of as history. Modernity installed the human perspective as the way in which the world was known and this in turn made "man" rather than God the author of history. This human-centered historiography underpins both modernist perspectivism and the cultural field in which such perspectives appear, with equally dramatic effects on science, religion, and art (see chapter 7). Importantly for reading Between the Acts, this modernist historiography equally affects the Great Names and the everyday versions of history that appeared in the wake of modernity.[7]

In A Room of One's Own, Woolf notes that, from the Great Names perspective, "A scene in a battle-field is more important than a scene in a shop—everywhere and much more subtly the difference of value persists" (4). This is taken up again in Between the Acts, when Isa compares the great version of history preserved in the library—war, science, politics, art—to pain-relief medicine that probably won't work: "What remedy was there for her at her age—the age of the century, thirty-nine—in books? Book-shy she was, like the rest of her generation; and gun-shy too. Yet as a person with a raging tooth runs her eye in a chemist shop over green bottles with gilt scrolls on them lest one of the may contain a cure, she considered: Keats and Shelley; Yeats and Donne. Or perhaps not a poem; a life" (8). Instead of great lives, it seems, Isa's age immerses itself in the tragically ordinary:

> None of them stopped her toothache. For her generation the newspaper was a book; and, as her father-in-law had dropped *The Times*, she took it and read: "A horse with a green tail . . ." which was fantastic. Next, "The guard at Whitehall . . ." which was romantic and then, building word upon word she read: "The troopers told her the horse had a green tail; but she found it was just an ordinary horse. And they dragged her up to the barrack room where she was thrown upon a bed. Then one of the troopers removed part of her clothing and she screamed and hit him about the face. . . ."
> That was real. (8)

History, art, and life here are inseparable. Even the opposition between everyday history and Great Names history is too neat when both are equally important in the above vignette. And the evolutionary history with which Lucy is so fascinated in fact fits on both sides, and thus neither side, of this opposition, caught between the great name of Darwin and the popular and public dissemination of his ideas. Evolution, as Lucy understands it, is a fantasy of permanent presence and an allegory for her own redundancy and immanent extinction, juxtaposed in the opening scenes with her brother's pride in military tradition, the long history of the house, and Isa's uncertainty and empathy for change.

What we might call the "popular public" sphere of history is also in some senses the most modernist form of history, for reasons suggested in chapter 3. The history of *The Times* newspaper that Isa is reading could exemplify the interdependent constitution and representation of modernity that comes to form this field. The adoption of *The Times* as the newspaper's title in 1788 (having been called *The Daily Universal Register* since 1785) speaks to a sense of modernity that people often place much later. It communicates almost the same image of its content and readership as the much later title of *Time* magazine: invoking both "the now" and efficient reflection on it. The newspaper was always a claim to disinterested skimming of whatever was contemporary, which is why, for Benjamin, "The social base of *flânerie* is journalism" (Benjamin [1927–40] 2002: 446). *Time* magazine was launched by Henry Luce and Briton Hadden in 1922 as a weekly news digest, with the claim that "People are uninformed because no publication has adapted itself to the time which busy men are able to spend on simply keeping informed" (quoted in Tungate 2004: 158). This claim is premised on a specific understanding of relationships between mass production and daily life, the national and the global, the state, the citizen, and the public sphere. As newspapers developed their modern form in conjunction with the Western institution of normative literacy, the history stretching from the abstract reflection of *"The Times"* to the imperative of *"Time"* also makes explicit an intimate relationship between mass culture and modernist historicity. Newspapers distribute a shared sense that one is, with every passing day, becoming more out of date. In its mesh of sensation and information measuring out a passing cultural history, the newspaper constitutes its presumed reader rather as evolutionary history does Lucy—caught between fantasies of presence and fears of redundancy.

Isa is too old for the present and too late for the past. One genealogy for this modernist "belatedness" comes through Friedrich Nietzsche. Nietszche's distinction between monumental history, antiquarian history, and critical history might also be identified with the tensions in *Between the Acts* between the historical claims made by the great lives or the army, the watch or the paintings, and the gramophone or the pageant. Nietzsche claims that monumental history enables an individual to find inspiration in history, encouraging one to "gain strength through reflecting on past greatness" (Nietzsche [1876] 1997: 69). Antiquarian history refers to the process of looking back on a solid foundation that articulates belonging and thus enables "love and loyalty" (72). But Nietzsche emphasizes the importance of *critical* history because "man must possess and from time to time employ the strength to break up and dissolve a part of the past" (75). This is another manifestation of the "critical" in modernism's critical attitude. Modern culture, Nietzsche argues, is too concerned with history and modern man is lost, adrift, and incapable of happiness due to his inability to forget history. But the importance of this text is also in its foregrounding multiple forms of modernist history, even allowing them to be more entangled than discrete. In the early scenes of *Between the Acts*, Isa's brushes and her hair seem antiquarian and the library monumental, but the history of the present relayed by the newspaper provides a space for each of these and, as Isa suggests, for critical history as well.

Baudelaire, Nietzsche, and Benjamin, all foreground the importance of time as something that constitutes us by passing us by. For the shopgirls, factory workers, and businessmen like Isa's husband Giles, modern life is timed. George Simmel's 1903 essay on this subject claims that "the technique of metropolitan life is unimaginable without the most punctual integration of all activities and mutual relations into a stable and impersonal time schedule" (177). But for the rural gentry, like Captain Oliver and Lucy, this again positions them as echoes of something past. Oliver's understanding of history cannot encompass Miss Latrobe's pageant and its discordant alignment of scenes lifted from fiction and fact in an erratically selective history of England. Nor could Oliver incorporate the moment-by-moment unpacking of cinema as a temporal experience in Marcel Duchamp's *Nude Descending a Staircase*. But Oliver's oppositional stance to what he sees as modernization is itself modernist, just as his antiquarian attachment to the pocket watch still situates him as a subject of modernity. As Simmel notes, the "universal diffusion" of watches already represents modernity's assemblage of experience into a whole life relative to many others (177). Nevertheless, although Oliver has a watch he seems set apart from modern life as city life. Metropolitan life and its associated cosmopolitanism are powerful modernist themes and, counter to these and thus just as pivotally, Oliver is associated with the rural.

If the rural emerged as the nonurban defined by modernity's processes of urbanization, Jean-Jacques Rousseau, William Blake, or even Matthew Arnold could still write from "the country" without a sense of being excluded from modern life. It is through writers like Baudelaire, and their equation of modernism, as the cultural self-consciousness of modernity, with the city, that the country becomes marginal to modernism. In the core representations of modernism—in Heidegger or Woolf, from Baudelaire through Agatha Christie's mysteries to horror films like John Boorman's *Deliverance* (1972), "the country" is a mesh of rural rusticity and anti-modernization. This urbanization of modernity persists in Cultural Studies, tied to a modernist investment in the changing present negotiated amid a dense field of others. For Simmel, "intellectuality" is a necessary response to the metropolis:

> With each crossing of the street, with the tempo and multiplicity of economic, occupational and social life, the city sets up a deep contrast with small town and rural life with reference to the sensory foundations of psychic life. The metropolis exacts from man as a discriminating creature a different amount of consciousness than does rural life. Here the rhythm of life and sensory mental imagery flows more slowly, more habitually, and more evenly. Precisely in this connection

the sophisticated character of metropolitan psychic life becomes un-
derstandable—as over against small town life which rests more upon
deeply felt and emotional relationships. (175)

Marx and Friedrich Engels' reference to "rural idiocy" in *The Communist
Manifesto* (1848) is a more extreme version of Simmel's opposition, which
itself draws on Engels' depiction of rural weavers as a class that "had remained sunk in apathetic indifference to the universal interests of mankind" (Engels 52). By the time Raymond Williams published *The Country
and the City* (1975)—which has never been the central Cultural Studies text
it deserves to be—the nonmetropolitan had come to stand for the past in
Cultural Studies, and in particular for the past persisting in the present.

There is in fact no straightforward binary opposition in modernity between metropolitan and rural time, however routinely modernism may
continue to conjure it. As the rise of "holiday-making" and "leisure" within
modernity indicates, what has emerged is rather a construction of metropolitan time as the too-rapid but barely-up-to-date standard, compared to
which there are several alternatives. The movie *Deliverance* was marketed
with the tagline "This is the weekend they didn't play golf," and in this juxtaposes at least five relevant temporalities: the city, structured leisure, "nature," the rural, and the "barbarian." In *Between the Acts* we can also find
an interleaving of different increasingly distinguished uses of time: work,
news, war, leisure, holiday travel, the festival, the pastoral, nature, and gen-
erationalization. Nevertheless, what happens at Poyntz Hall seems at least
as detached both from uses of time that are intimate with the city and from
the public, rather than private, sphere of action. This is not a representation
of transition, or still less of commuting, but of exchange between differently
located perspectives on (experiences and representations of) modernity. As
my example of rural picture theaters in chapter 1 suggests—and figure 4
manifests the displacement of modernity in both the car and the theater
despite the ubiquity of both in 1939, the same year as the action in *Between
the Acts*—being the first to undergo technological change does not necessarily fix one's degree of modernity. By the same token, the equation between
the rural and the premodern is the stuff of myth. Modernism is not a *zeitgeist* more or less up to date in central or peripheral parts of the world but
a field of attitudes and of questions, many of which are being asked by Miss
Latrobe's "country" audience.

Such perspectives on modernity are not always geographically defined.
Turning the progress of history into a critique of history is particularly evi-

dent in the long series of modernist utopian and dystopian narratives. I have gestured toward this history in both of the preceding chapters and, as I mentioned in the introduction, Fredric Jameson, among others including Benjamin, has claimed utopia as one of the foundational concepts of modernity (2002; 2004). This claim is often used to associate "late" modernity with dystopia as a reaction against the utopian social or aesthetic projects of modernity proper. Certainly some key Modernist dystopias have become cultural touchstones, but modernism routinely interweaves utopia and dystopia.

Futurism is the most visible Modernist figure in this regard. The Futurist embrace of the machine and speed is an attempt to find an articulation of culture that exceeds history by removing its human factors. Futurism should thus be distinguished from the utopian and dystopian science fiction writers before and after it because, for the Futurists, avant-gardism is an end in itself: they are not stepping outside what was visible as history to this point in order to examine the present. Instead, Futurism steps outside the present by fixing it in an attitude of speed, a progress for its own sake and thus speed without change—"presentist" rather than "futurist," perhaps. F. T. Marinetti declares that Futurists stand "on the last promontory of the centuries! . . . Why should we look back when what we want is to break down the mysterious doors of the Impossible? Time and Space died yesterday. We already live in the absolute, because we have created eternal and omnipresent speed" (119). But what is most spectacular in writers like Marinetti is suggestive for modernism more broadly. Utopianism is always, according to Benjamin, tied to its dependence on "the new," which is "the quintessence of that false consciousness whose indefatigable agent is fashion" (Benjamin [1927–40] 2002: 11), and is "as little capable of furnishing [humanity] with a liberating solution as a new fashion is capable of rejuvenating society" (15). The "people of the nineteenth century," Benjamin further claims, are "natives" of this "region" in which the pains of the new are the "latest novelty of all time" (26).

Dispersed Are We

Woolf's style in *Between the Acts* is no longer shockingly new, and nor was it in 1941. But her narrative in no way prioritizes the future. Bonnie Kime Scott stresses the variety of different sounds, emotions, and roles for the now also-no-longer-shockingly-new gramophone in Miss Latrobe's pageant (2000: 105ff). One of the gramophone's most crucial roles is providing a refrain for the pageant's assemblage: its production, experience, reception, and distribution across a *duration*. The way in which "today" automatically raises the specter of yesterday and the prospect of tomorrow depends on modernity's awareness of what the modernist philosopher Henri Bergson referred to as "duration" (Bergson [1899] 2001). The ticking of the gramophone is neither an event nor a pause but an irregular continuity: "The music chanted: *Dispersed are we*. It moaned: *Dispersed are we*. It lamented: *Dispersed are we*, as they streamed, spotting the grass, across the lawns, and down the paths" (Woolf [1941] 1992: 95–96). The gramophone is thus far from background noise, countering the looming events signaled by news from the city and the planes overhead with a different sort of temporality.

The new place for the figure of the scientist in modernity, and thus in modernist popular and public culture, brought with it not only new ideas about space and time but new currency for those ideas. This is spectacularly exemplified in media coverage of Albert Einstein's theory of relativity and its renovation of physics in the 1920s. Einstein won the Nobel Prize in 1921 and toured the United States that year, becoming the first mass-media scientist superstar. But this stardom in itself is not more important than the popular interpretations and derivations of Einstein, including the attempts by J. W. Dunne to assimilate something like Jungian comparative religion with relativity in books like *The Serial Universe* (1934), in which space and time are more or less interchangeable. As I suggested in chapter 3, and as the dissemination of interpretations and summaries of Freudian and Marxist theory also attests, modernism includes an expanding range of conversations between experts in a popular public realm. This context becomes important for part 3 of this book, so I want to pursue one instance of it in Woolf's novel.

In *Being and Time*, Heidegger argues, "It is repetition that first reveals to Dasein [Being] its own history" ([1927] 1962: 386). But repetition can only reveal history because something stretching between the repeated instances and experiences brings them together. Between the acts there is, to begin with, an interval. The interval is pregnant with waiting and resonant with effects and draws attention to nothing but duration. This something between the acts forms the context for each event. Such time is never empty but filled with memory, expectation, and other affects (even in the experience of the same old thing or nothing in particular); it is filled with the continuity of consciousness. In *Time and Free Will* (1889), Bergson argues that the objects we perceive as being in the world are only part of reality because we are always also perceiving *time*. If this seems a headily philosophical proposition it is worth noting that Bergson was not an obscure writer unknown outside of philosophy. In fact, Mary Ann Gillies claims, "The period of 1909–1911 saw over two hundred articles published on Bergson in English journals, newspapers, and books" (28). Like Marinetti, Bergson was a successful public speaker in England before World War I and his texts were quickly translated, a success Gillies suggests "stems from the ways in which he engaged with the dominant issues of the day. His was a voice raised in many debates about the nature of life" (30). She also suggests that whether or not Woolf read Bergson hardly matters, given the overlap between their conceptions of both reality and representation (Gillies 130).

Bergson's impact certainly depends substantially on the fact that he addressed science, art, and morality together. Bergson saw time as the dimension in which life was lived and in which experience makes sense: life and consciousness "need not be entirely absorbed in the passing sensation or idea; for then, on the contrary, it would no longer *endure*" (Bergson [1889] 2001: 100). Peter Childs also makes the link between Bergson and Woolf (Childs 48–50), following a discussion of the importance of psychoanalysis for Modernism. This connection is useful because Bergson's "duration" allows for varying individual experiences of time and thus stresses that individuals perceive history always from the perspective of the present. Bergsonist duration, as Gilles Deleuze puts it, coincides with consciousness. The whole (duration, time, continuity) "constantly creates itself . . . 'in the manner of a consciousness'" (Deleuze [1983] 1986: 8, quoting Bergson). Chronological time is not the same as this experience of time: "for a conscious being, to exist is to change, to change is to mature, to mature is to go on creating oneself endlessly" (Bergson [1911] 1944: 10). While this can be usefully cross-referenced to the discussion of maturity in chapter 2, it also exposes a problem behind the frequent claims that modernism (or even Modernism) "took on multiple perspectivism and relativism as its epistemology for revealing what it still took to be the true nature of a unified, though complex, underlying reality" (Harvey 30). For Woolf, as much as for Bergson, reality was not something underlying the experienced time and space of the world—even the landscape in *Between the Acts* is here a view and there a pasture and somewhere else just dirt for grubbing in. From this influential modernist standpoint, time and space are assembled, like representations of the past, from competing and unstable perspectives. And continuity is established in this process of assembling meaning amid other assemblages.

In *Cinema 1*, Deleuze uses Bergson's philosophy of temporality to elaborate a theory of cinema (which I take, given my argument in chapter 1, as a theory of modernism). Here Deleuze uses Bergson's distinction between a sensory-motor image, which he aligns with the cliché (Deleuze [1985] 1989: 19), and the time-image, which makes "time and thought perceptible" (17). *Between the Acts* clarifies the inextricability of these images in perspective: "As Bergson says, we do not perceive the thing or the image in its entirety, we always perceive less of it, we perceive only what we are interested in perceiving, or rather what it is in our interests to perceive" (Deleuze [1985] 1989: 19). The commonality between Bergson and Woolf, like the potential of Bergson for thinking about cinema,[8] suggests that we should not be too quick to read Woolf's disruption of linear temporality and critique of the accumulative progress of history as proto-postmodern. Let one example stand in for a case that has been made many times—and paradoxically about so many different modernists that it ought to be redundant: "Woolf speaks to us as a postmodern, not in terms of her specific historical moment, but in the way she approaches truth and subjectivity; she makes us read history as a series of unrelated moments, moments whose unity comes through a narrative that tells us more about its own construction than it does about the past" (Rosenberg 1128). This aspect of Woolf, whether it is read through Bergson or through Lyotard, is integral to her modernism, but it also provides an alternative to the most usual deployment of gender to talk about modernism, time and history.

Summarizing the narrative about history against which "postmodernism" is supposed to turn, Julia Kristeva claims that "the time of history . . . can be characterized as a *linear* time: time as project, teleology, departure, progression and arrival. This linear time is also that of language considered as the enunciation of a sequence of words" (Kristeva 187). This is the "grand narrative" (or meta-narrative) of history understood to represent Enlightenment thinking. But Kristeva's elaborations of the modernist revolution in art— from *Revolution in Poetic Language* (1974) to *Powers of Horror* (1982)—generally mounts this critique of linear history with references that are clearly modernist and usually Modernist. This critique is explained in her accounts of either modernism or postmodernism as a "feminine" subversion of or irruption from within a linear order associated with patriarchy. Kristeva argues that the modernist aesthetic revolution, which she begins with the Symbolists, accesses the "feminine" outside of history and language. Alice Jardine calls this critical move, in the work of Kristeva, Lyotard, Deleuze, and others, *gynesis* (Jardine 324–25). *Gynesis*, Jardine argues, deploys "woman" as modernity—as that which the man of modernity strove to understand.

This "woman" is a place for experience rather than a knowable experience, but it is also compatible with a Kristevan model of "women's time" that resembles Nietzsche's "monumental time": history determined by relations of *re-production* "and its representation" (Kristeva 189–90).[9] One of my aims in focusing on the shopgirl in chapter 4 was to set aside presumptions about what kind of feminine is central to modernism, if indeed modernism deploys gender to explain its difference the way so many critics claim it does (see Felski; Jardine). Certainly, many of the writers and artists pivotal to modernism have employed images of femininity to play out their disruption of old orders. It is not just that the changes and challenges to gender roles that are part of modernism offered up "the feminine" as an excellent canvass for new ideas about universal truths, cultural difference, and historical change.[10] Woolf again is exemplary. A lot has been written about the feminist analysis of history and culture that Woolf was producing around the time she wrote *Between the Acts*. *Three Guineas* (1938), in particular, is frequently juxtaposed with the novel to explore Woolf's links between fascism, masculinity, and patriarchy. But in Woolf "woman" is not a story about the unknowable exterior or anterior of culture—neither Kristeva's *chora* nor Jardine's *gynesis*. The pageant in *Between the Acts* begins with the birth of modernity and reorganizes the many layers and strands of modernity as a historical experience only available through its present-tense reception. There is no claim to refer outside of history, despite there also being no single coherent historical narrative.

In "The Metropolis and Mental Life," Simmel claims that "Man" as "a differentiating creature . . . is stimulated by the difference between a momentary impression and the one which preceded it" (175). The effect of this, he claims, is an ongoing sense of instability in the face of change. This is widely accepted as an integral modernist experience—from the violent proclamations of the Futurists, through the ephemeral present tense of ready-to-wear fashion, to the holding pattern of *Between the Acts*. The juxtaposition of multiple possibilities in *Between the Acts* is, like Miss Latrobe's pageant, only grasped at the edge of things. After the pageant, the audience considers:

> *Dispersed are we*, the gramophone triumphed, yet lamented, *Dispersed are we.* . . .
> "But you must remember," the old cronies chatted, "they had to do it on the cheap. You can't get people, at the time o' year, to rehearse. There's the hay, let alone the movies. . . . What we need is a centre. Something to bring us all together . . . The Brookes have gone to Italy,

in spite of everything. Rather rash? . . . If the worst should come—let's hope it won't—they'd hire an aeroplane, so they said. . . . But I was saying: can the Christian faith adapt itself? In times like these . . . At Larting no one goes to church . . . There's the dogs, there's the pictures . . . It's odd that science, so they tell me, is making things (so to speak) more spiritual . . . The very latest notion, so I'm told is, nothing's solid . . . There, you can get a glimpse of the church through the trees . . ." (Woolf [1941] 1992: 198)

As Marshall Berman famously argues, "To be modern is to find ourselves in an environment that promises adventure, power, joy, growth, transformation of ourselves and the world—and, at the same time, that threatens to destroy everything we have, everything we know, everything we are. . . . To be modern is to be part of a universe in which, as Marx said, 'all that is solid melts into air'" (159, quoting Marx).

And yet, since the canonization of Modernism, Western culture seems to be routinely caught up in discovering that the world is moving too fast for people to live in. Cultural Studies has engaged in this ongoing conversation, in recent decades often using the term "postmodernism" for this discovery. David Harvey's discussion of postmodernism as "time-space compression" has been influential. In response to Berman's reference to Marx, Harvey outlines yet another understanding of this "maelstrom of perpetual disintegration and renewal" (Berman 15; quoted in Harvey 11). According to Harvey, the modernist "transitoriness of things makes it difficult to preserve any sense of historical continuity" (11). This requires segmenting capitalism into epochs with their own requirements for the organization of time and space, and although Harvey acknowledges that when viewed from different perspectives modernism looks different, he nevertheless claims that in postmodernism time has annihilated space (Harvey 238) and—ironically this too is an argument he borrows from Marx—"the present is all there is" (240). From *Between the Acts*, however, I think we might take the useful suggestion that the modernist present is always saturated with various pasts and futures.

Woolf's critics have sometimes seen the smallness of the worlds she writes about, as well as the cultural milieu with which she is associated, as a sophisticated sort of provincialism. So much of what she writes focuses on individual perspectives or circulates in networks that are so culturally specific as to be almost stifling. And yet this apparent narrowness does not lead to any sharp focus. Simone de Beauvoir regretted this, claiming that she couldn't read Woolf's novels because "there isn't any thesis" (Bair 154). But it is because Woolf's worlds are so clearly located and yet so unfocused, so tied to particular experiences and so overwhelmingly aware of the rest of the world, that they offer such an exemplary feeling for the what is repeatedly claimed to be a pivotal modernist experience. Without claiming broad social and political commentary after the manner of D. H. Lawrence or George Orwell, Woolf's novels can be unfolded in many directions that reveal the specific conditions of the text's production. "Like quicksilver sliding, filings magnetized, the distracted united," *Between the Acts* encompasses and unfolds out into Woolf's own *oeuvre*; the outbreak of World War II; the impact of new scientific and psychological theories; modernist and more specifically feminist aesthetics; popular cultural and art currents of the time; shifting ideas about public and community; new philosophies and sciences of temporality and "culture"; and critiques of all of the above. None of these are subordinated to a single overarching thesis and thus *Between the Acts* also gestures toward the broad terms of reference, if not in fact also the interdisciplinarity, that dominate Cultural Studies. And if Cultural Studies makes its great claims to relevance through a similarly inassimilable web of the contexts that shape and express cultural meanings, that is crucial to its modernism.

In conclusion I return to the presumed opposition between time and space, and the associated opposition between modernism and postmodernism, by way of another return. Foucault's lecture "Of Other Spaces," which I considered in the last chapter, offers us Foucault's clearest argument for a distinction between the nineteenth and twentieth centuries in terms that might fit a break between modernism and postmodernism. Here he claims that the nineteenth century is obsessed "with history" (Foucault [1967] 1986: 22) and the "present epoch" (this lecture was delivered in 1967) with space, and particularly with simultaneity and juxtaposition: it is "the epoch of the near and the far, of the side-by-side, of the dispersed" (22). But the dominant discourse of the present to which Foucault is referring is structuralism, and thus a modernism typified by Saussure as much as Claude Lévi-Strauss. Even then Foucault acknowledges, "it is necessary to notice that the space which today appears to form the horizon of our concerns, our theory, our systems, is not an innovation" (22). I have tried to show here how modernists related time and space to one another in very diverse ways. In Foucault's essay, the changing forms of both utopia and heterotopia do not involve the kind of epistemic discontinuity he associates with the shift from a Classical view of time and space (Galileo) to the modern. Foucault's examples instead refer once more to the emergence of modernity—the appearance of illness in the language of the cemetery, of museums as the public collection of time, of the "colony." This discourse on space thus also marks the emergence in modernity of the spatio-temporal realm of modernist representation that the last part of this book will call "culture."

3

THE SPECTER OF MODERNISM

7

The Age of the World Picture

"We get the picture" concerning something does not mean only that what is, is set before us, is represented to us, in general, but that what is stands before us—in all that belongs to it and all that stands together in it—as a system. "To get the picture" throbs with being acquainted with something, with being equipped and prepared for it. Where the world becomes picture, what is, in its entirety, is juxtaposed as that for which man is prepared and which, correspondingly, he therefore intends to bring before himself and have before himself, and consequently intends in a decisive sense to set in place before himself. Hence world picture, when understood essentially, does not mean a picture of the world but the world conceived and grasped as picture.

Martin Heidegger, "The Age of the World Picture"

In part 3, my focus shifts to modernism more than Modernism, particularly to the modernist conditions that mark the emergence of Cultural Studies in theory and practice well before it had a disciplinary title. Cultural Studies is riven, sustained, and inspired by the field of modernist debates discussed thus far and, further, Cultural Studies depends on and elaborates a modernist model of culture entwined with an equally modernist model of subjectivity. Together these form the "critical attitude" of which I outlined Modernist forms in part 1. But Cultural Studies is also a quintessentially modernist discipline to the extent to which it remains a contested assemblage of methods, objects, and debates. The components of this argument are slightly more convoluted than the case studies that organized my previous chapters, in part because these three chapters pay more attention to the overlap between modernism and what is usually defined as postmodernism. In chapter 8, I trace a long modernist narrative in contestations over what culture is and what it is for. In chapter 9, I explore some examples of the refrains that characterize modernist Cultural Studies. These discussions, however, depend on understanding the modernist experience as itself a representation of modernity. To this end, chapter 7 focuses on a text in which the shape of Cultural Studies emerges in ways not usually attended to by readers and introductions. Martin Heidegger's essay "The Age of the World Picture," published in 1938, will serve as a jumping off point for several lines of discussion about age, world, and picture. But another return to the relations between Enlightenment, modernity, and modernism is necessary first.

Art, Science, Morality

Accepting "the Theodor W. Adorno prize by the city of Frankfurt" in 1980, Jürgen Habermas gave an address first published as "Modernity Versus Postmodernity" (1981) and then as "Modernity—An Incomplete Project" (1983). I will return to this essay throughout part 3 as a counterpoint to my use thus far of Michel Foucault's "What is Enlightenment?," which was itself composed in reply to criticism formed in and around Habermas's essay. In this essay, Habermas understands what he calls *cultural modernity* "as the separation of the substantive reason expressed in religion and metaphysics into three autonomous spheres. They are: science, morality and art" ([1981] 1983: 9). Thus far, Habermas's tripartite structure follows Max Weber's elaboration on Immanuel Kant, but he wants to extend this argument to the fate of such "cultural modernity" in the late twentieth century. He sees each of these spheres as being produced in modernity according to specialized assessments of validity, "handled as questions of knowledge, or of justice and morality, or of taste" and thus institutionalizing discourses that can professionally know them, "each of these in the control of specialists who seem more adept at being logical in these particular ways than other people are" (9). But while Enlightenment thinkers, Habermas argues, "wanted to utilize this accumulation of specialized culture for the enrichment of everyday life," Modernism shatters this "optimism" and increasingly insists on the autonomy of these spheres and their separation from "the *hermeneutics* of everyday conversation" (9, my emphasis).

In this essay, Foucault is one of Habermas' antimodernist "young conservatives": those who claim "as their own the revelations of a decentered subjectivity, emancipated from the imperatives of work and usefulness, and with this experience they step outside the modern world," combining modernist attitudes (such as an emphasis on a model of subjectivity that is not self-identical) with what Habermas sees as "an irreconcilable antimodernism" (paradigmatically removal from the common life-world). For Habermas, these "young conservatives" oppose reason with "a principle only accessible through evocation, be it the will to power or sovereignty, Being or the Dionysiac force of the poetical" (14). Regardless of whether this is a useful reading of Foucault—certainly it resembles Julia Kristeva's key arguments (see chapter 6) rather more than Foucault's—it demonstrates yet again that there are multiple and contradictory modernist traditions. Here, Habermas opposes the hermeneutics of modernist "critical theory" to an alternative—including Heidegger and Friedrich Nietzsche—that most commentary would agree is also modernist. This observation is important quite simply because synchronic "breaks" fail to explain such differences *within* modernism and thus require a reader to consign writers like Heidegger and Nietzsche to a foreshadowing of postmodernity, obscuring the many ways in which they need to be thought alongside their contemporaries.

For Habermas, will, Being, the body, nonidentity, power, and difference are successive names for the mystical theology of counter-modernity. Habermas dismisses as antimodernist, for example, what David Harvey calls Heidegger's "counter-myth of rootedness in place and environmentally-bound traditions as the only secure foundation for political and social action in a manifestly troubled world" (Harvey 35). At the same time, he dismisses trajectories like surrealism as having undermined the only modernism worth having—in effect as anti-"modernity" Modernism. Interestingly, Walter Benjamin also understands surrealism as exposing the shattering of "wish symbols of the previous century," but not in the same pejorative sense. Habermas in fact simultaneously aligns Foucault with Modernism (surrealism) rather than modernism (Enlightenment), but his charge of "antimodernism" is usually translated as "postmodernism," including by the incorporation of this essay in Hal Foster's famous collection on postmodernism. This undoubtedly glosses why Foucault in "What is Enlightenment?" takes such pains to stress the links between his own attitude and that of both Kant and Baudelaire.

Foucault's essay on Enlightenment and Habermas' essay on incomplete modernity are two documents in a debate that exceeds them (see Kelly 1994) and indeed reaches out to Heidegger's relation to modernism and modernity. While Foucault's response doesn't mention Heidegger, Habermas' wider critique of "specialization" in his "Modernity" essay provides a new context for Foucault's debt to Heidegger. Habermas sees the specialization of aesthetics (as in surrealism) and of philosophy or theory (as in Foucault) as abandoning its location in the material and rational world. But reading Heidegger's "World Picture" essay suggests that the opposition between the Heidegger-Foucault line and Habermas must be something else. Heidegger here is just as scathing about the specialist.[1] He sees specialization as taking many, and never positive, forms, for example the rise of modern "method-ology" in the university system (Heidegger [1938] 1977: 125) that becomes "not the consequence but the foundation of the progress of all research" in such a system (123). This detachment of knowledge-as-research from life and experience is only one element of modernity's specialization Heidegger criticizes in this essay. In an argument that is foundational to Foucault's work, Heidegger sees modernity as distributing knowledge according to discrete *objectifying* fields that are, at the same time, implicitly *subjective*: morality becomes a set of rules to which personal experience relates (116); art becomes a matter of perspective (116); and science becomes a field of experiments defined by their own hypotheses.

Where Modernism claims to continue an Enlightenment "project," it usually stresses a transhistorical and transcultural humanism. Adorno and Horkheimer—writing at the same time as Heidegger and partly in conscious dialogue with him—argue that Homer's *Odyssey* (c. 700 BC) "as a whole bears witness to the dialectic of enlightenment" because "the Homeric spirit takes over and 'organizes' the myths, but contradicts them in the process" (Adorno and Horkheimer 43). In *The Odyssey*, they contend, "The venerable cosmos of the meaningful Homeric world is shown to be the achievement of regulative reason, which destroys myth by virtue of the same rational order in which it reflects it" (44). They claim this "reason," representing and destroying myth at the same time, is singularly prescient in Homer but centers Enlightenment thought about modernity. The same dialectic is also apparent for them in Nietzsche's writing of "both the universal movement of sovereign Spirit . . . and a 'nihilistic' anti-life force"—both the revelation of ideology at all levels and "the reduction and malleability of men . . . worked for as 'progress'!" (Adorno and Horkheimer 44). Modernity, they suggest, gives rise to its own critique, and film, adolescence, modern love, urbaniza-tion, fashion, and the sense of the contemporary itself are all examples and components of this—of what I have called modernism.

But of all this, Heidegger is in fact more skeptical. He understands mo-dernity's break with the past as transforming what counts as human values. Such a position often leads to charges of "relativism"—claims that seeing human values as something other than universal undermines any possible truth or value—but Heidegger is not denying the importance of human values or of thinking in terms of foundations and origins. For Heidegger, things do have an origin, and a meaning defined by it, but this is located neither in the subject's perception of them nor in the subject's production of them but, instead, in the field in which they are produced. For instance, "The artist is the origin of the work. The work is the origin of the artist. Neither is without the other . . . artist and work *are* each of them by virtue of a third thing which is prior to both, namely that which also gives artist and work of art their names—art" (Heidegger [1931] 1971: 17). While this excerpt may seem far removed from that use of reason to benefit everyday life on which Habermas insists, Heidegger's claim that we need to conceive of a field in which a cultural object or practice is meaningful before we can analyze it in fact meets up with Habermas in Cultural Studies.

Heidegger insists that we think always through our own period's knowledge of the world, so that the origin of ideas like "truth" is only relevant if those origins are still residually present without any attempted return to a past point of view. While "World Picture" is usually read for its discussion of science, a topic to which I will return, this essay also considers modernism's impact on how the world is known more generally. Heidegger proposes as his central claim that

> Man makes depend upon himself the way in which he must take his stand in relation to whatever is as the objective. There begins that way of being human which mans the realm of human capability as a domain given over to measuring and executing, for the purpose of gaining mastery over that which is as a whole. The age that is determined from out of this event is, when viewed in retrospect, not only a new one in contrast with the one that is past, but it settles itself firmly in place expressly as the new. To be new is peculiar to the world that has become picture. ([1938] 1977: 132)

This emphasis on both mastery and novelty in modernity extends, for Heidegger, not only to science but also to aesthetics, morality, and religion.

In his discussion of how this has transformed religion, Heidegger identifies two trajectories brought together in modernism: perspectivism and mass culture. The idea that religion has become a matter of perspective, and is thus relegated to another type of mass production, recalls Nietzsche's discussion of "the death of god" but also looks forward to Roland Barthes' discussion of "The Death of the Author." In both of these arguments, any unified constant authority is undermined in modernism by the separate empowerment of every individual:

God is dead. God remains dead. And we have killed him. How shall
we comfort ourselves, the murderers of all murderers? . . . Is not the
greatness of this deed too great for us? Must we ourselves not become
gods simply to appear worthy of it? (Nietzsche [1887] 1974: 181)

[A] text is made of multiple writings, drawn from many cultures and
entering into mutual relations to dialogue, parody, contestation, but
there is one place where this multiplicity is focused and that place is
the reader, not, as was hitherto said, the author. (Barthes [1977] 1999:
148)

Heidegger argues that, instead of understanding the world through standards like God and Beauty, modernity depends on "culture" for a relative
set of "values." Heidegger thus sets out the terms of a debate over what "cultural relativism" means including, in another essay in the same collection
as "World Picture," the self-interestedness with which this debate will be
carried out. In an aside that aptly summarizes what many decades later we
sometimes refer to as the "culture wars," Heidegger says: "Those standing
about in the marketplace have abolished thinking and replaced it with idle
babble that scents nihilism in every place in which it supposes its own opinion has been endangered. This self-deception, forever gaining the upper
hand in relation to genuine [Nietzschean] nihilism, attempts in this way to
talk itself out of its anguished dread in the face of thinking. But that dread
is dread in the face of dread" ([1954] 1977: 112). This dread is an alternative
perspective on the ephemerality and speed elsewhere used to characterize
the experience of modernism (see chapters 4 and 6) but it is also, of course,
often used to characterize "postmodernism" for writers inclined to use that
term.

The World

Heidegger understands "the world" as that which organizes and knows "the
earth" ([1931] 1971: 66ff), but this is only one element of the age of the world
picture, as the epigraph to this chapter indicates. The possibility of representing the world is nevertheless integral to being equipped to "get the picture" and in this context we can approach the problem of relations between
modernity, modernism, and postmodernism through a crucial instance of
representing *the world*: "globalization." Discussion of globalization is often
associated with postmodernism.[2] As Benedict Anderson's canonical text on
nationalism suggests, however, the "global" and the "national" it is often as-

sumed to have displaced are entwined concepts. In *Imagined Communities* (1991), Anderson accounts for how the nation and nationalism "came into being" toward the end of the eighteenth century (4), at the height of the Enlightenment and as part of the emergence of modernity. He argues that the uncertainty "rationalist secularism" left behind required "a secular transformation of fatality into continuity, contingency into meaning," and the idea of the nation served this end (11). It is not that no one talked about "Japan" or "France" before this time, but that "states were defined by centres, borders were porous and indistinct" (19). The "nation" was not only always tied to traffic across borders but its borders were constructed to facilitate and manage such traffic, emerging among the new mobilities of modernity and their mapping of the world. The new chronometer, which mapped time and space onto each other at the foundation of modern cartography, overlaps here with other kinds of maps: "Like censuses, European-style maps worked on the basis of a totalizing classification, and led their bureaucratic producers and consumers towards policies with revolutionary consequences" entwining "explorers, surveyors and military forces" in a project of filling in the grid (Anderson 172).

The modernist ideas about the city I discussed in chapter 4 extend and refine this placement on a global map. In 1903, George Simmel could claim that Weimar was not truly metropolitan because it lacked "the decisive nature of the metropolis[—]that its inner life overflows by waves into a far-flung national or international area" (182). This modern city and this nation-state are both modernist concepts insofar as they are experiences and representations of modernity tied together by the concept of culture. Through culture, modernism reflects on relations between nation and world encompassing colonialism, transnational exchange, cosmopolitanism, and what we could call "modernist travel": industrialized travel for the purposes of cultural experience. Modernist travel encompasses new modes of travel for work and lifestyle: the iconic Modernist figures of the American émigré and Paris' "multicultural" Left Bank are only the more noticeable accumulations in a field of crisscrossing paths. Albert Einstein or Leon Trotsky in Mexico, and Paul Gauguin in Tahiti or Margaret Mead in Samoa, are, respectively, celebrity and expert versions of this field but it also encompasses banal holidays, traveling salespeople, and commodities like traveling clothes—whether these were designs for mass-produced patterns or the singular white bathing suit of an F. Scott Fitzgerald heroine.

Anderson attributes such shifts to new forms of mobility (railways, steamships, motor transport, aviation) and to the need for common management skills and modern perspectives shared by colonial empires and capitalist interests bound together in the spread of "modern education" (115–16). This set of connections easily interwove with narratives about modernization and blurred into the label "Americanization," which, in the 1920s, was the first term to link transnational trade with cultural homogenization in ways we now associate with globalization. There were many critics of American-ization at the time, but Rudolf Kayser's essay "Americanism," published in 1925, disdains such widespread dismissal: "it would be wrong to want to recognize the epoch only in the external phenomena of economy and ex-change, thereby passing over the new orientation of the spirit" (Kayser 396). For Kayser, Americanism is not reducible to Fordist cultural production and not solely about the transnational distribution of commodities. It is also not only "the new European catchword" (395) but "a new European method," encompassing new active lifestyles as much as opposition to tradi-tionalism and religiosity in art and other fields. "Americanism is fanaticism for life," Kayser writes, "for its worldliness and its present-day forms" (396). Americanism was thus another name for emphasis on the present (and thus even for modernism) and incorporated American pragmatism as well as popular forms like cinema.

In the cultural, economic, and political emergence of "the nation" in "the world" discussed by Anderson, both the colonial and the postcolonial—reflecting on and constituting culture and identity in this age of the world picture—become modernist concepts. While I could refer to the Modernist texts of Frantz Fanon that discuss the colonial situation and decolonization through the specializing institutions of modernism, and with a telling em-phasis on breaking with the past of "native culture" (see Fanon [1952] 1999: 225–26), it will be more useful at this point to notice the extent to which Arjun Appadurai's recent theories of postcolonial globalization are continu-ous with modernism. In his text on the cultural dimensions of globalization, significantly titled *Modernity at Large* (1996), Appadurai argues that the na-tion-state has been undermined and displaced by other (deterritorializing) forms of power: by ethnoscapes, mediascapes, technoscapes, financescapes, and ideoscapes (1996: 33). In fact, versions of each of these scapes could be located in Anderson's account of modernity's nation-world formation. Ap-padurai's model is of course pointing to changes in each of these fields, but as its debt to Gilles Deleuze and Felix Guattari's model of deterritorializa-tion suggests, this is another mode of the modernist assemblage. Elsewhere, Appadurai insists that these "scapes" show how identity and tradition are no longer linked to place, but rather displace "trait geographies" with "process geographies" (2000: 6). This is only a singularly postmodern narrative if we ignore its continuity with, for example, Anderson's recognition that the nation-state was never tied solely to territorialized traits or opposed to mobility. And while Appadurai's scapes are fluid and irregular "landscapes," they are also continuous with what Heidegger calls the "age of the world picture" in being "deeply perspectival constructs" (Appadurai 1996: 33).

An example that does not replicate the usual discussions of globalization in terms of trade might be helpful here. When Le Corbusier was appointed to finish designing the Indian city of Chandigarh in 1950 he was already internationally famous, but what "international" meant in this sense, and what the "International Style" he represented meant by employing the term invoke very specific modernist discourses on the world as coherent and knowable. Thus when Corbusier called a house "a machine for living in" he was making simultaneously aesthetic, scientific, and moral claims that positioned him as knowing the spirit of an age relevant to the world as a whole. The age known by Corbusier was the age of Corbusier, and International was the Style proper to it. Kenneth Frampton defines the International Style as the child of Corbusier and Frank Lloyd Wright—characterized by emphasis on volume, planes and surfaces, and lightweight fabricated building materials—but the exemplary International Style is not Wright's hand-wrought materials and integration of the natural environment but the precast look exemplified by Stuttgart's 1927 model "workers' housing" exhibition (Frampton 1992: 248–61).[3] While Corbusier and Appadurai seem entirely incompatible in some ways, they not only agree in important respects about a disjunction between what Heidegger would call "earth" and "world" but where they differ they are in fact taking up equally modernist trajectories.

Corbusier's manifesto approach to architecture recast how built form intersected with life by relegating cultural specificity to geographical constraints and thinking instead of "modernity at large." Walter Gropius' claim that "A modern, harmonic and lively architecture is the visible sign of an authentic democracy" (in Welchman 246) is explicitly tested in Chandigarh: the first planned city in the brand new nation-state of India. Frampton sees the failures of Chandigarh as representing the Enlightenment's "inability to nurture an existing culture or even to sustain the significance of its own Classical forms, its lack of any goal beyond constant technical innovation and optimum economic growth" (1992: 230). And yet, in 2008, the now somewhat dilapidated drama that is Chandigarh is the subject of a world heritage listing application based on the same rhetoric that aimed to manage the lives of its citizens from the beginning: paint colors, street trees, leisure activities, world view. In its summary of modernist planning and architecture, from Enlightenment politics to Modernist public art, Chandigarh literally both concretizes and shuts down contentions that help define modernism.

Learning from Disneyland

Thinking about modernist architecture returns us in another way to the problem of modernism's relation to postmodernism. Architecture is one of the most influential sources of our ideas about the postmodern aesthetic. However, across its fullest range from Corbusier's monumentalism and Wright's play with both the natural and the built through Antoni Gaudí's flowing shapes and Louis Sullivan's skyscrapers to Bauhaus utility and Deco motif, Modernist architecture and design is anything but redundant. Moreover, the modernist task of designing a "look" that represents a cultural moment remains as entrenched for Frank Gehry and Mark Newson as it was for Corbusier and Chanel. This doesn't necessarily dismiss the argument that postmodernism, as a periodization for architecture, rests on a sense of coming after the great stylistic extravagances, revolutionary fervor, and claim to coherent projects of the Modernists, and this warrants further consideration.

The modernist redistribution of aesthetics as a relation to both the popular and the public (see chapter 3) has meant that some of the best-known modernist experiments with built form take place in public art and architecture, of which one of the most telling instances is the art gallery. The concept of public art is itself a modernist one, and the public face of "Art" is a statement about this role, as the design and display parameters of public galleries make clear. And the provocation that is built into Wright's design for the Solomon R. Guggenheim Museum in Manhattan (1959) is no different in terms of its discourse on art, style, authority, and the public than Gehry's for the Guggenheim Bilbao (1997) or Jacques Herzog and Pierre de Meuron's for the Tate Modern extension (projected completion in 2012). "Postmodern" architecture, rather than manifesting the end of design or intention, appears on the same conceptual terrain as that which occupied the Modernists. If some famous postmodern designs tend to dehistoricize architecture and undermine representation of singular intention, then these are extensions of some rather than other modernist debates. Charles Jencks, Robert Venturi, and others make compelling arguments for a major conceptual break in post-World War II architecture. This thesis, exemplified by Venturi, Denise Scott Brown, and Steven Izenour's *Learning from Las Vegas* (1977), is outlined in Scott Brown's earlier essays. In "Learning from Pop" (1971), Scott Brown extols the difference between the intentional posturing of Modernism and "learning from what's there," meaning not only from the context the design is intended for but from popular and mass culture indications of what is desired in that context. Learning from advertising, which is one of her key examples, might require engaging with its bias, "But at least it's another bias, an alternative to the architectural navel contemplation we so often do for research; i.e. ask: What did Le Corbusier do?" (Scott Brown 63). But if Corbusier was only interested in some elements of what was "there" and rarely who would use it, then the "Las Vegas" thesis has selected precisely and only that element of modernist architecture as the Modernism to which it will be "post," ignoring Wright's "Fallingwater" (1936–39), for example, or Sullivan's office buildings.

More problematic still, Jencks' exemplar of "multivalent" postmodern architecture is Gaudí, a pivotal figure in the Catalan "modernisme" movement. Gaudí can hardly be assimilated to a periodization that is useful for postmodernism and yet, as Jencks notes, "There wasn't a communicational mode Gaudí didn't use at least once" (Jencks 313). Jencks also concedes, "The more one analyses [Le Corbusier's *Unité d'Habitation*], the more one finds link after link between the different levels of experience. . . . Not only does this [multivalency] allow the architecture to become alive in different ways to each generation and thus result in a lasting architecture, but it also stimulates each generation to reach beyond its familiar abstractions" (quoted in Hays 305). This is less a paradox, as K. Michael Hays puts it (306), than a contradiction revealing how little difference is marked by "postmodernism" as a style at the level of experimental architecture. Gaudí's Casa Milà (1905–7) and Jørn Utzon's Sydney Opera House (1957–73) also speak "nonsynchronously" to different audiences, as does that lasting icon of Exposition culture, the Eiffel Tower (1889). And between Gaudí and Utzon, between Corbusier and Venturi, we have Disneyland. By considering Disneyland's modernism, I contest claims about postmodernism that are used to distinguish Cultural Studies from modernism not only at the level of periodization, because I do not only mean Disneyland on its opening in 1955 but Disneyland today, but also at the level of content, because "Disneyland" has come to serve as a particular image of what Cultural Studies does.

The "unification of disparate material" (Jencks 309), which is postmodern architecture's most compelling evidence in support of its break with modernism, also continues what I have called the assemblage strand of modernism. In much the same way as Chanel reorders existing fashion elements, "postmodern" architecture reorders the significance of elements, assembling its pastiche style after the manner of surrealists. Even the revalued multiplicity of cultural reference points in Las Vegas casinos or Disneyland draws not only on the displays of modernist shopping and the cultural pastiche of the modernist Exposition, but also on modernist planning more generally. Disney's EPCOT Theme Park (1982) makes some of the most obvious references: the "Experimental Prototype Community/City of Tomorrow" echoes Corbusier in several key respects; its "World Showcase" mirrors the national pavilions of the Modernist Expositions; and its central globe mirrors the once famous "perisphere" at the center of the World's Fair of 1939.[4] Included as figure 14, the perisphere, with its accompanying "trylon," stood at the center of the walking paths carefully mapped through the mix of international cultural display, sideshow alley, and futurist utopia that constituted the World's Fair.[5] Maps of the various versions of Disneyland, and images of its attractions, make entirely clear its debt to the design, planning, and content of such hugely successful and quintessentially modernist Fairs and Expositions. The mapped experience of Disney theme parks, designed around movement, attention, distraction, and sensation, equally derive from the Exposition concept. In fact, the permanent carnival spaces of Las Vegas or Disneyland also make them much more like the multi-pavilion cultural mélange of the Expositions than like a building. Las Vegas casinos that work as iconic cultural digests—like the small-scale partial "Paris" and the selective façade of "New York–New York"—or as compressed citations of historically impossible locations—like the ancient Egypt of "Luxor" or collage of mythical Europes in "Excalibur"—are conceptually contiguous with Disneyland, perhaps especially in their symbolic rather than mathematical picture of the world.

If Disneyland and Chandigarh are contemporaries, then so are the broader fields of "Disney" and Vegas, even if the success of theme parks took some time to manifest as the mega-resorts of Vegas today. Vegas extends the theme park into "adults only" as well as family play, but the idea of the theme park is the leisure industries' version of a modernist manifesto on social hygiene. Disneyland extends the Taylorist time management of childhood, families, shopping, and cultural education into the arena of "tourism." The educational utility of the "tour"—reflecting on the world as a process of reflecting on the self—is itself a product of modernity. In this context, Dean MacCannell's comments on architectural souvenirs are helpful. MacCannell

Figure 14. "World's Fair Views: The Perisphere Bisected by Ramp," 1939, New York World's Fair, published September 29, 1940. Photograph from the Library of Congress, Prints and Photographs Division, Gottscho-Schleisner Collection (reproduction # LC-G613-T01-38526 DLC).

sees Giovanni Piranesi's eighteenth-century "Views of Rome" as a new form of documentation that stressed symbolic meaning as much as physical fact. Piranesi's views represent the experience of visiting "Rome" rather than the things that are there, via a perspective that mimics "a camera or a human eye" (MacCannell 29). This representation gestures to the emergence of a modernist idea of culture in the way "the so-called subjective view point has been entirely constituted outside itself" (29). As MacCannell notes, this further constructs a "tourist viewpoint or attitude (in the pejorative sense)" (29); an attitude supplemented by increased nineteenth-century merchandising to create the tourist experience. Tourist agencies and other travel vectors were converted into an industrialized hierarchy of travel in which the tourist was a holidaymaker and a sightseer as well as (at least sometimes) a student of culture, which also meant that culture needed to be expertly compiled for him or her.

For MacCannell, these experiments with perspective culminate in Disney, where the "historic past and childhood are overwhelmed by fantasy versions of themselves" (33). He positions Disney firmly on the side of anti-symbolic (anti-hermeneutic) tourist architecture, seeing in Piranesi, Disney, and Gehry's Guggenheim not only a mythic historicity that occludes origins but also an invocation of the commonality we "lack" (35). While Piranesi-Disney has "killed and cooked" this crisis "for consumption by tourists" so that "there is no recognition of historical dialectic" (35), Gehry's Guggenheim seems to MacCannell to bring this dialogue about common culture somewhat back into play (36). MacCannell's argument draws on Jean Baudrillard's and Fredric Jameson's critiques of Disneyland as representing what postmodernism does to the real and to history. Baudrillard insists that Disneyland's "digest of the American way of life, panegyric to American values . . . is presented as imaginary in order to make us believe that the rest is real, when in fact all of Los Angeles and the America surrounding it are no longer real, but of the order of the hyperreal and of simulation" (Baudrillard [1981] 1988: 174). Jameson concurs that reframed quotation displaces any authentic history in Disneyland, arguing that postmodernism is historicist rather than historical (1991: 118). But these plausible arguments slight Disneyland's modernist context.

Disney's initial success lay in "interwar" cinematic cartoons logically aligned with surrealism. As Herbert Muschamp suggests, "There are clear formal resemblances between Surrealistic painting and some Disney designs. . . . The supernaturally tidy Main Street, the Matterhorn rising in a suburban Southern California desert, the tropical river flowing in the shadow of a Bavarian castle: these display characteristic Surrealistic techniques of displacement, juxtaposition, and the uncanny. Even Dali never contrived to put a whole nation in mouse ears" (Muschamp 1998). Benjamin also saw in Mickey Mouse the kind of critique of life and commodification—and the commodification of life—for which surrealism was famous:

> In such films it is not worthwhile to have experiences. . . . Not since the first fairy tales have the most important and vital events been evoked more unsymbolically and unatmospherically. . . . All Mickey Mouse films are founded on the motif of leaving home in order to learn what fear is.
>
> So the explanation for the huge popularity of these films is not mechanization, their form, nor is it a misunderstanding. It is simply the fact that the public recognizes its own life in them. (Benjamin [1931] 1996b: 545)

Walt Disney's own statements about the inspiration for Disneyland emphasize its relation to orderly public life and focus on both keeping disrepu-

Figure 15. "Disney Saucer Ride, Tomorrowland," 1961. Photograph from the *Los Angeles Examiner* collection, University of Southern California, Regional History Collection.

table people out and providing entertainment for adults while their kids wait safely in time-managed queues. This formula for "happiness" managed the routine before the moment of pleasure as much as the incitement of thrilling new experiences, and while Disney acknowledged the impossibility of conceiving of "the world" in real life and real time, he nevertheless attempted it. Learning from the "World of Tomorrow" at the 1939 World's Fair (see figures 14 and 15), Disney acknowledged that "right when we do Tomorrowland, it will be out dated" (in Aldridge 2002). The utopian language of the World's Fair, with its rocket ship crossing the earth and its sparkling vision of tomorrow equipped with cars, dishwashers, and television, seems to be displaced in Disneyland by what Jameson and Baudrillard recognize as a nostalgia for something that never existed. But this imperative to bind technological innovation, corporate success, and ideal familial citizenship together around the capture of cultural diversity is also an Exposition thematic continued in Disney today. If the picture of "Tomorrow" taken in 1961 (see figure 15) seems to have pushed through futurism and into kitsch, Disney's "The House of Tomorrow" tells another story. This Disneyland attraction, which opened in 1957, was deemed no longer futuristic and closed in 1967, only to be reconstructed and relaunched in 2008 as a "retro-future" feature that stresses the ongoing refurbishment of fantasies of the past and future, complete with the hygienic erasure of any messiness where the two come together.

The Human Sciences

The concept of the world picture is also a starting point for thinking about the human or social sciences. For this, I want to draw two important implications from Heidegger: first, that the human sciences are among the most pervasively influential products of modernism; and second, that modernism in this respect, as much as through the various aesthetic histories more usually discussed as Modernist, is the context for "the turn to representation" that is sometimes called "the cultural turn" in discussions of twentieth-century theory. Both these phrases have been used to attack "postmodernism" and post-structuralism in the academy, often with reference to Cultural Studies. But we cannot understand this "turn" without acknowledging the extent to which modernism itself comprises it and the extent to which academic critics of this "turn" are also constituted by it. Heidegger's discussion of how all modern sciences have representation as their object and practice is not the only way to make this point. A history of the sources of "the turn to representation" also demonstrates its modernism. We can trace a line from Marx to Louis Althusser to Foucault to Judith Butler that would gloss this "turn," to cite Butler's *The Psychic Life of Power* (1997), as recognizing and articulating the complexity of one's attachment to the conditions of one's own existence. This turn is at the foundation of what I called in the introduction modernism's critical attitude. It refers to analysis in which "Social categories signify subordination and existence at once" (Butler 1997: 20) and any theory of the subject is "always double, tracing the conditions of subject formation and tracing the turn against those conditions for the subject—and its perspective—to emerge" (29). Butler thus might also show us exactly why the same turn Heidegger objects to in modern science constitutes his own work.

Modern science is crucial to the world picture that turns man into a "world-knowing" subject. Heidegger claims modern science presents the world as a world picture with highly specific contents and limits. By this he does not only mean the physical sciences. The *subiectum*—"Man" as both subject and object of modern knowledge—is also produced in the human sciences:

> The interweaving of these two events, which for the modern age is decisive—that the world is transformed into picture and man into subiectum—throws light at the same time on the grounding event of modern history, an event that at first glance seems almost absurd. Namely, the more extensively and the more effectually the world stands at man's disposal as conquered, and the more objectively the object appears, all the more subjectively, i.e., the more importunately, does the subiectum rise up, and all the more impetuously, too, do observation of and teaching about the world change into a doctrine of man, into anthropology. (133)

This "anthropology" is, in the broadest sense, a combination of humanism and perspectivism, "which has set in since the end of the eighteenth century" and "finds its expression in the fact that the fundamental stance of man in relation to what is, in its entirety, is defined as a world view" (133). The modernist sciences that called themselves human or social, or both, remain exemplary of this shift.

Jameson also argues that the concept of modernity "traces its lineage back to the founding fathers of sociology" and that "sociology itself is conterminous" with studying modernity (2002: 7). Jameson's claim stresses the emergence of "disciplinarity" in modernism, but such formal specialization was always in dialogue with what we might now call interdisciplinarity. To think about Stanley Hall's influence on sociology, for example, we would also need to consider his mainstreaming of psychoanalysis as a "social science" in the United States, his teaching of anthropologists, and the alternative paths to sociology via quite different forms of expertise, like journalism, in relation to which his sociology took effect. To take another example, and as Habermas argues, Simmel is too philosophical to be a sociologist and too sociological to be a philosopher (Habermas 1996: 404). Simmel's neo-Kantian model of culture is in fact a very familiar one for Cultural Studies, encompassing "buildings and educational institutions," "the wonders and comforts of space-conquering technology," "the formations of community life" and "the visible institutions of the state" (Simmel 184). And he deploys a critical attitude commensurate with this breadth, concluding his essay on the metropolis with the caution that "it is not our task either to accuse or to pardon, but only to understand" (185). Numerous writers have pointed out the continual revival of attacks on, and defenses of, one image of humanism or another. Similarly, modernist interdisciplinarity gives rise to an ongoing narrative of "new" disciplines. While specialization and categorization dominate modernity, the critical attitude of modernism impels the equally ongoing creative destruction of both.

There is thus also an anti-disciplinary strand in modernism. Heidegger argues that the specialization of knowledge into discrete methods and fields that is associated with "the prearranged and limited publication of books and periodicals" ([1938] 1977: 139) establishes self-validating categories for research projects that can only succeed by proving their own terms and remaining separate from any connection to the life-world. Here he clearly sounds a great deal like Habermas, but I want to consider his critique as it pertains to anthropology itself. The discipline of anthropology occupies two key places in Heidegger's problem with what he calls anthropology: in its specification of "culture" as an area of institutionally verifiable expertise, and in its removal of thinking about "culture" from the culture experienced as the life-world of the anthropologist. When Raymond Williams, in his definition of "culture," names Edward Tylor's *Primitive Culture* (1871) as a "founding text" of anthropology, he indirectly points to both of these tendencies: "This runs back, in one line, to [Johann von] Herder's distinction of plural *cultures*—distinct ways of life, which needed to be studied as wholes, rather than as stages of development towards European *civilization*. It runs back also, in another line, to concepts derived from this very notion . . . of 'stages' of *development*" (Williams [1976] 1985: 39). While the latter line is taken by Tylor, wider debates around science's capacity to understand culture and experience brought forth anthropology itself at a nexus of travel writing, colonial trade, and administration, as well as modernist philosophy and science.

According to Anderson, the anthropological perspective on those Others who occupy the grid of the world was impelled by a complex mix of capitalist interests, colonial experience, and new systems of managing life and citizenship through education (Anderson 113ff). Anthropology extends a humanist narrative to this mapping of the "new world," which is itself a "new synchronic novelty" possible "only when substantial groups of people were in a position to think of themselves as living lives *parallel* to those of other substantial groups of people" (188). Anthropology was caught up in the tension between equivalence and difference that capitalism, colonialism, and humanism depended on, but was also framed by an agenda to better the condition of humanity. Tylor closes *Primitive Culture* with the declaration that "The science of culture is essentially a reformer's science" (Tylor 410)—a phrase that becomes the title of an important Cultural Studies text by Tony Bennett—and Franz Boas closes *The Mind of Primitive Man* (1911) with a call for "greater tolerance of forms of civilization different from our own" (Boas 278). While Tylor's cultural evolution positioned all cultures relative to European modernity, Boas can be credited with the anthropological version of relativism (Bennett 87–89) as well as with its interpretation as environmental determinism. Between Boas and Bronislaw Malinowski, anthropology developed a model of fieldwork that was scientific in the sense of being formally repeatable and yet also reliant on an experience that was never entirely repeatable.[6] In 1922, Malinowski published the texts, *Argonauts of the Western Pacific* and *The Scientific Theory of Culture*, that together laid out his view of culture. The progress narratives of Tylor and James Frazer, and a certain reading of Freud, were set aside as ignoring how each culture worked as a functional system in which every piece had its own purpose. But Malinowski, as a precursor to Claude Lévi-Strauss and "structural anthropology," nevertheless understood his own observations of experience as scientific generalizations based on the equivalent of experimentation.

Heidegger acknowledges that the style of the age also defines what is meant by science, and he sees modern science as having been shaped by both "machine technology" and the subiectum into a process of research and experimentation. While he extends this critique to all the human sciences, including history (Heidegger [1938] 1977: 123), Heidegger also emphasizes the emergence of modern experimental science. This science, he argues, detaches discrete areas of inquiry from the rest of the world, delimiting what will be noticed about it. It then seeks the total explanation of that delimited area by a process of falsification—seeing mistakes in other theories and eliminating variations in the process of the experiment. Heidegger argues that modern science is thus opposed to experience, which is what one knows of Being. Instead, experimental science "constructs empirical findings outside the realm of such experience" (Glazebrook 84) and replaces experience "generalized over many instances" with "the observation of single instances that can support or undermine a hypothesis which is held by the scientist in advance" (Glazebrook 84–85).

If striving to understand how the world works was the real good of science, scientific "research," Heidegger argues, defeats this good by being confined to the paradigms and hypotheses it sets up. This approach turns the "incalculable," which we cannot comprehend, into the shadow of something merely too gigantic to calculate. But Heidegger does not think a return to classical science is possible: "The flight into tradition, out of a combination of humility and presumption, can bring about nothing in itself other than self-deception and blindness in relation to the historical moment" (135–36). This genealogy of science explains science as a struggle between dominant or victorious knowledges and subordinate or "outdated" ones:

> Hence it makes no sense whatever to suppose that modern science is more exact than that of antiquity . . . No one would presume to maintain that Shakespeare's poetry is more advanced than that of Aeschylus. It is still more impossible to say that the modern understanding of whatever is, is more correct than that of the Greeks. Therefore, if we want to grasp the essence of modern science, we must first free ourselves from the habit of comparing the new science with the old solely in terms of degree, from the point of view of progress. (117–18)

The Experience of Technology

This brings me to Heidegger's well-known account of technology, in which he defines *modern*, as distinct from pre-modern, technology as shaping or managing nature rather than responding to it. By technology, Heidegger is not strictly referring to the changes wrought by mechanical production. For Heidegger, the definitions of technology as "a means to an end" (i.e., instrumental) and as "a human activity" (i.e., anthropological, in the sense of being centered on human activity) necessarily "belong together": "For to posit ends and procure and utilize the means to them is a human activity" ([1954] 1977: 4). Foucault takes up this idea of technology as a *techne*, which implies not only certain apparatuses for doing things but the disposition of such an apparatus within regimes of knowledge. If we understand technology as a set of tools, skills, and literacies that intersects with systems of power, then technology refers to a very wide range of human practices—to cinema, for example, but also to fashion. Heidegger's approach is more concerned with culture than with technical progress. Heidegger's insight into the visibility of the redundant or malfunctioning tool—or, in the inverse, the visibility of the *new* tool—is also useful for thinking about theoretical and methodological tools such as ethnography.

Novelty, as Tom Gunning insists (see chapters 1 and 5), is a key driving force in modernism. It drives the flâneur, for either Baudelaire or Benjamin. In fact, Benjamin selects for the flâneur the following "maxim": "In our standardized and uniform world, it is right here, deep below the surface, that we must go. Estrangement and surprise, the most thrilling exoticism, are all close by" (Halévy quoted in Benjamin [1927–40] 2002: 444). While the flâneur was of his moment, and is only with a problematic sleight of hand translated neatly to other conditions, estrangement continues to be a crucial modernist strategy. The more a "tool" depends on being a mechanism of "wonder," the more easily it can be become redundant in the work of articulating new modes of sociality. This is apparent in the reliance of certain modernist technologies like cinema, Exposition, ethnography and Cultural Studies on defamiliarization. Defamiliarization can be seen in the desire or dissatisfaction expressed in interdisciplinarity and the continual emergence of new disciplines (both always on the verge of redundancy). But Gunning also usefully foregrounds how a range of social experiences were derived from changes at the level of technology but given their "newness" by cultural processes.

Gunning aligns this defamiliarization with Carolyn Marvin's argument in *When Old Technologies Were New* (1988), whose organizing themes outline key modernist continuities in debating technology: expertise and literacy, community and progress, location of the body in space and time, media spectacles, and cultural homogenization. Marvin's account of new technology starts with the nineteenth-century telegraph, but she quickly adds a comparison to printing even before this, stressing that the "structure" of our experience of new technology "is characteristically modern" (3). With reference to Marvin's reflections, Gunning finds himself feeling hesitant "about terms like post-modernity" (2004: 51), pointing out that both ends of the twentieth century "generate inventions revolving around reproduction and communication and, perhaps even more clearly, both mine these new technologies for theoretical and aesthetic implications" (51).

In "The Question Concerning Technology" (1954), Heidegger claims we are "chained to technology, whether we passionately affirm or deny it. But we are delivered over to it in the worst possible way when we regard it as something neutral; for this conception of it, to which today we particularly like to do homage, makes us utterly blind to the essence of technology" ([1954] 1977: 3–4). It is not tools or machines that comprise technology here, but technology's modes of assemblage, either "enframing" or "revealing" (Heidegger [1954] 1977: 20–21). Heidegger sees technology as making the world strange, both when it is habitual—"At bottom, the ordinary is not ordinary; it is extra-ordinary, uncanny" (Heidegger [1931] 1971: 32)—and when it is unfamiliar. While Cultural Studies has inherited "defamiliarization" as a positive aim, Heidegger stresses its intimacy with alienation. He focuses on the way technology "alienates" us from our "native habitat by bringing the world within our grasp," as when films draw their audience "away into realms of imagination—often strange, often quite ordinary; they feign a world which is no world" (Heidegger quoted in Inwood 117). This alienation thus also compromises our "rootedness," in an "entirely new position of man in and towards the world," and suggests how technology produces its own mysteries that thus "might provide a new rootedness" (117). The modernist imagination and experience of technology as an orientation to the world is apparent in modernist science fiction from the nineteenth century to today in just these ways.

Modernist science fiction refers not only to the popular genre that links short stories, novels, comics, films, radio, and eventually television, but to all reimagining of the world via technology, such as the General Motors "Futurama" display at the World's Fair of 1939, set in a mythically clean car-centered 1960. The fair's displays around everyday life were specifically American but conceptualized as the whole world of tomorrow: from the "rocket port," which imagined inter-planetary movement, to "The Hall of Electrical Living," which presented a domestic science fiction. Such examples are needed to counter the more famously dystopic science fictions of the Modernists, such as H. G. Wells' *The Time Machine* (1895) and Aldous Huxley's *Brave New World* (set in a "Futurama" where everything is periodized as A.F.—that is, After Ford and After Freud). The World's Fair of 1939, with its gleaming people, houses, and lives, occupies the same cultural space as the broadcast, in 1938, of Orson Welles' radio adaptation of H. G. Wells' *The War of the Worlds* (1898), which famously caused public panic by simulating a newscast reporting an alien invasion. Although accounts disagree about the size of the audience, Richard Hand notes that *reports* of the broadcast being misunderstood as real were widely circulated, derided by cultural critics (including politicians) as proof of modern gullibility in the face of technology, and reproduced as a sensational story about the challenges of life today. While "The War of the Worlds" made the strange power of the media and special effects explicit, it also relied on familiarity: on the now habitual consumption of radio, including as a political medium. The banality of news reporting and political addresses to the nation is what made the fantastic credible. For Heidegger, such popular culture is a shadow of the technologized masses and of the objectified subject. But many of his concerns are represented in the popular science fiction texts I am discussing here because they share a cultural history in which technology both articulates and demands an "entirely new position of man in and towards the world."

Let me explore this intersection further as a way back to the question of "culture." Modernist anxiety about human dependence on technology and, at the same time, the threat of redundancy built into the technologization of life and experience seem to be as continually recycled as Marvin suggests. The same themes are endlessly redeployed with new technological reference points, endlessly returning to the question of what comprises the human in the experience of technology. In this way, the Modernist icon of the doll or mannequin I discussed in chapter 5 influences modernist science fiction: Mary Shelley's *Frankenstein*, Fritz Lang's *Metropolis*, Hans Bellmer's dolls (see figure 13), Phillip K. Dick's *Do Androids Dream of Electric Sheep* (1968). Ridley Scott's film *Blade Runner* (1982), an adaptation of Dick's 1968 novel, has been positioned as a "postmodern" reply to this tradition, but the precursor texts were also responding to each other and to a broader discursive frame. As Rainer Maria Rilke notes with reference to Lotte Pritzel's doll exhibitions of 1913, this quintessentially modernist idea of the doll, is a frustration and a disappointment if not a horror, because we cannot make it "into a thing or a person" (Rilke 29). *Blade Runner*'s Rick Deckard, thrown into a familiarity with the "replicant" he never wanted, is exposed to a more fully objectified subject—able to be traded, remodeled, and made, in the end, completely redundant, but in ways that clearly speak to his own experience.

The term Heidegger uses for the complex relation between the objectified subject and the subjectified object in modernity is subiectum: "In such producing, man contends for the position in which he can be that particular being who gives the measure and draws up the guidelines for everything that is" ([1938] 1977: 134). The subiectum is the subject who represents something—by setting it out in front of him- or herself and thus actively composing what it means—but the subiectum is also, because the modern subject is always representing its own capacity to know the world, at the same time the passive creation of this process. This is also a version of the notorious "death of the subject" understood to follow from "the turn to representation," because the subject is no longer the author of representations but a representation itself. But subiectum does not describe the end of the self any more than of consciousness, but rephrases the self as a "necessary interplay between subjectivism and objectivism" (Heidegger [1938] 1977: 128). Following Hegel and Marx, a long tradition of modernists see the fundamental problem of the modern subject as alienation—objectification of the self in one's own experience. But in foregrounding Heidegger's perspective on the situation of Cultural Studies in this chapter I want to add to this familiar reference point the importance of a phenomenological tradition for Cultural Studies. Just as clearly sourced in the Enlightenment and refined by modernity in ways that are still ongoing, the mediated self-reflexivity articulated by phenomenology shares a great deal of common ground with Cultural Studies as a named discipline. Lawrence Grossberg suggests as much when he insists that "the beginning of modern philosophy" should not be located with Cartesian self-reflecting consciousness but with Kant's identification of this consciousness "with the mediating position of experience (giving rise to both phenomenological and structural theories of culture and knowledge)" (Grossberg 1997: 16).

I see both phenomenology and these structuralist approaches to culture as facets of the broader modernist foregrounding of "culture." Heidegger's claim that modernity "has, as a consequence of the liberation of man, introduced subjectivism and individualism" but, at the same time, has "produced a comparable objectivism" ([1938] 1977: 128) constitutes another recognition of what I have called the modernist critical attitude. Heidegger argues that the modern subject expects "culture" to provide us with an "experience." And among the pervasive specializations of modernity it seems culture becomes the field in which experience is known.[7] "Culture" is thus a sign of the world picture Heidegger would contest and yet, at the same time, names that to which philosophy should attend because culture is also "the lifeworld" of both experience and representation (unlike the objective "world picture" of the experiment). In this double sense of culture—experience and representation—we come to why modernism warrants its *ism*. Modernism has a ground and an object and an audience, which are all the same thing: culture. And for this reason it is possible to think of modernism as the "cultural turn" in modernity.

8

The Invention of Culture

What the expert is tired of today the public will be tired of tomorrow.

Ezra Pound, "A Few Don'ts by an Imagiste"

Cultural Studies did not so much develop out of a mesh of modernist influences as within and alongside them. While it took some time and required some particular catalysts for any academic institution to name something "Cultural Studies," I think it is clear that we cannot begin Cultural Studies with the Birmingham School. Thinking about the origins of what now looks like "the Birmingham School" needs also to begin with this understanding. The ongoing difficulty of defining Cultural Studies—for me a productive difficulty—also draws on this longer history, intersecting a range of new modernist discourses on culture.

We Other Victorians

As I suggested in the introduction, writers on Modernism often struggle to pin down what seems to change about modernity in the mid-nineteenth century, often relinquishing the struggle entirely for the more spectacular benchmarks of one war and then another. But even if we accept that modernism does not break with modernity, the familiarity for us today of the cultural fields and practices at the end of the nineteenth century, compared to those at the beginning, is striking. In this chapter I suggest that it is in fact an idea of "culture" that forms this continuity: that modernism is the "cultural turn" in modernity, as I put it at the end of the last chapter. This "turn" began in the Enlightenment but took impetus from the long nineteenth century, drawing on but not reducible to changes to democracy, capitalism, and industry and specially shaped and apparent in what we could called the emergence of "cultural expertise."

Although there are many important events to take into account in such a story, such as the European revolutions of 1848 and the 1867 expansion of male suffrage in England, none dramatically provides a story for all the others. What becomes singularly more visible across the long nineteenth century and holds shape over the equally dramatic changes of more than a century after is a distinct field we can call "culture." Lawrence Grossberg understands the modernism of culture this way: "the modern notion of culture, a notion which continues to animate cultural studies, involves, on the one hand, the projection of a position constituted by a temporal displacement from some other (eg, tradition) from which change can be comprehended and, on the other hand, the equation of that position with a standard of judgement from which one can offer a 'total qualitative assessment' of such changes" (1997: 14). This model of culture does not make "culture" another word for "art" in Max Weber's account of the modern specialization of art, science, and morality. That culture does encompass art in any credible attempt to sustain this taxonomy is clear, but it may even displace morality and has a very complex relation to science.

I argue that modernist culture is always double, comprised, first, of representation—an objectified form that varies as to contents and homogeneity (sometimes art, sometimes the spirit of a people or ethnic custom manifest in particular institutions or practices)—and, second, of an experience, which varies both in importance and in its relation to representation. This doubled culture is accounted for differently in different contexts, such as Branislaw Malinowski's functional approach to native culture, Martin Heidegger's anxiety about the rootlessness of modern life, or Stuart Hall's analysis of contemporary blackness and ethnicity. The doubleness of modernist culture is also manifest in its comprehension, its constitution, of both the subject and object of reflection on the world. This idea of culture is sourced, as Grossberg suggests, in the Enlightenment. Culture for Hegel is already a "self-alienated spirit" (Hegel 294ff): "Spirit constitutes for itself not merely *a* world, but a world that is double, divided and self-opposed" (295), composed of, on the one hand, "the world of reality or of its self-alienation" (297) and, on the other, a consciousness that is antithetical to that alienation but "is for that very reason not free from it" (297). Always implicit in modernity, the modernist cultural turn expands in some crucial ways in the nineteenth century, drawing on and affirming the necessity of new cultural institutions and forms of expertise supported by them. This, I contend, is the emergence of Cultural Studies, translating and transforming the modernist critical attitude through the public and popular fields it helped form, largely through the constitution of cultural expertise.

Grossberg takes his understanding of "the modern notion of culture" from Raymond Williams' authoritative history, *Culture and Society* (1967). Here, Williams argues that, until the nineteenth century, the idea of culture was generally tied to religious tradition, at which point new conceptions of culture and society began to evolve. Through the reconceptualization of democracy and industry, these new conceptions brought forth a new kind of writer: the cultural critic. Like Williams, I take Matthew Arnold as exemplary of this new cultural criticism, but I want to add another element to Williams' story. The reconceptualization of democracy at this time particularly centered on new discourses on citizenship, attached in various ways to the expansion of literacy and new modes of cultural distribution that grounded and reflected that literacy. The cultural critic, therefore, emerged only with new audiences for cultural expertise.

In the wake of the Enlightenment, newly authorized critics sought to understand how society should be judged and guided in terms that were not exclusively religious. As Arnold's famous *Culture and Anarchy* (1869) attests, this often still prioritized religious standards. Arnold's famous definition of culture as "the best which has been thought and said in the world" ([1869] 2006: viii) is a judgment based on inherited values shaped but not defined by secularization. The challenge posed by secularization that critics like Arnold faced was that if "God" does not directly determine values like *beauty* and *truth*, then these values can be more multiply and contextually defined. *Culture and Anarchy* preserves for us a key moment in—although not an exclusive point of origin for—the separation of culture as a way of understanding human endeavor.

The Arnoldian ideal of "culture" sets a new standard against which value will be determined and yet, in order to function as a standard, there must be an authoritative system by which it is maintained. Arnold sees this as the work of cultural criticism. In his essay "The Function of Criticism at the Present Time," Arnold defines criticism as "The endeavour, in all branches of knowledge, theology, philosophy, history, art, science, to see the object as in itself it really is" ([1864] 1962: 258). Such criticism, however, is also the exercise of curiosity: "to try to know the best that is known and thought in the world, irrespectively of practice, politics, and everything of the kind; and to value knowledge and thought as they approach this best, without the intrusion of any other considerations whatever" (268). While here Arnold sets the terms of much more than a century of debate about textual analysis, for Arnold criticism was as significant as art itself, communicating distinctions necessary for the production, circulation, and consumption of art. It also, paradoxically, considering this exclusion of "other considerations," had a social mission. For Arnold, culture is essentially opposed to anarchy and will teach citizens not to disturb social order no matter how worthwhile their motives (Arnold [1869] 2006: 257). This proposition is clearer if we move beyond an aesthetic frame of reference, as Arnold often did.

Contextualized by the Second Reform Act of 1867, which gave suffrage to the urban working class, *Culture and Anarchy* opens up the terrain on which, to trace the most direct line, both the Leavisite interest in the social context of art and the Williamsian interest in the meaningfulness of art across different contexts appear. While "culture" for Arnold is defined as that which has the amorphous qualities of "sweetness and light," he is equally clear that it is the experience of such qualities that matters—cultural engagement that is "permeated by thought, sensible to beauty, intelligent and alive" ([1869] 2006: 48). From Arnold's perspective, this operates differently for each of three contemporary cultural classes: the Barbarians (upper class), the Philistines (middle class), and the Populace (crowd). For most men, he claims, the ongoing enlightenment of culture is accessed through art and religion. However, "If a man without books or reading, or reading nothing but his letters and the newspapers, gets nevertheless a fresh and free play of the best thoughts upon his stock notions and habits, he has got culture. He has got that for which we prize and recommend culture; he has got that which at the present moment we seek culture that it may give us. This inward operation is the very life and essence of culture, as we conceive it" (ix). Arnold stresses that culture is not the "spirit" of a people, as some around him proposed—although this is a proposition far less opposed to Arnold than he suggests, and one to which I will return. Instead, for Arnold, culture was the process of perfecting life, in other words, the force invigorating such a spirit. Arnold's vision of culture is a refinement of Kantian Enlightenment, forestalling unrest but nevertheless begetting "a dissatisfaction which is of the highest possible value in stemming the common tide of men's thoughts in a wealthy and industrial community, and which saves the future, as one may hope, from being vulgarised, even if it cannot save the present" (20). This culture is both "the humane instinct" and "a principle of authority" (111), which differs from "what one's ordinary self likes" (108). As both dutiful enlightenment and inspirational life course, culture is the ground and the means for Arnold's argument in favor of compulsory education, which lead directly to the pivotal Education Act of 1870 that mandated universal education.[1]

Pound's aphorism quoted as the epigraph to this chapter depends on a relationship between art and the public that radically differs from Arnold's, but only in the fact that what is valuable might change—a prospect already dimly apparent in Arnold as the force against which he argues. By Pound's time, the tendencies Arnold sees around him are more visible. The voice of the "public" was presumed to be more audible in a range of ways, including in commodified cultural consumption. Cultural expertise was now more publicly in dialogue with consumers clustered around different definitions of value. Taking Arnold as his model in many respects, at this time F. R. Leavis saw "culture" as working toward a good threatened less by anarchy than by the mass culture Arnold certainly saw it as heralding. Leavis blamed industrialization—and associated shifts in democracy and in popular and public culture—for severing key continuities Arnold had been trying to shore up. What Leavis means by culture is still "the best that has been thought and said," but many of the texts Leavis put forward for his own educational agenda differed from those Arnold would have chosen, largely because of the greater importance Leavis placed on *cultural* context.

A telling clash of expert interpretation between Leavis and C. P. Snow over the relationship between science and literature fleshes out this expanding importance of culture. In 1959, Snow gave a Rede lecture, entitled "The Two Cultures," on the relationship between science, on the one hand, and literature and art, on the other. Leavis was present at the lecture and responded to it angrily. Lionel Trilling, commenting on this clash in 1962, noted the irony that Snow's assertion in this lecture, that "literary intellectuals" and culture in general must come to value science as the great cultural way forward, took the opposite line to Matthew Arnold's Rede lecture in 1882 entitled "Literature and Science." "In essential terms," Trilling claims, "the issue in debate has not changed" (10), adding that Leavis' "admiration of Arnold is well known" and that his "position in respect to the relative importance of literature and science in education is much the same as Arnold's" (9). Both Arnold's lecture and Leavis' response to Snow were confronting a claim that science rather than "culture" was the foundation of knowledge and morality in modernity, but in doing so they were responding to the claim that "science" could be, or rather provide better guidance for, culture.

This was not a debate between "reason" and "imagination" but rather over the kind of reason that should guide culture. According to Trilling, in "response to the modern situation," Arnold affirmed G. W. F. Hegel's claim that "Reason—or Idea, or Theory or Creative Imagination" was now "decisive in human destiny" insofar as it was deployed to "shape the conditions of [man's] own existence" (Trilling 19). The debate between Leavis and Snow implicitly contests whether or not reason should be defined this way, assaying the relative capacities of science and art—discourses long forced apart and now fragmented internally—to speak of morality (Trilling 14). Blaming "culture" rather than "science" for Auschwitz, Snow even argues, to Trilling's bemusement, that a "traditional culture," one especially associated with the literary, "manages" the Western world (Trilling 17). But for both Snow and Leavis, "culture" is not only that *against* which science should be revalued but also that *within* which it should be revalued, because for both of them culture means much more than art. It is in culture that science should or should not be appreciated more fully—a field extending to newspapers, school curricula, movies, and conversations at parties.

In his response to this conflict, Trilling notes that Arnold did not use the word "culture" "in the contemporary sense in which it is used by anthropologists, sociologists, and historians of thought and art; this is, more or less, the sense in which it is used by Snow. For Arnold, 'culture' was 'the best that has been thought and said in the world' and also an individual person's relation to this body of thought and expression. My own use of the word in this essay is not Arnold's" (Trilling 10n). Trilling himself is a key figure in institutionalizing literary Modernism, a process which would not have been nearly so effective if there had not been multiple voices pressing for particular inclusions and exclusions and thus for the importance of the category under contention. While opposed to the New Critics and "Leavisism," Trilling himself distinguishes Modernism from what he deems more banal forms of cultural activity. He accuses Snow not of disrespecting art but of neglecting politics (22) and himself sees "the culture of literature in relation to politics" (24) as its great necessity. This is not, for Trilling, because people learn politics from authors but because they learn to criticize life through art. For both Arnold and Trilling, "culture" taught "us" the way life should be, although their understanding of what it taught were crucially different.

This idea of "culture" comes, for Trilling, at a cost. He contends that, if "all things are causative or indicative of the whole of the cultural life," such a mode of thought validates the importance of "intensities of moralized feeling" by making it seem that everything "good in life is at stake in every cultural action" (30). He credits this attitude to the influence of Karl Marx and Sigmund Freud, but also references phenomenology through Hegel and existentialism, uniting these through "all that the tendencies of modernity imply of the sense of contingency in life, from which we learn that the one thing that can be disputed, and that is worth disputing, is preference or taste" (30). While Trilling does not dispute that culture names life in this way, he also sees this mode of thought as the triumph of "style" as understood by advertising (see chapter 5): "In our more depressed moments we might be led to ask whether there is a real difference between being The Person Who defines himself by his commitment to one or another idea of morality, politics, literature, or city-planning, and being The Person Who defines himself by wearing trousers without pleats" (30). Trilling's alternative is the disinterestedness of philosophy. If everything in life—radium, skyscrapers, pleats—becomes culture, then nothing can be detached enough to reflect on everything in life. What would seem to him the more substantial contribution of Martin Heidegger as opposed to Chanel may not be appreciated.

A Partisan Review

In the popular story about Modernism with which I opened this book, Modernism was more or less over by World War II and followed by a period of recovery from aesthetic as well as social upheaval until new revolutions again overturned Western culture in the 1960s. It is from this latter context that Cultural Studies seems to take its impetus. But what is framed in this story as a period of recovery was not in fact a hiatus but an escalation of the speed and power with which new institutions for cultural education became the cultural establishment. This is a period in which galleries and museums became not just archival spaces and public displays but cultural "centers"; "cultural" disciplines appeared in newly compulsory secondary schools and spread more widely through universities; and the canon of Modernist art and criticism was concretized in all these places. There is also more continuity to debates over culture before and after World War II than this story supposes. Amid his remarks on Snow and Leavis, Trilling positions his own reputation as exemplary. The opposition between the "Barzun-Trilling syndrome" and "the Book-of-the-Month Club" opposes the latter as "middlebrow" cultural expertise to his position at Columbia University, where he was central to a renowned "Great Books" course, and to *Partisan Review*, where Trilling participated in a circle of partisanly respected cultural commentators. While the Chicago School is often positioned as a crucial U.S. contribution to Cultural Studies for its conjunction of ethnographic analysis and attention to marginalized (subcultural) urban life, I think this has obscured other influences, including pragmatism and the changed vision of culture in American criticism that appeared in parallel and through direct exchanges with key European influences.

In 1939, *Partisan Review* published Clement Greenberg's "Avant-Garde and Kitsch," which claimed nineteenth-century painting was as generic as mass cultural kitsch in order to hold up "modernist" art and its associated criticism as the proper mode of cultural commentary. In this essay, Greenberg provides another account of the production of culture as a specialized activity. He sees "avant-garde culture" as an unprecedented development, one made possible by a "superior consciousness of history—more precisely, the appearance of a new kind of criticism of society, an historical criticism" (9). For Greenberg, avant-garde art emerges from the intellectual renovations of the 1840–60s, coincides with "scientific revolutionary thought," and involves a withdrawal from the public as well as the popular into "art for art's sake" (10). This process alienates art from both "the mass" and "the ruling class" that had traditionally patronized art. *Kitsch*, on the other hand, is opposed to specialization—"chromeotypes, magazine covers, illustrations, ads, slick and pulp fiction, comics, Tin Pan Alley music, tap dancing, Hollywood movies, etc., etc." (11) he sees as produced at an intersection of industrialization, urbanization, and "what is called universal literacy" (12). Greenberg's kitsch demands nothing more than money and its apparently democratic form is irrelevant because it is, using a term deployed to the same end by Leavis and the Frankfurt School, "predigested."

Leavis was far less interested in experimentation than many modernist literary critics—often positioning himself as opposed to "the Bloomsbury set"—but he too stressed the importance of a "minority culture" defined against "mass civilisation." His own *Mass Civilisation and Minority Culture* (1930) attacked narrow-minded elitism at the same time as he lectured the general "reading public" about the necessity of becoming "critically adult." In 1933, with Denys Thompson, Leavis published *Culture and Environment: The Training of Critical Awareness*, which sought to directly advise a general readership and train immature minds against manipulation in ways that would seem very familiar to high school students today who learn about the exercise of power in popular culture under the influence of Cultural Studies.[2] While this should remind us of Immanuel Kant's "Enlightenment," this training aimed to defend culture against a new environment: "There are thousands who will day-dream and night-dream in a cinema while idly allowing meaningless clap-trap to float pictorially before them, thousands to one who will make the intellectual and moral effort to read a hard book or hear a symphony concert, where he will encounter real thought and feeling formally expressed" (Leavis and Thompson 107). With such principles Leavis helped shape the new university Literature departments after the war(s), by which culture was supposed to offer both solace and skills for a changing world.

As Leavis formed his position on "culture" alongside and at odds with Eliot and the New Critics, Williams formed his alongside and at odds with Leavis, inspired by Leavis' efforts to "make English grow to its place as a central subject in a contemporary human education, with the emphasis on criticism and on cultural history rather than on academicism and the vagaries of taste" (Leavis quoted in Williams et al. 246). But if Williams maintains a distinction between culture understood as "a whole way of life" and culture as the "special processes of discovery and creative effort" (Williams [1958] 2002)—only the latter being compatible with Arnold's or in many respects Leavis' sense of "culture"—he also finds in the value ascribed to the latter in everyday life a point of intersection between these different conceptions of culture. His insistence that "culture is ordinary" is thus followed by the Arnoldian remark that "An interest in learning or the arts is simple, pleasant, and natural. A desire to know what is best, and to do what is good, is the whole positive nature of man" ([1958] 2002: 95). Tony Bennett argues that the role credited to Williams in "a 'cultural studies creation story' . . . both exaggerates the degree to which" his concept of culture "involved a break with the Arnoldian heritage just as it also obscures other pedigrees which might be claimed for this key concept of cultural studies" (88). Bennett places Arnold, Edward Tylor, and Williams all in a longer modern(ist) tradition defined by a progressive search for "the aesthetic and moral conditions for a common culture" (Bennett 100). This is the context in which Williams opposes the "angry young men" at university to the reactionary types personified by the ladies in a "tea shop" and, most urgently, the advertising types who deride "any serious standards whatever."

When Richard Hoggart's Centre at Birmingham gave the first major institutional place to Cultural Studies, its practices were already well established under the general rubric of modernist critique by this range of influences. Andrew Goodwin, in his introduction to Hoggart's *The Uses of Literacy* (1957), describes its project as transitioning between Leavisism and Cultural Studies (Goodwin in Hoggart xvii). For Hoggart, culture is a field that has reform as its effect if not as its object—another echo of Arnold, as Bennett suggests—and Williams' influence is clear in Hoggart's analysis of the "wish for entry into the cultured life" (238). This "culture" is manifest not only in literature and literary taste but equally in rooms that are furnished as displays of cultural expertise, echoing "a thousand others who sought cultural graduation at the same time" and thus were relieved of "healthy untidiness, natural idiosyncrasy, straight choice of what is personally liked" (24). This also draws out the individualization of culture as a *project*, which Arnold, Leavis, Trilling and Williams all furthered. Walter Benjamin also saw the nineteenth-century rise of the private individual mirrored in the rise of the "interior" in this way: "he brings together the far and away and the long ago. His living room is a box in the theater of the world" (Benjamin [1927–40] 2002: 9].

Such rooms are places to represent "culture" as "ornament" (and ornament as signature, Benjamin stresses), rather than constituting what Hoggart, much like Friedrich Nietzsche, would see as an authentic cultural life. But at the same time, for Hoggart, these rooms are aspirational, specially associated with uprooted "scholarship boys" who pursue perfection and are characterized first of all by their "humanity" (Hoggart 241). The experiences these rooms represent matter "since they have to do with the importance of roots, of unconscious roots, to all of us as individuals; they have to do with those major social developments of our time towards centralisation and a kind of classlessness; and they have to do with the relationship between cultural and intellectual matters and the beliefs by which men try to shape their lives" (244–45). Ben Highmore's account of Williams' "structures of feeling" suggests that what is at stake in such analysis is "a perspective from which to view anthropological culture saturated by a mass of representations" (Highmore in Williams [1958] 2002: 91–92). But before turning to anthropological culture I want to place the general terrain mapped by these voices in relation to some other familiar reference points.

Martin Halliwell and Andy Mousley stress an overlap between the model of culture being produced here and Habermas' claims for a Weberian public sphere that can distinguish: "the objective, the social and the subjective (understood by Habermas as 'the totality of facts' about reality, where facts correspond to truths), morality (defined as 'the totality of all interpersonal relations that are recognized by members' of the social world 'as legitimate') and art (characterised by Habermas in terms of a Romantic aesthetic of individual expression which 'delimits from the objective and social worlds a domain for each member of *what is not common*')" (Halliwell and Mousley 88, quoting Habermas). In fact, the Weberian taxonomy is too rigid to describe the way Cultural Studies approaches these elements through their interaction in the field of culture. As John Frow and Meaghan Morris put it, the post-Birmingham School model of culture is "a contested and conflict-

ual set of practices of representation bound up with the processes of formation and reformation of social groups" (Frow and Morris xx). *Resistance
Through Rituals* (1975), edited by Clarke, Hall, Jefferson, and Roberts, is the
exemplary collection, gathering together many of the Centre for Contemporary Cultural Studies' key voices to discuss working-class youth subcultures.
Their analysis is predominantly historical, structural, and ideological. It belongs to the post-1968 public concern with the identifications, practices, and
limits of youth as (yet another) sign of the times and to the same concerns
in popular culture (as manifest, for example, in Stanley Kubrick's *A Clock-
work Orange*, 1971). But the historical specificity of this content can be ex-
aggerated as an entirely new vision of culture. If Cultural Studies' "culture"
refers not only to superior and enlightening forms but also to "the totality of
symbolic life within a given social space" (Mulhern xvii), then this is no dramatic break from Arnold or Williams insofar as it understands the work of
"culture" to be both a specialized activity and something held in common.
Nor is it a break from the Modernists who spurned mass culture or from
those modernists, like Nietzsche and Heidegger, as well as Theodor Adorno
and Max Horkheimer, who were dismayed at the separation of culture as an
object to be studied.

The Object Culture

Another key Modernist influence on the Birmingham School's understanding of how culture works as a limit is Antonio Gramsci's concept of hegemony. As Jean and John Comaroff note, the Cultural Studies take on hegemony as "a dominant system of lived meanings and values, relations and
practices, which shapes experienced reality" is a more coherent understanding of hegemony than Gramsci's own texts produced. Whether adapting
Gramsci's theory of "social hegemony"—"the 'spontaneous' consent given
by the great masses of the population to the general direction imposed on
social life by the dominant fundamental group" (Gramsci 1971: 12)—into a
more overarching model or deploying the term more loosely to mean the
ideological maintenance of the status quo, Cultural Studies is attracted to
Gramsci precisely because the term is not a universal. As Comaroff and
Comaroff put it, citing Dick Hebdige's discussion of Gramsci, Gramscian
hegemony is always unstable and uncertain, "realized through the balancing
of competing forces, not the crushing calculus of class domination" (Comaroff and Comaroff 385). Gramsci used hegemony to oppose an economic
determinist version of Marxism and to articulate how experts (intellectuals)

could address and improve the life-world around them. Gramsci provides new tools for discussing the complex imbrications of culture and power, but insisting on the new relevance of cultural expertise was integral to this.

Marxist analysis in Cultural Studies more generally is mediated by Cultural Studies also falling into that group of modernist discourses that Halliwell and Mousley call "civic humanism" (88). "Civic humanism" links analysis of society and culture with an investment in "on the ground" politics that comprehends both Habermas and Stuart Hall. Workers' education is Habermas' example of a dissemination of the aesthetic that does not detach itself from the other spheres of modernity ([1981] 1983: 13) and this "outward-looking civic consciousness" is also evident in Stuart Hall, despite Bennett's important caution about overstating the importance of politicized cultural education to the Birmingham School (Bennett 47–48). Halliwell and Mousley stress that Hall's version of civic humanism must be seen as "post-Enlightenment": "pragmatic rather than grounded upon a systematic theory of human nature" (Halliwell and Mousley 81). This is in fact a crucial distinction, because despite the importance of ideology critique to Cultural Studies it for the most part understands ideology in relativist terms. The label post-Enlightenment, however, can easily obscure the continuum from Kant to Arnold to Williams to Hall and misrepresent Hall's emphasis on thinking about subjectivity in both ideological and relativist terms, or his insistence that the subject is a representation and that representation is subjective, as very recent and therefore more easily dismissed developments.

This returns me to uses of the phrase "the cultural turn" that are very different to mine. For many critics, the "cultural turn" is more or less synonymous with postmodernism and opposed to "science." As the echo of Snow and Leavis might also suggest, Stuart Hall rightly sees in this debate a return to "modern" themes. As David Morley notes, there is a cogent argument in which, in just this resurrection of old debates, "cultural studies stands not against sociology per se, but rather against one particular, long dominant positivist tradition within it—and as the rescuer of a 'lost' tradition, the recovery of which has done much to reinvigorate contemporary sociology" (Morley 17–18). Morley also suggests a similar relationship between Cultural Studies and anthropology, arguing that where Cultural Studies is viewed as a superficially successful threat to disciplinary seriousness, this threat is fed by the turn to representation within anthropology itself (20). The sense that Cultural Studies is reclaiming an anthropological project is also invoked by Hall, citing Claude Lévi-Strauss' claim that "the centerpiece of Social Anthropology should be the study of 'the life of signs at the heart of social life'" and that this was "the resumption of the forgotten part of the Durkheim-Mauss program" (Hall quoted in Morley 19).

These different claims to the parameters and provenance of "culture" can be recovered from a degree of self-serving territorialization by recognition of their long history. Francis Mulhern sets aside differences between figures like Arnold—for whom culture represented the ideal values of humanity— and those like Johann von Herder—who saw the values of culture as histori- cally relative—to claim they are equally dependent on the idea that cultures could co-exist and indeed be hybridized (Mulhern xvi-xvii). While his claim that Cultural Studies has more or less abandoned "the historic privileges of 'culture with a capital C'" (Mulhern xviii) is overstated, as I discuss in the final chapter, Mulhern is undoubtedly right to see the formation of the discipline as "both a continuation and a displacement of English Kulturkri- tik" (xvii) because it maintains culture as "the object also, and crucially the subject, the ideal subject, of discourse" (xviii). Mulhern particularly dis- tinguishes this from an anthropological model of culture he summarizes as "ethnic custom" (xvii). But this distinction deserves more caution. The imperative to capture, retrieve, preserve, name, and manage culture links the mode of cultural criticism stretching from Arnold to Stuart Hall (and beyond) with the emergence of anthropology and with comparable moves in popular and public culture, such as Howard Carter's expedition to Egypt, James Frazer's mythologies, and modernist Exposition culture.

One of the crucial factors in Franz Boas' development of anthropological theory was his appointment to the World's Fair in Chicago, held in 1893.[3] There, in a rejection of the evolutionary schema (associated with Tylor) that dominated anthropological display, Boas and others arranged for "na- tives" to live in a mock village where they imitated their own daily lives—or at least an anthropologically edited performance of them—for the enjoy- ment and education of visitors. Set within the purview of the first "Ferris Wheel" on a carnival midway, these ethnic displays with timed ceremonies collated from different historical periods resemble Disneyland more than the lives of particular people, even if they were a radical departure from the "village nègre" of the Paris exposition of 1889, in which people them- selves, rather than their culture, were the object on display. Benjamin notes, "World exhibitions glorify the exchange value of the commodity. They cre- ate a framework in which its use value recedes into the background. They open a phantasmagoria which a person enters in order to be distracted" ([1927–40] 2002: 7). In this context, anthropology produced both a "culture" that could be put on display like a spear or a pot and a marvel to be enjoyed like a Ferris Wheel. The difficulty of viewing this critically at the time amid the wonder of a new discipline is apparent in comparison to the reception of anthropologist Zora Neale Hurston's fictional and non-fictional vernacular cultural histories. Hurston worked under Boas and with Margaret Mead and Ruth Benedict, and her collection of Black Southern traditions, stories, and games in *Mules and Men* (1935) was widely praised in anthropological circles and can even now be seen as innovative (see Gambrell 99). Her novel, *Their Eyes were Watching God* (1937), was more ambivalently received as, to quote Richard Wright: "not addressed to the Negro, but to a white audience whose chauvinistic tastes she knows how to satisfy. She exploits that phase of Negro life which is 'quaint,' the phase which evokes a piteous smile on the lips of the 'superior' race" (in Henderson 58). Regardless of Boas' or Hurston's intentions, this brings culture into view as a field of debate between experts. Thus debates around such exhibition practices led Boas to stress the necessity of a theoretical anthropology to outline and affirm its necessity, just as contestations over cultural value bought the "cultural critic" to the foreground to outline and affirm the necessity of cultural value.

The evidence Hoggart presents in *Uses of Literacy* is a blend of textual and historical analysis with reflection on his own experience.[4] A similar mode of reflection on experience is built into the Birmingham School blend of literary analysis, ethnography, and sociology and is more generally crucial to Cultural Studies' bricoleur approach that writers like Grossberg were, early on, eager to praise as well as question (Grossberg et al. 2). Contemporary overlaps in practice between anthropology and Cultural Studies—a fraught issue on some institutional battlefields—arise not only because anthropology has learned from Cultural Studies new ways of analyzing culture as a field of power as much as Cultural Studies has learned methodological and ethical debates from anthropology. They also arise because, as Renato Rosaldo suggests, both share a fundamentally modern idea of culture as that which mediates "between the person and reality as the realm of experience and knowledge" (quoted in Grossberg 1997: 15).

Malinowski's new model of "participant observation" required ongoing everyday contact to record the "imponderabilia of everyday life" (Malinowski 18) that comprised the fabric of native culture and thus permitted access to their perception of the world (25). The interpretation of culture for Malinowski cannot proceed, for example, from observing eleven boys squatting in a line, to calling that a game based on an interpretation of their attitude as "game-like," or even by knowing a word for "game" and being told it is one. Instead, Malinowski claimed, only in participatory experience could he understand the complex significance of, in this example, the idea of games, the timing and placement of games, the particular game's rules and tendencies, or its relation to observation. While many questions have been asked about what is perceived in participant observation, and with what degree of accuracy, culture for Malinowski was manifest in the perspective, desire, and consciousness of individuals and groups. Perhaps, as Morris puts it, "the ethnographic present is used to extract the same moral ('life is complex and some good comes of everything') from endlessly diverse situations" (1998: 20). But, as a range of recent revisions of ethnography suggest, the paradigmatically contingent culture construed by anthropological ethnography manifests less what mediates between individual and society, as Rosaldo suggests, than the gap between the anthropologist's and other individuals' experience of that mediation.

The sometimes dubious pleasures derived from "ethnic" performance should not distract us from noticing how modernism understands both "familiar" and "other" cultures as requiring education and expertise. This also suggests that we bring the less-cited modernist field of "pragmatism" into a history of Cultural Studies. The proliferation of intercontinental trade that shaped modernism did not stop short of philosophy. The pragmatists drew on Enlightenment thinkers and on the transnational emergence of modernist reflection on "how we live today." For William James' "radical empiricism," every analysis is a particular observation, and consciousness, perception, and the perceivable world are inseparable. But the impact of pragmatism on the "human sciences" is not confined to acknowledging the diversity of human experience. Pragmatism coheres around the question of usefulness: "what definite difference it will make to you and me, at definite instants of our life, if this world-formula or that world-formula be the true one" (James 20). This differs from Heidegger's phenomenological reflection on the space opened up by the broken or new tool because it is entirely "a matter for the individual's appreciation" (James 25). For pragmatism, something is true or good when it is perceived as benefiting the individual, rather than being determined by a field that defines both the object and the subject of such perception. This may well be a crucial distinction in understanding some of the variations in Cultural Studies practice, since the phenomenological, anthropological, and pragmatist modes of modernist relativism bring with them different ethical and methodological tendencies. Nevertheless, as Grossberg claims, Cultural Studies is always "radically contextual and this is true of its theory, its politics, its questions, its object, its method and its commitments . . . context is everything and everything is context" (7).

This context, however, is usually in the service of bringing some definite object (culture) into view. Cultural Studies has a great deal still to learn from the fullest range of its modernist contemporaries, including from those who objected to this objectification of culture. Nietzsche, for example, objects because of the subjectivity this "culture" produces. Modern culture, he contends, is "not a real culture at all but only a kind of knowledge of culture, it has an idea and feeling for culture but no true cultural achievement emerges" ([1876] 1997: 78). Such knowledge has no real hunger behind it, he argues, and cannot act "as an agent for transforming the outside world but remains concealed within a chaotic inner world which modern man describes . . . as his uniquely characteristic 'subjectivity'" (78). For Nietzsche, knowledge of objectified culture allows the modern subject to maintain a comforting attachment to home, state, and the masses. It is important to bring this caveat to the image of Nietzsche as the high priest of "cultural modernism" in his elevation of culture over "science, rationality and politics" (Harvey 18). Avoiding David Harvey's (and Habermas') term "cultural modernism" thus helps us to see the "cultural turn" in Nietzsche's own work as a turn to a criticism of culture that does not only refer to aesthetics—that culture that might just be collected and known about as something like Pierre Bourdieu's "cultural capital"—but also to a critical attitude toward life.

The Place From Which One Deals With Culture

I am not arguing that there is a single conversation being undertaken by all modernists. Modernist cultural analysis is a web of conversations, not all of which meet up. At stake here is not whether Heidegger agreed with Nietzsche, what Mikhail Bakhtin said about Ferdinand de Saussure, or whether Williams read Michel Foucault. Instead, this is a field of sometimes continuous and sometimes disjunctive conversations in which Cultural Studies names an attitude—and to say this attitude is critical is of course not to imply it is negative. The experience of modernity is always a representation of modernity because of how modernity centers on an individual perception that cannot be removed from the field of "culture" that gives that point of view its meaningfulness. Whether this is primarily understood as being dangerously complicit with oppression, as for Marx; as opening up possibilities for change even as it also continually fragments possible foundations, as for Woolf; whether there is much to regret in this, as Heidegger believes; or whether we want to dispute its most romantic interpretations, like Foucault; both modernism and Cultural Studies, as an aspect of modernism, consist in taking up a particular (expert) place from which to deal with this situation. Cultural Studies deploys to this end those classic Modernist traits of self-reflexivity and perspectivism combined with the classic modernist tools that put these into action: ideology, dialectics, phenomenology, pragmatism, ethnography, semiotics, and dialogic analysis. It also employs those modernist tools that enable a critical position by the conscious disavowal of their own position (a consciousness that speaks to it), such as "impersonality" and "formalism." This is not an exhaustive list but it demonstrates the crucial modernist conjunction of an "expert" position and a "culture" that invites analysis or requires defamiliarization.

This attitude requires historical context in order for its specific practices to be made visible, but it is not the product of a linear evolution. Benjamin, is a key example. The extensive now-published archive of Benjamin's works and notes comprise not an astonishingly prescient vision of what would become Cultural Studies, but rather Cultural Studies in practice. Fragments like "The Cultural History of Toys" (1928) and "The First Form of Criticism That Refuses to Judge" (1930), as well as Benjamin's notes on particular texts or events as indexes of contemporary thought and feeling, supplement his published works to bring forth Cultural Studies as a form of analysis that juxtaposes the everyday with a defamiliarizing perspective on contemporary life. Different histories of this attitude do not undermine the need for a longer historical view tied, in part, to the transnationalization of cultural forms and practices, including cultural critique and expertise, itself propelled by modernism. In the process of its canonization Modernism often seemed exclusively Anglo-European, but Benjamin's first "exposé" of the arcades project, for example, includes an epigraph from Nguyen Trong Hiep, a Vietnamese poet reflecting on Paris, which clearly summarized for him the reflexive attitude of modernity (Benjamin [1927–40] 2002: 3; 14).

The "New Culture Movement" in China, which fed the May Fourth Movement and nurtured the nascent Communist Party, demonstrates that reflection on a newly objectifiable "culture" in China was contemporary with related European discourses, as it was in equally but differently nationalist forms in, for example, Japan and Mexico. The New Culture Movement was manifest in magazines like *Xin Qingnian* (see chapter 2), published also with the French title *La Jeunesse* to signify, as much as did its references to Western science, its place in transnational intellectual and cultural conversations. Elisabeth Croll describes it as "eagerly awaited each week by students and teachers who flocked to the new bookstores" (80; see also Lee 120ff). We should not incorporate this into avant-garde stories about "little magazines" in search of a single Modernist narrative any more than we should imagine that Chinese modernism today is the same as that in the United States. Such magazines were directly shaped by political programs like those of Chen Duxiu (first secretary and chairman of the Communist Party and founder of *Xin Qingnian*) as well as by new dialogues between public and expert manifest in letters pages, and between science and art manifest in the writing and editorial work of scholars like Lu Xun, most of whom, like Chen, had studied abroad.[5] Because of its direct dialogue with macropolitical action, *Xin Qingnian* is not a "little magazine"—that is, it does not aspire to be "little" and, in Western terms, it has a public voice more like a newspaper—but it does overlap with such magazines, including in its calls for aesthetic and cultural revolution as the most crucial forms of revolution.

Xin Qingnian speaks to a transcultural trade in culture that does not define it as derivative, even if there were obviously imports (see Lee 44).[6] The discontinuities between discourse on the urban and the rural in Chinese Modernism and English Modernism, alongside the crucial intersections, would alone be a fascinating and complex study. But whatever the difference of its Modernism, the modernist emergence of expertise on culture is still tied to a modernity that unfolds there around (very different) discourses on secularization, urbanization, and industrialization. What makes *Xin Qingnian* particularly modernist is its simultaneously objectified and subjective model of culture as defined by a field of experts, and noticing this should also help us to notice the crucial importance of expert judgment to magazines more familiar to histories of Modernism, like *Blast*, *The Free-woman* (later *The New Freewoman*, and then *The Egoist*), and *Cahiers du Cinéma*. As Leo Lee's study of Modernism and modernity in China, *Shang-hai Modern* (1999), brilliantly captures, modernism in China cannot be tied to particular political discourses (by representing the "Chinese enlightenment" as comprehended and exhausted by May Fourth, for example), nor is it compatible with the familiar Modernist story about European aesthetic revolutions. If, for Lee, this particular urban and cosmopolitan incarnation of Chinese modernity was shut down by subsequent events, the importance of culture as a modernist field of contestation in China was not foreclosed on, as the revolution itself made very clear. New ideas about culture continued to emerge in tension with one another, forming and reforming the modernist terrain for what we might call "culture wars" in order to see its extension into contemporary mediaspheres.

Although there are many ways to claim cultural expertise, the specifically modernist mode of expert reflection on culture sustains them all. Arnold, Nietzsche, Adorno, Heidegger, and Trilling all see cultural expertise as an appropriation from philosophy that has (or at least might have) deleterious effects. The terms of this debate have been remarkably persistent, including the much-recited call for an authentic culture that enables both the best art and the right critical history. If it seems that Cultural Studies has broken with this tradition, a claim I will return to in the next chapter, what authenticates culture has never been straightforward. The cultural expert, like any expert, requires an authorized place from which to speak, but such authorized places are far more varied for cultural than for other forms of modern expertise, ranging across little magazines, academic journals, newspaper columns, government reports, talk shows, and many more authenticating platforms. Nikolas Rose points out that modern "expertise" permeates everyday life. "For the majority," he notes, "expertise operated not through social planning, paternalism and bureaucracy, but in terms of a logic of choice" (Rose 88) between forms of advice "by knowledgeable persons." Individuals "could thus become the object of proposals and strategies for reform or prevention by expertise. The quotidian lives of the masses became gridded by regulatory codes" (113). Culture, just like medicine or the rule of law—indeed, more so because of the greater accessibility of some forms of cultural expertise (expressed as taste, for example)—manifests multiple and competing forms of expertise, even if their regulatory codes are often self-selecting.

It is not only that individuals are all subjects of culture and may form what Rose calls "counter-expertise," but that, in the modernist context, across media punditry, academic analysis, political pronouncements, the practices of art or meta-cultural institutions, and other calls to cultural affiliation, culture becomes a site *defined* by competing expertise. As Zygmunt Bauman puts it, modernist culture required the cultural expert:

One cannot even explain the meaning of the concept [culture] without reference to human "incompleteness," to the need of teachers and, in general, of "people in the know" to make up for this incompleteness. . . . The idea of culture, in other words, establishes knowledge in the role of power, and simultaneously supplies legitimation of such power. . . . Whatever their other ambitions, modern intellectuals always saw culture as their private property; they made it, they lived in it, they even gave it its name. (99–100)

Thus in critics' ongoing redefinition of "culture" and its value, in unfolding possible allegiances like Marxism or psychoanalysis, *Partisan Review* or the Birmingham School, modernism gives rise to what we might now call "the culture wars." Modernism as an institutional category quickly became a tool in these wars as Greenberg, Georg Lukács, Snow, and Leavis all make clear. Authorized cultural expertise emerged, as Heidegger suggests, as a saleable position in a particular market place: modernist lecture tours from Arnold to T. S. Eliot to Jacques Derrida evidence this as clearly as the emergence of magazines that evaluate and diagnose "culture today" for diverse constituencies.

If contemporary media experts on culture, from the British Prince of Wales through well-known movie critics to conservative U.S. pundit Bill O'Reilly, seem to much more clearly mark a commercial space for the culture warrior,[7] the earlier example of Eliot is telling. As editor of several influential journals (including *The Egoist*), from his desk at Faber and Faber, on his lecture tours speaking to crowds of students, artists, and the general public, and in his essays commenting on peers and canonical greats, Eliot's taste was deployed as expertise. Expertise for, of course, others deemed to be in need of it—which is all expertise can ever be *for*. With reference to the critical tradition that had already emerged around Charles Baudelaire, Benjamin notes, "Taste develops with the definite preponderance of commodity production over any other kind of production" ([1938] 1996a: 81). Taste, he argues—and we can see the same argument in Trilling or Bourdieu—"has the value of a more or less elaborate masking of [a] lack of expertness" (Benjamin [1938] 1996a: 82). Tension between the public and the expert, as well as between experts, is at the forefront of the modernist field of culture and ingrained in the popular itself as contentions over, for example, digest or "eclectic" magazines, new public buildings, or television genres.

On the terrain of the culture wars, a postlapsarian or "belatedness" narrative is characteristic: the natural or otherwise proper state of culture is often represented as having been lost or thwarted in new cultural complexity. A vocal participant in these debates since Kant, let alone Arnold, the trajectory I am calling modernist Cultural Studies is no exception. Internally, the presumed political project of contemporary Cultural Studies work is treated as something lost—as a cultural potential for more authentic critical engagement that has always only recently slipped out of reach. Mike Featherstone points out that "the sense that there is a cultural crisis, that we need a 'diagnosis of our times,' has long been the meat and drink of cultural specialists (artists, intellectuals and various types of cultural intermediaries)" (2). Culture wars are struggles with a sense of *zeitgeist*, itself a modernist term (usually attributed to Herder), mostly employed to bemoan whatever it is the *zeitgeist* is supposed to be. Certainly "culture wars" seems a very specifically contemporary U.S. phrase and, as Bill Readings suggests, its U.S. manifestation does have a particular nationalist history (Readings 112ff). In this history, Cultural Studies is positioned both as a force for retrieving lost cultural value and as one of the forces responsible for such a loss. But the public and popular spectacle it refers to extends to modernism in general. I have taken my subtitle here from Michel de Certeau's essay, "The Place From Which One Deals With Culture," where he points out that we "cannot discuss culture or its global aspects without, first of all, recognizing the fact that we are . . . dealing with it from only one site, our own" (1997: 123). Certeau argues that speaking of culture at all raises the partiality of any expertise and thus articulates the field of culture as one in which exclusion and contestation is inevitable. From this recognition he is not seeking consensus, but a place for dealing with culture that is open to dialogue.[8]

The practical complexity of achieving such a goal demands more careful consideration of how we know culture, a problematic that is unfolded in an interesting way by Foucault's history of the emergence of modern knowledge. In his preface to *The Order of Things*, Foucault suggests there are three "regions" in which the (modern) world is known. The first is comprised of the "fundamental codes of a culture . . . the empirical orders with which [the subject] will be dealing and within which he will be at home" ([1966] 1973: xx). These codes are, in Foucault, more or less equivalent to the Althusserian model of ideology: apparatuses and dispositions that constitute "concrete individuals as subjects" (Althusser [1971] 1994: 159) even as they necessarily involve subjects in ideological practices as "the practical rituals of the most elementary everyday life" (160).[9] As Althusser's model of *interpellation*, by which we recognize ourselves in some ideologically framed statement (160), suggests, we manifest ideology by recognizing it—by being sufficiently well trained to do so. Consequently, we become subjects of our own shifting cultural context in the same process. This is also the constitutive reflection (or turning back) on the self that Judith Butler calls "complicity."[10] These are not orders open to dialogue in the sense desired by Certeau or Cultural Studies, however fundamental they are to the modernist experience.

The second of Foucault's regions is science: "scientific theories or the philosophical interpretations which explain why order exists in general" (Foucault [1966] 1973: xx). These are the analytic processes that look like modernism in action: ideology critique, semiotics, ethnography, experiment, phenomenology, and so on. Cultural Studies might appear here as one of the diverse and changing systems for classifying and managing the world. This region *claims to know* the first as the world in which subjects come to be. But Foucault also refers to a third region that seems crucial to the intimacy between modernism and Cultural Studies. This region, "imperceptibly deviating from the empirical orders prescribed for it by its primary codes, instituting an initial separation from them, causes them to lose their original transparency, relinquishes its immediate and invisible powers, frees itself sufficiently to discover that these orders are perhaps not the only possible ones or the best ones" (xx). This region is a mingling of experience and analysis. This is where heterology can appear in the context of Foucault's argument: the first region as it is lived inseparably from the classifications of the second, where people order the world and know that they are ordering it. As much as this extends Althusser's recognition that awareness of ideology is part of both conforming to or resisting it, this is also the "culture" Cultural Studies aims to study. While this tripartite structure echoes and refines a familiar distinction between morality, science, and art, this third region, especially in its imperceptible deviation from real life, would be better understood as culture itself—as coextensive in any subject's experience with the world as they know it.

This understanding of culture as the entwinement of experience and representation central to modern knowledge provides a useful reply to Grossberg's concern about the fate of Cultural Studies as it is challenged by the move beyond "modern thought" to postmodernism (1997: 30). Grossberg rightly wonders how the discipline would negotiate such a demand, having been so closely tied to modernity through ideas like consciousness, ideology, and nation and to a "grand epistemological revolution" (30) it both participates in and critiques. Given this model of culture, Grossberg's insistence that Cultural Studies now needs to focus on "articulations between discursive alliances, everyday life and machineries of power" (31) is in fact a restatement of Cultural Studies' intrinsically modernist form. Just as Modernism often imposed a false coherence on the Enlightenment, the label "postmodernism" often imposes a false coherence on modernism. In this respect, postmodernism and Cultural Studies as a named discipline are products of the same historical forces, because the relegation of modernism to a closed, past Modernism produces both of them. This relegation gradually solidified many facets of modernism into discrete "disciplines," eventually including the academic mode of Cultural Studies. Cultural Studies is not a mode of analyzing "cultural modernism" because there is no modernism that is not "cultural." Cultural Studies rather appeared as one name for modernism's critical attitude—an attitude crucially unanchored by specific methods and objects and always at the vulnerable edge where scholarly expertise meets public and popular debate.

9

On Popular Music

How can we break with a program that makes a value of crisis (modernism), or progress beyond the era of Progress (modernity), or transgress the ideology of the transgressive (avant-gardism)? . . . [Modernism] may have "lost a fixed historical reference" (Habermas), but the ideology has not: modernism is a cultural construct based on specific conditions: it has a historical limit.

Hal Foster, "Postmodernism (a preface)"

Insisting on the modernism of Cultural Studies is not only a theoretical or historiographical proposition but important for thinking about how students respond to the central concerns and approaches of Cultural Studies. This final chapter explores the modernism of contemporary Cultural Studies through the example of popular music. But it also discusses the potential of and obstacles to teaching Cultural Studies through modernism and vice versa. One of the merits of using Cultural Studies to think about modernism is that, while such an approach makes large claims about the longevity of modernism, it also rescues modernism from being a vague historical abstraction by attending to how modernism is experienced. Cultural Studies' analysis of popular music can serve here as an example of its attention to economic, social, and technological conditions that materially inflect modernism in many different situations. Popular music also provides an opportunity for considering what is at stake in identifying the modernism of Cultural Studies, including whether there is an imperative to "go beyond" modernism.

Reprise

Many commentators have stressed links between Modernism and Cultural Studies, although usually in terms of the former influencing the latter, with standard reference to Antonio Gramsci and the Frankfurt School. Some stronger connections, however, have also been made. Lawrence Grossberg's argument that the postmodern critique of master narratives like "ideology" and "nation" requires that Cultural Studies find new ways of articulating identity, state, and culture (Grossberg 1997) with which I closed the last chapter is a good starting point here. While it identifies Cultural Studies with postmodern critique, it also sees Cultural Studies as confronted by postmodernism—as in fact a modernist discourse that must be renovated by postmodernism. But I want to qualify even this more tangled relation between the terms Cultural Studies, modernism, and postmodernism with a discussion of John Hartley's *A Short History of Cultural Studies* (2003), which explicitly sets out to write a history of Cultural Studies for the early twenty-first century.

Hartley begins his history with Allen Lane's Penguin and Pelican imprints and their relationship to Modernist narratives on the popular, the public, and cultural education: "After a weekend spent with Agatha Christie in Devon, Lane searched Exeter station's bookstall for something to read on his journey back to London, but found only popular magazines and reprints of Victorian novels. Following this, he recognised the need for good quality contemporary fiction at an attractive price. Lane was determined that the new range be available not just in traditional bookshops, but also in railway stations and chain stores such as Woolworths." Drawing heavily on Penguin's own website history (Hartley 20ff), Hartley's account of this Modernist project implies that it produced Cultural Studies. He stresses the importance of the selections that made up the early Pelican range of new and reprinted non-fiction titles, from George Bernard Shaw's *The Intelligent Woman's Guide to Socialism, Capitalism, Sovietism and Fascism* (1928, Pelican 1937), through Raymond Williams' *Culture and Society* (Pelican 1958) and E. P. Thompson's *Making of the English Working Class* (1963, Pelican 1968), to Pelican's hundredth title: Richard Hoggart's *The Uses of Literacy* (Pelican 1957). What makes Hoggart, but not Shaw, an early practitioner of Cultural Studies is something Hartley never clarifies.[1]

In Hoggart's own account, the Penguin and Pelican texts signify the cultural aspirations of a new type of student/scholar, one freed by the same new educational system that produced "Modernism" from the class systems that produced them: "they own the Penguin selection from [T. S.] Eliot, as well as some other Penguins and Pelicans; they used to take *Penguin New Writing* and now subscribe to *Encounter*. They know a little, but often only from reviews or short articles, about [James] Frazer and [Karl] Marx; they probably own a copy of the Pelican edition of [Sigmund] Freud's *Psycho-pathology of Everyday Life* [1901, Pelican 1938]" (Hoggart 239). Hoggart's simultaneous disdain and attachment here might extend by association to the aims and methods of Cultural Studies, which are indirectly positioned as, like these readers, uprooted and cynical but still the place where what matters continues to be discussed. Hoggart says they know "Just enough about the social sciences, about anthropology, about sociology, about so-cial psychology . . . to supply a destructive reference on most occasions. 'What about the Polynesians?' has now succeeded the political 'What about the Russians?' as the key-question. They take up the game of finding clay feet. . . . They are the poor little rich boys of a world over-supplied with popularised and disconnected information" (243). Acknowledging the plea-sure in such games, Hoggart claims that while they represent "a nostalgia for belief" (243) it is one needed to oppose the "obediently receptive passivity" of the masses with "their eyes glued to television sets, pin-ups and cinema screens" (244). In this snippet from one of Cultural Studies' canon-forming texts we can see a combination of critique and pastiche, of evaluation and documentation, and of commitment and disconnection that continues to characterize Cultural Studies. The same sequence of terms, however, is also used to distinguish between Modernism and Cultural Studies.

The most consistent argument in Hartley's history is that, from the Pelican paperbacks to the contemporary proliferation of specialist academic texts, Cultural Studies is a publishing venture. The same could be said of Modern-ism, from its small circulation publishing ventures through its spectacular trials and successes to the ongoing reprinting and anthologization traced by the publication dates in my bibliography. Hartley's history repeatedly refers to Modernism, without ever reflecting on the significance of that associa-tion. While Hartley may be right to see the birth of the Cultural Studies "reader" as the moment of its commercialization (151–52), his own history demonstrates that its institutionalization clearly precedes those textbooks. My difficulty with Hartley's history is not its (overwhelmingly Modernist) components but their integration into a continuum that nevertheless breaks at the Birmingham School. Cultural Studies proper, he implies, relegates the Modernist history before it to a parent culture archive. The central special-izations of Cultural Studies, such as "everyday life," are thus disconnected from modernism. Invested in its own endlessly claimed newness, this Cul-tural Studies, like Hoggart's readers, is free to wander without declared allegiances through the backlogs of other disciplines and to reinvent old debates as new ones. Both of these freedoms might be virtues at times, but they also come at a dehistoricizing price and leave Cultural Studies open to charges that it contributes to no ongoing intellectual or cultural necessity and that it is (or even should be) a populist "teaching machine" (see Hartley 161).

It seems, after reading Hartley and others, that Cultural Studies has definitively abandoned the thread of modernist cultural analysis committed to preserving a public and personal value for culture as enlightenment. This shift has been closely aligned with Cultural Studies' attention to popular culture, rather than with any methodological tendency. This attention to popular culture as a means of exploring everyday constraints and opportunities has been at the forefront of attacks on Cultural Studies within and outside the academy, particularly wherever the opposition between enlightenment and popular culture is presumed to be self-evident. Cultural Studies is often represented in such attacks as uncritically populist, producing analysis that anyone could produce and determined to reject any value that might exclude the pleasures of "the people." In this context, Graeme Turner provides a useful map of a populist tradition in Cultural Studies (Turner 187ff). He cites Jim McGuigan's complaint that "what starts out" in Cultural Studies "as a retrieval of particular class experiences of everyday life," as in Hoggart's analysis of working class culture, "ends up . . . as 'an uncritical celebration of mass-popular cultural consumption'" (Turner 188). According to Turner, what McGuigan attacks here is a phase of Cultural Studies that was exhausted by the early 1990s (Turner 188), which in turn positions "populist" Cultural Studies as contemporary with the emergence of postmodernism as a dominant academic category.

The most sophisticated version of equating Cultural Studies, postmodernism, and populism sees Cultural Studies' refusal to define both its own discipline and the content of "culture" as its main weakness. Exemplarily, in *The University in Ruins* (1996), Bill Readings argues that the institutionalization of Cultural Studies embraces a "culture" that refers to nothing at all and that "The ambivalence of Cultural Studies' relation to the academy is apparent in the appeal to 'ordinary people' as legitimation" (100). Elsewhere, although this set of equations is very contradictory, "Cultural Studies" and "postmodernism" are treated as terms that are interchangeable with the labels "post-structuralism" and even "theory." But what coheres these accusations is the assumption that Cultural Studies abandons something vital—"traditional values," "humanism," or academic "rigor" (terms that are not synonymous and in fact have different relations to Modernism).[2]

Such accusations focus on *what* is studied by Cultural Studies, arguing that emphasis on the popular both abdicates the responsibility of humanities disciplines to maintain culture as an index of value and voids the possibility of critique: "Rather than posing a threat, the analyses performed by Cultural Studies risk providing new marketing opportunities for the system. Practices such as punk music and dress styles are offered their self-consciousness in academic essays, but the dignity they acquire is not that of authenticity but of marketability" (Readings 121). This critique constitutes another Modernist history for Cultural Studies. Readings claims that Modernist "culturalism" had a center that both Cultural Studies and postmodernism have evacuated or "dereferentialized."[3] Students of Cultural Studies are familiar with this set of equations, taking them from representations of Cultural Studies in the media and the academy but also from their teachers' courses and reading preferences. Nevertheless, equating Cultural Studies with postmodernism because the latter insists on relativism, values play as much as structure, and is vulnerable to charges of both populism and abstraction relies on a very strange picture of Modernism, which is signally defined by each of these things. The "postmodern" characteristics of Cultural Studies in fact draw out one thread of its modernism—the one most concerned with undoing coherence (gathering in surrealism rather than Futurism and Walter Benjamin rather than F. R. Leavis). Only in some versions of Cultural Studies has this thread has been dominant and it is neither equal nor opposed to the strand of Cultural Studies in which the critical potential of popular culture is particularly celebrated.

Such celebration has been as controversial in Cultural Studies as in Modernism. James Joyce's commonness was derided by Virginia Woolf for disregarding why Homer mattered more than banal ablutions or advertising. And while the critical flashpoint was not the same, a related debate was ignited when John Fiske's late 1980s texts on the "carnivalesque" potential of popular culture divided the academic field of Cultural Studies. While the controversy around Fiske focused on his analysis of popular culture in terms of its resistance to dominant values, it depended on his more precise claim that popular discrimination "is quite different from the critical or aesthetic discrimination promoted by schools and universities to evaluate the quality of highbrow texts" (Fiske [1989] 1990: 122)—a claim that this chapter generally addresses. This approach was both lauded and vilified and brings me to the example of popular music, both because Fiske highlights it and because the debates ranged around Fiske not only preceded him but have continued to be important to studies of popular music since.

If we begin our history of Cultural Studies where Hartley does, and where

Grossberg and Readings imply we should, that is, in the Modernist frame, then we can argue that Cultural Studies has always prioritized popular music as part of its endeavor to engage with culture as it is lived in the present. Popular music offers, and Grossberg sees in this an "echo" of Hoggart's aims, "unique insights into and perspectives on the question of how people live their lives in a particular time and place" (Grossberg 2002: 27). At the same time, as Simon During argues, institutionalized Cultural Studies' "own claims to being a dissident discipline have, in part, been borrowed from the rock rhetoric which vernacularized transgression" (During 128). Cultural Studies' interest in popular music is thus tied to the public authority of the cultural critic as well as to ideology critique and other perspectives on what popular culture means for participants. The disciplinary expansion of Cultural Studies in the late 1980s to mid-1990s when "postmodernism" was at its zenith thus also involved new studies of popular music.

The anthology *On Record: Rock, Pop and the Written Word* (Frith and Goodwin 1990), which gave new pedagogical coherence to the field of popular music studies, was promoted with the tagline, "Did you know that Jean-Paul Sartre once wrote an essay on the Top 40?" This question is a tease designed to surprise readers with the serious relevance of talking about popular music. Sartre's piece is not actually included in the collection. The piece that comes closest to fulfilling the promise of surprising the reader with philosophical attention to popular music is Theodor Adorno's essay "On Popular Music" (1941). I could have devoted the rest of this chapter to comparing the way the Frankfurt School, the Birmingham School and contemporary Cultural Studies discuss popular music. Instead, I want to focus on the continuity of themes and approaches deployed in popular music studies from Adorno to the present. I think this approach reveals a set of definitively modernist questions that are constantly being reestablished as both imperative and irresolvable concerns for Cultural Studies.

Teaching Adorno

Almost every year since 1996 I have taught Adorno's "On Popular Music" to undergraduate and (post)graduate students in courses on cultural theory, popular culture, youth culture, or modernism. I have several reasons for doing so, the first of which can be summarized by Dave Laing's opening to a review essay on the early 1990s' expansion of popular music studies: "I sometimes wonder what course popular music studies might have taken if Theodor Adorno had turned east to Moscow instead of west to New York when he fled from Nazi oppression in the 1930s" (Laing 223). Adorno's essay is foundational, establishing both the necessity of thinking seriously about popular music and some influential parameters for doing so. My second reason is to provoke a response that never fails to appear and be, for many students, both entertaining and eye-opening. Adorno's tirade against "pre-digested" popular music is highly recognizable to my students, lining up easily with familiar dismissals of pop music with which they often agree. It is with some shock, then, that many students encounter the fact that Adorno is talking about "jazz," which they have received as a form of institutionally supported art and, at the same time, a musical "parent culture."

Henry Jenkins, Tara McPherson, and Jane Shattuc begin their essay "Defining Popular Culture" with an anecdote about musical exchanges between "art" and "the popular":

> When Miles Davis improvised "My Funny Valentine" at Lincoln Center in 1964, jazz stood as an unquestionable art form. Jazz has not always had such respect. In the 1920s the reception of [the] form stood somewhere between "moral opposition and primitivist celebration." Theodor Adorno condemned much of jazz in the 1940s as a form of "pseudo-individualization," or a false attempt at originality. . . . In the years since Adorno's critique, jazz did not become somehow "better." Rather the definitions of high culture and popular culture changed to accommodate new tastes. (26)

Adorno's "jazz" included the swing big bands, like Glen Miller's, which were then jazz's most successful commercial form, but also the improvisational music we now more often call "jazz."

Adorno opposes all popular music to "serious" music, which is instead dialectical: "As much a cryptogram of the unreconciled antithesis between individual fate and human destiny as it is a presentation of the bonds, however questionable, that tie the antagonistic individual interests into a whole, and as it is finally a presentation for the hope of a real reconcilement" (Adorno [1932] 1976: 68–69). Popular music he understands, by contrast, as a vacuous and banal reflection of the capitalist system that produces it (Adorno [1941] 2002: 428), although only the distraction of the audience accounts for why something that corresponds to the system that produces it would not also reflect its inequities and contradictions (443, 458). As "pure commodity," popular music is represented by Adorno as "the most alien of all music to society; it no longer expresses anything of social misery and contradiction, but forms rather in itself one single contradiction to this society . . . falsifying the cognition of reality" (425).

In *Aesthetic Theory* (1970), Adorno's fuller elaboration of this argument concedes that all art is constrained by economic conditions. Under capitalism, not only does art never entirely escape its bourgeois reception as "a reconciling glow enfolding the world" ([1970] 1984: 2) but "there is no contesting the cliché of which cultural history is so fond, that the development of artistic processes, usually classed under the heading of style, corresponds to social development" (6). Nevertheless, art proper for Adorno "can no more be reduced to the general formula of consolation than to its opposite" (2). My students are right to be suspicious that Adorno's tools might be as blunt as they seem. Proper artworks, he says, "participate in enlightenment because they do not lie" (6).[4]

Robert Witkin's *Adorno on Popular Culture* (2003) is one secondary source that elucidates Adorno for my classes. As Witkin notes, "The category on which Adorno fixes to distinguish what he might call good serious music from popular music is *standardization*," which in fact involves "an entire theory of popular culture in itself" (98). The opposition between serious and standardized music is one my students recognize from the mass media and very often also in their own interpersonal negotiations of taste. It is therefore a consistently useful exercise to explore what this opposition implies. While Adorno saw "mass culture" in general as a pervasive threat to social good, popular music was a particularly telling instance of the ways in which the culture industry produced not only consistent forms but also standardized subjectivities. These are structured in "a system of response-mechanisms wholly antagonistic to the ideal of individuality in a free, liberal society" (Adorno [1941] 2002: 442).

Adorno argues that "the culture industry" produced a deceptive balance between differentiation and familiarity that attracted without surprising. This in turn manufactured an image of creativity and choice within popular music he called "pseudo-individualization." It is precisely because popular music claimed to access the audience's pleasures, desires, and aspirations that such pseudo-individualization could also standardize consumers themselves (see chapter 3). This standardization is not about the formal recognizability of love songs, for example, or songs limited to a certain musical range. Instead it refers to the determination of each instance of popular music by its field (which in turn points to a crucial continuity between Adorno and Pierre Bourdieu that can be useful to more advanced students).

In the face of this culture industry, Adorno stressed the importance of a dialectical relation between art and life that could make music "serious." He argued that "only when the artist develops" music's formal elements "in contact with the life-world on which they reflect can meaningful form be constituted" (Witkin 100). Popular music is, by contrast, a polished product without such contact. Adorno describes it as "ready-made," a "mechanism," and, as Witkin puts it, "a schema that clicks automatically into place when cued" (Witkin 100).

The term "ready-made" here is telling in our context because Adorno's dismissal of the possibility that popular music could reflect on the world in any significant way can thus be referred back to Duchamp's found objects (see chapter 5). While the everyday was both invoked and made strange by the readymade, Adorno insists that popular music is instead contained by its field, which is what gives every song its standardized meaning. This is how what looks like innovation in popular music, whether in improvised solo breaks or other unexpected musical effects, in fact works to continue that standardization. Such innovation recognizably differs from the expected, but in a way that is constrained by and reinforces those expectations. In invoking the field in which it is "different," the variation belongs to the field rather than to the music itself.

In every class of mine that reads this essay, some students inevitably object that popular music can be very complex, even musically difficult, and that not only do popular songs differ from one another but the field of popular music itself changes. Adorno would clearly respond that while "The original patterns that are now standardised evolved in a more or less competitive way," the industrial shape of popular music distribution "institutionalises desiderata which originally might have come from the public" (Adorno [1941] 2002: 444). This response rarely satisfies my students, who, while they often recognize or even sympathize with this argument when it comes to "pop," are just as often interested in differentiating the (popular) music they personally prefer from such condemnation. In this regard, my students use a similar argument to Adorno's, distinguishing an authentic critical relation to the world as the attitude which transforms musical originality into serious or important music.

Perhaps the two key figures in unfolding a canon of popular music studies after Adorno are Simon Frith, in the United Kingdom, and Grossberg in the United States. In his pivotal essay, "Towards an aesthetic of popular music" (1987), Frith argues that "The question we should be asking is not what does popular music reveal about 'the people' but how does it construct them." This claim is largely consistent with Adorno's work. But Frith continues: "popular music is popular not because it reflects something, or authentically articulates some sort of popular taste or experience, but because it creates our understanding of what popularity is" (1987: 137). Frith suggests something important here about why popular music has been so widely discussed by cultural critics, and one of the most challenging elements of this classroom conversation is to map the multiple ways in which music might be defined as "popular." But these are not the terms for defending the value of popular music that my students' own cultural training has offered them. Instead, they either use Adorno's terms, more or less, for sectioning off some music as serious (popular) music, or they defend the value of any music whatever on the grounds of its physical or emotional impact. Certainly, the latter argument is also often made by Cultural Studies of popular music. Susan McClary and Robert Walser, for example, part company with Adorno when he sets aside the "rhythmic" and "emotional" responses to music as respectively reliant on the primitive "beat" and sentiment. Musical experience of the rhythmic type, he argues, "is based upon the underlying, unabating time of the music—its 'beat'" that will override all differentiation (Adorno [1941] 2002: 460). Adorno associates musical experience of the emotional type with girls in particular and while he does not represent such fans (to use a contemporary term for this figure) as entirely passive dupes, he represents them as being satisfied with these standardized pleasures (see chapter 4).

Thus, while inspiring debates about how to assess the value of the music they love and hate, via Adorno I can also raise with my students the context in which we come to have such investments in popular culture. It is more difficult, however, to explain to them that such distinctions between the popular and the enlightening, entwined with distinctions between commodities and art, are intrinsic to modernism. Modernism is a term they have been socialized (well before university but certainly also there) to associate with now irrelevant ideas. In fact, the terms of this debate are established by modernism. As Renato Poggioli suggests, in modernism art no longer means the human production of beauty but instead infers a range of other improving values such as enlightening challenge and defamiliarizing originality (Poggioli 80–81). In this context, art becomes part of an evaluative system in which experts discriminate between forms of novelty, difficulty, and affect to adjudicate what will be valuable. The "popular" is a term with some force in this evaluation because it signifies what is already known and received as common and thus neither new nor requiring expertise.

Let me reiterate here that stressing the modernism of our conversations about the popular is not the same as claiming that nothing changes in these debates. What counts as popular, as music, or as popular music has been shifted many times—for example, by the dissemination of the personal computer, as my students are well aware. But the conditions that produced mass-distributed popular commodity culture are entwined with ways of talking about them. Among broad technical, economic, and discursive changes, by the 1920s and 30s the mass-consumption of commodities as leisure appeared in an array of now familiar forms and venues and were attached to particular discourses on popular culture. The *Middletown* studies are exemplary: the Lynds argue that "The rise of large-scale advertising, popular magazines, movies, radio, and other channels of increased cultural diffusion from without are rapidly changing habits of thought as to what things are essential to living and multiplying optional occasions for spending money" (1929: 81–82). This is not merely a side effect of modernization although, as Adorno always stresses, the types of popular culture that succeed cannot be separated from the broader life-world of consumers.

Modernist discourse on popular culture turns on newly shared focal points for cultural expertise. Popular music is just one example of this expansion, but its selection is not arbitrary. From Adorno's "On Popular Music" we can draw a range of key modernist exchanges that Modernism makes spectacularly visible and Cultural Studies continues. Through them Adorno's tirade offers my students both a critical perspective on the analysis of popular culture and a fuller history of such analysis. The fraught distinction between "the popular" and "culture as enlightenment" is one such dimension, the tension between commodification and art is another, but behind these are still more that pervade the public, popular, and academic spheres in which my students orient themselves. The foundational modernist debates over the constitutive, necessary, and desirable relations between individual subjects and society underlies these contestations over popular music and is much more accessible to my students in Adorno—despite how difficult he can seem to some—than, for example, in G. W. F. Hegel. Via Adorno I can thus connect them to competing models of how the relation between "culture" and "the masses" should be conceived.

I can ask my students to compare Adorno's argument, for example, to Sigmund Freud's *Group Psychology and the Analysis of the Ego* (1921). In this text, Freud postulates that there are two sorts of groups with different relations to individuality: the organized, hierarchized group (e.g., a church or army), and the amorphous, shifting group (e.g., the herd or crowd). This double sense of the group is another consistent modernist theme, within which, as in both Adorno and Freud, the unorganized group is often feminized. When José Ortega y Gasset or Matthew Arnold figure the masses as masculine it is because they want to attach agency and discrimination or choice to them. Adolf Hitler's view of the masses gives texture to this distinction. For Hitler too, there are two kinds of masses. One is the "Nietzschean" herd—"The people in their overwhelming majority are so feminine by nature and attitude that sober reasoning determines their thoughts and actions far less than emotion and feeling" (Hitler quoted in Reich [1942] 1978: 87)—and the other is a *Volk* resembling the "organic community" of Leavis. One reason Adorno rejects the idea that jazz is folk music—a thesis put forward by Winthrop Sargeant, with whom Adorno understands himself generally to agree—is because he feels there is no longer any "folk" with unmediated access to a culture identified with them to produce such music. He would undoubtedly make the same argument about reggae or hip hop, which are examples my students often want to use to counter Adorno in this respect. At the same time they often endorse Adorno's dismissal of a group-identity construed as herd, crowd, or mass and as connoting youth, femininity, and malleability. My students' received image of the pop music fan is precisely that of consumers collected into "contagious" peer groups (see Freud [1921] 1922: 64–65).

It is worth observing as well that stressing the modernism of Cultural Studies is just as productively disjunctive viewed from the classroom where "Modernism" is being taught. Clement Greenberg's essay opposing "Avant-garde and kitsch" (1939) is made newly accessible by thinking about his opposition between transnational commodity culture and the authenticity of "folk" culture through a Cultural Studies framework. For Greenberg, kitsch is "Another mass product of Western industrialism . . . on a triumphal tour of the world, crowding out and defacing native cultures in one colonial country after another, so that it is now by way of becoming a universal culture, the first universal culture ever beheld" (18). Seven years earlier, Adorno had also used the term "kitsch" as a commonplace for what is not genuine: "In music, at any rate, all real kitsch has the character of a *model*. It offers the outline and draft of objectively compelling, pre-established forms that have lost their content in history, and for which the unfettered artist, cast adrift, is not able to fashion the content on his own" (Adorno [1932] 2002: 501). And kitsch also describes, for Adorno, the "culture-trash" to which even philosophy is reduced in the plays of Samuel Beckett: "Culture parades before him as the entrails of *Jugendstil* [roughly *art nouveau*] ornaments did before that progress which preceded him, modernism as the obsolescence of the modern. The regressive language demolishes it. Such objectivity in Beckett obliterates the meaning that was culture, along with its rudiments. Culture thus begins to fluoresce" ([1961] 2005b: 1116). This demolition of culture that is also its fluorescence represents modernist culture as destructive regeneration, an image that returns in the "progress by attrition" narratives of popular music and popular music studies alike.

For Greenberg and Adorno, kitsch is popular exactly to the extent that the popular cannot be "folk." Greenberg continues with an account of "global culture," which my students are likely to think appeared much more recently: "Today the native of China, no less than the South American Indian, the Hindu, no less than the Polynesian, have come to prefer to the products of their native art, magazine covers, rotogravure sections and calendar girls" (18). Like Adorno, Greenberg believes the "irresistible attractiveness" of kitsch depends on its leveling formula. "Rembrandt" could be reproduced as cheaply as calendar girls, he notes, and so neither cultural imperialism nor economics provide a better explanation for why the calendar girls are more popular. My students might summon up the "modern" here, claiming that popular mass culture, being opposed to art that requires training—whether in "taste" or "understanding"—can more effectively invoke the changing force of the contemporary.

The range of possible responses to popular music is not defined for my students by folk culture on the one hand and commodity culture on the other, or by the individual on the one hand and the undifferentiated masses on the other. In fact, in harmony with Adorno, they tend to dismiss claims about a geographically specific relationship between an audience and the music they identify with—this seems to them obviously out of date—and they rarely make claims for wholly individual relations to the popular. Instead, between the masses and the individual they position the group, particularly via a recognizably Birmingham School model of subcultures. Like the Birmingham School studies surveyed in *Resistance Through Rituals*, my students see the subcultural use of music as "symbolic"—and usually also as transitional in ways related to "youth" experimentation with identity and community.

As Stuart Hall suggests, the Birmingham School studies generally "reflected the lingering presence of the belief that the symbolic could not be anything but a second-order, dependent category" (Hall 293). But the aspect of these studies that stresses intimacy between popular music, community, and political commitment is very familiar to my students. To clarify what is at stake in this, I often set Adorno's "On Popular Music" alongside Grossberg on "the rock formation" and its claims to authenticity, which is another model my students recognize from their own experience in popular culture but do not always support. Magazine articles, radio stations, clubs, band posters, and music television programming all insist on the continuity of both these models in my students' experience of media culture. While Adorno excluded authenticity from his account of popular music by dismissing the possibility of either modern "folk music" or popular music that was also art, authenticity has nevertheless continued to be an important critical term in popular music studies, where it has become particularly associated with "rock" and "rebellion." As Grossberg notes, insofar as the rock-authenticity formation in popular music studies "has continued to speak as the dominant (whether or not it is) through the voices of many performers, critics, and scholars, the question of authenticity has been reproduced over and over again, albeit in slightly different ways" (2002: 39). An opposition between authentic rock and commodified pop that in many ways mirrors Adorno's dismissals has preoccupied popular music scholarship for decades (28–29; see also During 127–28).

The rock formation Grossberg refers to, like Adorno's jazz, has shifted its place in the terrain of popular music. His central examples are now "classics" that belong on dedicated "classics" channels and in "classic" or "best of" compilations, although they are also sometimes revived as images of coherent-because-past authenticity in the same manner as once contentious Modernist art. Moreover, Grossberg's classification of the field of popular music, which places "rock" as (at least once) intimate with youthful rebellion and political struggle, necessarily does not engage with the array of pop-rock hybrids, with the political claims of explicitly commercial "alternative" music, or with the diverse politicized constituencies of genres like hip hop, new country, and new metal with which my students are often familiar. And yet his account of a lost authenticity in relations between youth and popular music resonates with them. Their most common objection is to his periodization—in other words, they want to dispute *when* rather whether there was such an authenticity.

Grossberg claims that "postmodern" popular music is aware of its status as performance (1992: 201–41). This draws on his earlier argument in "The Deconstruction of Youth" (1994) that, in the era of MTV, the category "youth" no longer names any foundational social experience. Rock was a critical force for Grossberg largely because "the antidomesticity of the rock and roll apparatus is an attack on the place in which its own youth is constructed" (1994: 188), and the fragmentation of both "youth" and this anti-domestic "rock" is the same process that leaves behind only that self-aware performance. This argument never fails to outrage a significant percentage of my students, who want to insist on the equivalent significance of their own experience of "youth" through and around popular music cultures that they understand to represent their "generation." But even here a continuity can be useful because they sometimes do not feel the same degree of credibility should be attached to music popular with those younger than them; or at least they are willing to speak about popular music and authenticity in generational terms.

Most years, I also assign students in courses on modernism or cultural theory the famous "culture industry" chapter of Adorno and Horkheimer's *Dialectic of Enlightenment*, which also condemns the mass production of popular music. Here, as I have mentioned before, Adorno and Horkheimer reject all popular mass culture as a tool of deception designed by "the culture industry" to keep the populace generally passive. My students are familiar, from popular and public culture around them, with stark versions of this argument and its complement, a narrative about lost innate human values that strongly resembles the lost authenticity story. They have learned from these fields as well that "culture" is a battleground for defining and defending political philosophy (see chapter 8). While the polarized demagogic platforms that claim to know the absolute truth of culture under the aegis of one or another "culture war" usually rely on repetitive cliché at best and violent exclusion of any difference at worst, it can also encompass what my students recognize as a way of engaging with Adorno and Horkheimer. In fact, a range of current public and popular debates are summarized *and* set against each other once more in their claim that "The sociological theory that the loss of the support of objectively established religion, the dissolution of the last remnants of pre-capitalism, together with technological and social differentiation or specialisation, have led to cultural chaos is disproved every day; for culture now impresses the same stamp on everything" (Adorno and Horkheimer 120).

It is perhaps ironic that Adorno's dismissal of popular music retains most currency in popular music studies. As Frith argues, "In broad terms, the analytic response to Frankfurt pessimism has been to accept the organisational account of mass cultural production, to ignore the complexities of Adorno's aesthetic theory, and to look for the redeeming features of commodity culture in the act of consumption" (Frith 1996: 13; see also McClary and Walser 284). Adorno's judgments are first of all aesthetic. For Adorno, "Music is not ideology pure and simple, it is ideological only insofar as it is false consciousness" and the "Sociology of music is social critique accomplished through the critique of art" ([1932] 1976: 63). In his *Introduction to the Sociology of Music* (1932), Adorno makes a claim he seems to avoid in the "Popular Music" essay, namely that "there is still some good bad music left today, along with all the bad good music" (32). This reference also allows us to consider whether Cultural Studies participates in what Adorno calls the "intellectualizing" of entertainment, which undermines for him both productive "mindless artistry" in entertainment and the serious "sense in works of art at the top" (Adorno and Horkheimer 143).

My students are very invested in the possibility of value in popular music, and some elements of Adorno's analysis would be less clear to them were it not for the historical gap between his "jazz" and theirs. They want to talk about what might be "the best" popular music, and Adorno offers a sufficiently distant example of what is at stake in such judgment to help them place it within ongoing critical debates. While the blurb on Frith and Goodwin's *On Record* (1990)—"Did you know that Jean-Paul Sartre once wrote an essay on the Top 40?"—enticed readers with the promise of popular music's seriousness, the blurb on Frith's *Performing Rites* (1996) entices with a game of expert adjudication that is as central to the music cultures in which my students participate as it is to Adorno and Frith. Who is "better," it asks: "Billie Holiday or P. J. Harvey? Blur or Oasis? Dylan or Keats? And how many friendships have ridden on the answer?" My students routinely use popular music to periodize, to discriminate, and to assemble, and it is easier for them to notice that Adorno's "serious music" is not outside the realm of taste. Adorno would never have denied that, despite thinking his judgment was about more than taste, nor would he deny that the "classical music" he thought of as serious was as much a product of modernity as pop music. If Arnold Schoenberg's twelve-tone system is the modernist music Adorno preferred, it is still not any more transformative for "classical music" than the possibility of attaching it to new communities for music consumption and is in fact not separable from that change.

In unpacking Adorno's assumptions about what kind of "music" is avant-garde, and relative to what, my students learn to unpack their own related assumptions. Modernist avant-garde music is itself remarkably varied. Luigi Russolo's "The Art of Noises: A Futurist Manifesto" (1913) is hardly likely to have appealed to Adorno any more than jazz or later paeans to the poetic sound effects of radio.[5] Adorno consistently condemned the effects of radio on serious music. In fact, for Adorno, all sound recording was "an extraordinary threat to the life of artworks that emanate from it" ([1934] 2002: 280)—not a dialectical relationship between art and life but a representation of the relationship between modernity and technology: "phonograph records are not artworks but black seals on the missives that are rushing towards us from all sides in the traffic with technology; missives whose formulations capture the sounds of creation, the first and last sounds, judgement upon life and message about that which may come thereafter" (280). My students generally agree that mediation makes an artwork less authentic—in fact, it is an opinion they hold to very resiliently. But when they encounter everyday music that is mixed from samples of already electronically-produced recordings via an artistry primarily attached to a production company and primarily disseminated by televised film—which the music may have been altered or tailored to suit—or through online downloads of multiple kinds—which the music, again, may have been altered or tailored to suit—or even cut and twisted into a ringtone, the mere fact of being recorded does not seem to deprive music of much original artistic effort. They generally embrace a narrative in which live performance is proof of being outside some version of the culture industry and thus of both artistic credibility and cultural relevance. Adorno can help them to focus on what mediation means and what it means to them. Even "live" performance did not invest *popular* music with authenticity for Adorno, and thus he also provides a useful counter to a simplified version of the culture industry thesis with which they are familiar.

Refrain

Adorno also offers students a challenge. Explaining to students with varying facility with critical theory what Adorno means is itself a challenge, although this is less the case with "On Popular Music," which is written for a broader audience. But a greater challenge arises from the fact that while I think Adorno is wrong about popular music, my students' first response is to disagree, only to agree with him more often than not when brought to consider the components of his argument. They do, however, want to dispute what is defined as "popular music." This returns us to Frith's point that popular music is important for its explicit construction of popularity. Adorno's texts work so well in my classroom for two related reasons: first, they invite students to compare their own taste, and its significance and context, with that of Adorno and each other; and second, they open up both critical theory and modernism to conversations they agree are both socially and personally important. The dialogues Adorno enables thus have a longevity that challenges the "progress by attrition" that strikingly characterizes both popular music and popular music studies.

Frith and Goodwin's introduction to *On Record* stresses this logic of death and rebirth wherein "generations successively attempt to establish new paradigms that either incorporate or obliterate previous methodologies" (Frith and Goodwin ix). As we saw with the fashionability of Chanel (see chapter 5), this logic is tied to the modernist emergence of "the classic" because it is the logic by which the already successful might stave off redundancy in the system. When the editors of *Rock Over the Edge* (2002) ask "If 'rock' doesn't mean what it used to mean, then what does it mean now?" (Beebe et al. 3), their answer is a variation on old themes: one authenticity myth is called up to replace another; one articulation of the individual versus the masses through expressions of taste and style is ranged against many others; one negotiation of the copy through genre, cover, citation, or sample vies with others. In *Rock Over the Edge*, the label "postmodern" is particularly important, being used to dismiss as outdated Modernist assumptions presumed to dominate popular music studies. Robert Fink distinguishes "The New Musicology" from the old musicology's Modernist certainties, claiming that new musicology emerges from the ruins of the field's canon and its "ruling ideological assumptions" (Fink 63). His understanding of this "alternative aesthetic" must, however, still be awkwardly distinguished from Modernist musical avant-gardism (110) and from "the graduate student who can tell you how the Talking Heads act out the dissolution of the subject in postmodern society," whom Fink also thinks fails to understand the real plethora of contemporary art music (73). A range of essays in this collection are troubled by the persistent problem of modernism (see, for example, the pieces by Hill and Middleton). From mourning Kurt Cobain to wondering what happened to the politics of rock, "new" popular music studies are presumed here to require a postmodern cultural apparatus. At the same time, these essays position modernism as something in relation to which arguments still need to be mounted. Tony Grajeda finds the "decidedly modernist" image of "mass culture and its Other" in Simon Reynolds' portrait of post-rock (Grajeda 240), and Roger Beebe reconstitutes, in the same volume and in a context that gives it more power, Fredric Jameson's aside that "the Beatles and the Stones" are the "high modernist moment" in response to which punk and new wave arose (Beebe 315).

Using such narratives about attrition and renovation to illustrate my point, I can suggest to my students that it would be equally possible to think of postmodernism as relating to Modernism the way "new punk" relates to punk: an analogy within which postmodernism, while not the same as Modernism, should not be thought of as opposed to or outdating Modernism. The various incarnations of "new punk" are punk attitude in new contexts or for new audiences, overwhelmed at times by the institutionalization of that attitude as something past. If Green Day is not punk in the same way as The Sex Pistols, The Sex Pistols were a different punk to The Stooges and their attitude to popular music was not remote from that of The Troggs or Black Sabbath. The point, however, is not whether my analogy is unassailably better than Jameson's but that these and many other stories about the "break" in popular music are possible, surely produced with different biographical reference points. I invite my students to produce their own. What will ground a comparison of such analogies is the recognition that context and continuity are equally important in situating these bands in relation to one another. They will never resolve into a convincing break when viewed up close or at a distance but only in the middle ground of a particular taste regime.

The way in which such a critical scenario of "progress by attrition" is represented in both popular music and popular music studies also brings us back to exchanges between expertise and taste—two terms that reinforce one another. In "On the Fetish-Character in Music and the Regression of Listening"([1938] 2002: 288ff), Adorno famously claims that taste refers only to personal preference while aesthetic judgments are truth statements. In the practice of cultural analysis this is a rhetorical difference—judgment is distinguished from taste by mode of address. If Thorstein Veblen, George Simmel, and Adorno are all key precursors for Bourdieu's now famous ideas about taste and distinction, then so is Arnold, and this sequence of ideas needs to be seen as an unfolding strand of modernist debate rather than a new sociological intervention at one single point. In a piece on "Chambermaids' romances," for example, Benjamin asks, "when are works of literature categorized according to the class that consumes them?" He answers himself immediately: "Unfortunately, they are not—or all too seldom. Yet how much more illuminating this would be than hackneyed aesthetic appreciations!" ([1929] 1996b: 225). Despite Lionel Trilling's concern that talking in terms of taste reduces everything to personal preference on the order of one's preference for or against pleats, only some forms of taste will be deemed expert. Not everyone's call for attention to chambermaid's romances seems worth publishing—let alone sixty years after the fact—and not everyone's prefer-

ence for or against jazz will seem telling. When Fiske intimates the importance of taste to understanding popular culture, his comparison of a gallery
opening with a Grateful Dead concert (1990: 44) carefully stresses Cultural
Studies' capacity to not only see but expertly evaluate the "culture" at work
in both settings.

In the midst of such extensive recycling of oppositions and debates,
Adorno might also remind us that not all repetition is merely repetitious.
Even Deleuze and Guattari's famous post-structuralist argument against
the regulated repetition they see as "territorialization"—in every sphere
from the armed state to therapeutic discourses on the self—nevertheless
acknowledges that repetition can be both productive and challenging. In
a much-cited chapter on "the refrain" in *A Thousand Plateaus*, they argue
that the musical refrain is neither static nor inflexible. It is a repetition that
extends and changes one's place in and relation to the world and that links
people and places. Their argument is not confined to avant-garde composition, despite their preference for avant-garde examples, from John Cage
(294) to La Monte Young (380). The refrain is an experience of recognition,
a moment of familiarity, of coming home. Popular music's firm foundation
in the refrain is the means by which it routinely calls up cultural context
and at the same time invites immersion in the music, wherever one hears
it: "The motif of the refrain may be anxiety, fear, joy, love, work, walking,
territory . . . but the refrain itself is the content of music" (331).

Many scholars commenting on Deleuze and Guattari's use of music
stress, as Andrew Murphie puts it, the "deterritorialising potential in music" (1323). But, as Meaghan Morris suggests in her essay "Crazy Talk is Not
Enough," simple oppositions between home-making (territories) and travel
(deterritorialization) are singularly unhelpful for understanding their work.
This essay uses the film *Muriel's Wedding* (1994) as its central example but
the argument is also propelled by references to popular music. Morris takes
her epigraph from the opening of Deleuze and Guattari's chapter on the
refrain, in which a child comforts itself by singing in the dark (Morris 2006:
187; Deleuze and Guattari 343). But music is more broadly important in this
essay, which defends Deleuze and Guattari's work against narrow readings
as either the cynical (Nietzschean) critique of a Nick Cave "murder ballad"
or the "wide-eyed fey" (Spinozist) affirmation of a Hollywood "Old Man
River" (Morris 2006, 188). Such musical reference-points reverse the usual
alignment between, on the one hand, criticism and Modernism (citing the
famous 1938 film performance of "Old Man River" by "negro" activist Paul
Robeson) and, on the other, affirmation and postmodernism (Cave's *Murder*

Ballads album of 1996 mixes genres, periods, and texts in every track). But what matters in elaborating these connections is that both these misreadings are equally intent on creative destruction (see Morris 2006, 188)—they are, in other words, equally of modernist studies and of Cultural Studies.

In fact, "Deleuze plainly says, 'we can't assume that lines of flight are necessarily creative, that smooth spaces are always better than segmented or striated ones'" (Deleuze quoted in Morris 2006: 198). Murphie also points to the way territorialization is tied to deterritorialization (as smooth is to striated) in Deleuze and Guattari's thought. Taking up the claim in *A Thousand Plateaus* that "it is necessary to consider the effects of deterritorialization on a given species at a given moment," Murphie elaborates with the example of "the rave, both as song (both analogically and digitally sampled and dispersed) and as bower bird (always taking place somewhere else which is stratified socially as something else)—assisted by the mobile telecommunications network and provoking the attempts of the State to stratify or capture it" (Murphie 1323). The difficulty of reading the opposition between territorialization and deterritorialization as neither fixed nor moral, and opening popular music up in this way to more mobile accounts of value or popularity, is exacerbated by the common conflation of postmodernism and post-structuralism in which they are set together against Modernism.

Reading literature on postmodernism and popular culture, one might think it surprising that Adorno's arguments, as they apply to popular music, are so much more familiar to my students than those suggested by Deleuze and Guattari. But as Morris argues in her better-known essay "Banality in Cultural Studies," Cultural Studies' reflection on popular culture continues to see its own analysis as an expert action imposed on an inexpert populace and its tastes (see Morris 1990; chapter 4). Cultural Studies has not only taken up modernist assemblage and bricolage in its interdisciplinarity and eclectic array of objects, but has been equally shaped by the modernist emphasis on expert evaluative critique. In the "Banality" essay, Morris again draws many of her examples from popular music, contrasting the Fiske-style analysis of pop fans to the self-conscious critical attitude embedded in available audience positions for the rock band Midnight Oil. For Cultural Studies in general, she suggests, the kind of judgment that defines one as a critic is presumed to be unavailable to the popular and even to the public. Cultural Studies' attachment to a definition of culture that includes the ordinary and the popular necessarily means that its validating expertise will be grounded in being able to create from those objects something that can be spoken about authoritatively a coherent field. The question remains how.

My students, in their process of learning through Cultural Studies to re-fine the mode of their expert interpretation of "culture," are very aware of the distinction this involves between taste and expertise. But if it is true that popular culture "has been used as an instrument by the educated and middle classes to maintain their ideological authority by defining 'good' and 'bad' culture" (Jenkins, McPherson, and Shattuc 27), then this particular instrument is just as important for the consumption of popular culture on its own terms. That is, debating what is expertise and what is taste, and what is mediation and what is art, are not just refrains that cohere modernist cultural analysis but refrains that also cohere the popular culture it analyses. It is crucial to the modernism of Cultural Studies that it must be in dialogue with the kind of critical reflection that constitutes the subject of modernity. My students, mounting arguments for and against each other's popular musical commitments, can use Adorno to reflect on the way in which specific cultural fields make sets of values visible, or even possible, without imagining that this makes such value irrelevant. And in the refrains that cross the gap between their classroom and their tastes and Adorno's, they can also see the shape of a modernism that still concerns them.

Conclusion

Modernist Cultural Studies

People tax me very readily with being a revolutionary, but the equilibrium they try so hard to maintain is for vital reasons purely ephemeral: it is a balance which has to be perpetually re-established.

Le Corbusier, *The City of Tomorrow*

As my epigraph from Corbusier suggests, the vital terms of modernist cultural analysis and debate remain so because they constantly need to be re-established. This is the founding necessity of the modernist procession of claims to break with the past. Ezra Pound's exhortation to Modernists to "make it new" is heeded as carefully by the modernist cultural critic, including practitioners of Cultural Studies, as it ever was by aspiring modernist poets.[1] But Cultural Studies as it is defined and practiced at the beginning of the twenty-first century (at its best) takes "the new" as a task rather than a marvel, exploring the contemporaneity of culture as it is challenged and propelled by history and paying attention to the current, the ephemeral, and the marginal but always in relation to the equally modernist concept of a common culture. In combining this attention to how we live today with the modernist imperatives to, on the one hand, evaluate culture and, on the other, exhaustively document it, Cultural Studies is a perspective singularly attentive to the modernism that continues to define us.

Let me return to what has so often been used as the exemplar, if not the definition, of Modernism—namely, avant-garde art—and to the trouble with distinguishing between modernism and postmodernism. If *Modernist* art was, as writers as different as Jürgen Habermas and Nancy Troy suggest, quickly transformed into an institutionalized (and profitable) spectacle, *modernist* art has continued to struggle against what art means. Once officially deployed (if not captured) by what we could call the Guggenheim mode of Modernism, some other frame of reference for the modernist challenge to art seemed necessary. But to properly grasp this history we must recognize that modernism extends beyond an archive of aesthetic forms that can be closed precisely because it can be dated. Postmodernism emerged as a name for the continual struggle to challenge aesthetics when such a challenge was represented as something already dealt with. "Postmodernism," too, was quickly taken up outside aesthetics per se in other fields also seeking to maintain a critical attitude that institutionalized Modernism had confined to history. Cultural Studies undoubtedly shares some of this historical space and is "postmodern" in this sense.

The image of "the refrain" with which I concluded the last chapter can also return us to such periodizing narratives about modernism. The "break" itself is a powerful modernist refrain, and evidence for and against an array of breaks has appeared throughout this book. To avoid thinking in terms of which break is the correct break, I set out to think about modernism not primarily as a collection of dates and texts but as what Michel Foucault might call an "episteme." Foucault's histories search for the "network of analogies" between discourses, practices, institutions, and fields that give a certain character to an age. Despite the difficulties inherent in thinking about the operations of knowledge at such a scale, Foucault wants to ask if knowledge can "at a given time and in a given culture . . . possess a well-defined regularity" ([1966] 1973: x). I have tried to show that this question is itself a product of modernism, partly because of the idea of "given culture" on which it depends. It is of signal importance, then, that Foucault explores how to ask and answer this question in texts, from *The Order of Things* (1966) to *Discipline and Punish* (1973), which search for the "network of analogies" that brings modernity into view. David Harvey's *The Condition of Postmodernity: An Enquiry Into the Origins of Cultural Change* (1989) sets out, drawing on Foucault, to account for postmodernity in similar terms, and it is significant that his "postmodernity" finally sounds very modernist. We certainly find many Modernists embracing "fragmentation and ephemerality" (Harvey 44) and many more expressing "incredulity towards meta-narratives" (Lyotard xxiv, quoted in Harvey 45). Harvey's own summary implies something similar, positioning Foucault as an extension of Max Weber and Jean-François Lyotard as an extension of the language games of Modernism (Harvey 45–46).

Harvey's text refers to a narrative about postmodernism very much in vogue when it was written in 1989. Hal Foster published one of the influential collections defining postmodernism in 1983, with the decidedly modernist title *The Anti-Aesthetic*. It was then republished once under its subtitle, *Postmodern Culture* (1985), only to be republished in 2002 under the original title when postmodernism was no longer the height of fashion. In his introduction, Foster notes that while some writers in the collection "define postmodernism as a break with the aesthetic field of modernism" and others do not, all except Habermas "hold this belief in common: that the project of modernity is now deeply problematic" (Foster [1983] 1985: vii). This is so, for Foster, first of all because Modernism has now become "the official culture" (vii). Harvey concurs, locating the countercultural movements of the 1960s as part of the institutionalization of Modernism: "for the first time in the history of modernism, artistic and cultural, as well as 'progressive' political revolt had to be directed at a powerful version of modernism itself" (Harvey 37). In these arguments, postmodernism appears "Somewhere between 1968 and 1972," although it is still an "incoherent movement" at the time (38).

This is, of course, also the period in which those texts of Foucault's to which I referred above appeared, and this is another periodization of the "end" of modernism about which I wish to be cautious. Around the same time as Lionel Trilling was challenging the contemporary meaning of "culture" (see chapter 8), Adorno was looking back on the changes of twentieth-century modernism. His essay "Trying to Understand *Endgame*" ([1961] 2005b) has been used by Lawrence Cahoone and others to gesture to a shift from modernism to postmodernism. Here, Adorno focuses on a set of distinctions between Samuel Beckett and modernism as exemplified by Edmund Husserl, Marcel Proust, Charles Baudelaire, James Joyce, T. S. Eliot, and Thomas Mann, but also reaching back to William Shakespeare. With such a long view, the modernism that Beckett is "after" extends to modernity itself. The essay eventually turns to seeing in *Endgame* the confirmation or affirmation of modernist reflection on modernity—of Walter Benjamin, of Expressionism, and, for example, of Bertolt Brecht. The reasons for singling out Beckett as a break at all, then, are most effectively summarized in the changed face of institutionalized art in the 1960s, in a world where *historical* reference points like surrealism were staples of a cultured worldview. The entwined political action and cultural fragmentation of "the sixties" was certainly spectacular, but with the exception of its new forms of media memorialization it otherwise seems to resonate with, rather than against, the complex of utopian discourse and barricade struggle in the nineteenth century discussed by Benjamin ([1927–40] 2002), the ennui of Baudelaire, the refusal of Friedrich Nietzsche, or the disillusionment of Clement Greenberg.

Cahoone opens the second part of the anthology *From Modernism to Postmodernism* (2003) in which he includes this essay with the following gloss on the way "Modernity Realized" means the emergence of modernism: "The century from 1860 to 1950 brought the triumph of modernity, and simultaneously its greatest crises, both intellectual and social" (85). It is, Cahoone implies, the becoming ordinary of the great changes the first part of the anthology had defined as "modernity" that constitutes modernism as the simultaneous realization and critique of modernity. But Cahoone's focus is on a particular expert narrative about modernity in crisis, a narrative in which "radicalism became the *norm*" of philosophy (85). Opening the third part of this anthology, "Postmodernism and the Re-evaluation of Modernity," Cahoone notes that, unlike modernism, postmodernism "was not the child of crisis" (221), and attributes it instead to a sense of "prosperous disorder" (221) that encouraged disillusioned embrace of whatever contests universality. Cahoone's account of this shift implies a pervasive change at the level of both everyday life and expertise, and these are valuable touchstones in the light of my own argument thus far. But comparing Cahoone's introductions to modernity, modernism, and postmodernism again reveals more continuity than difference and thereby situates the claim that "On or about 1968 the world changed" as no more certain than Woolf's claim about 1910 that I discussed in the introduction.

Does it matter whether there is or is not a postmodern break with modernism? Given that, as subjects of modernity, we are specially attentive at all times to the difference of ourselves and of today, can it matter if there is more in common between Matthew Arnold, Theodor Adorno, and Bill Readings than some histories mention or some taxonomies allow? To put this rather differently, if the condition of modernity is a historicizing one and if we necessarily take up our place amid an array of ways to historicize ourselves (see chapter 6), does it matter which we choose?

I think it remains counterproductive to ignore the continuity of modernism, a continuity that questions whether postmodernism does more than ask why Modernism can no longer be produced. Perhaps it would be helpful to install postmodernism as a canonical shorthand parallel to Modernism: as a capitalized Postmodernism that can no longer be ignored because it is the subject of so many readers and exhibitions and is recognizable, however messy its forms, in public as well as popular culture.[2] But if this conceded Postmodernism works in some similar ways to Modernism—as an institutionalized field centered on a more or less discrete archive—it is not, in fact, a parallel concept. Or, rather, it is not a parallel concept yet and it is by no means clear that it will become one. The postmodernism posed as breaking with Modernism can't quite work as a Postmodernism because of its contemporary force—because it is still treated as the name for present tense activities, including the relegation of Modernism to the past and the unification of disparate arguments through their opposition to Modernism.

As Judith Butler points out, if postmodernism does unify the many disparate claims across methodological and political gulfs that it is often assumed to embrace—aligning, for example, Foucault and Jacques Derrida despite the crucial differences between them—then "it is a decidedly 'modern' sign, which is why there is some question whether one can debate for or against this postmodernism" (Butler 1995: 38). If writers like Fredric Jameson, including in Foster's collection, have continually stressed that postmodernism was never anti-modernism or un-modernist, such a term still needs to be held accountable for the ends it now serves. In 1996, Foster returned to the periodization of postmodernism with an equally telling title, *The Return of the Real*. There he reflects on *The Anti-Aesthetic* like this: "even within the left, especially within the left, postmodernism was a disputed notion. Yet not long ago there was a sense of a loose alliance, even a common project, particularly in opposition to rightist positions, which ranged from old attacks on modernism in toto as the source of all evil in our hedonistic society to new defenses of particular modernisms that had become official, indeed traditional, the modernisms of the museum and the academy" (Foster 1996: 205). This postmodernism is a way of talking about the installment of Modernism as a particular object to be attacked or defended: Culture in the Arnoldian sense; or "public art," that troublesome expert form of degraded culture for Adorno (see Adorno and Horkheimer 160). Postmodernism certainly provided a way to speak about changes to the place from which experts spoke of culture, but it neither invented nor radically disrupted that place.

I have tried to stress that such continuity does not equal homogeneity. As Nietzsche, Marx, and Freud each bring forth particular modernist threads in specific contexts, so too do Foucault, Deleuze, and Habermas. I have foregrounded two particular strands of modernism in this regard—hermeneutics and assemblage—not because they dichotomously encompass modernism in its entirety but in order to show the ongoing importance of contesting what modernism means. This modernism cannot be synthesized into one project any more than "modernity" can be—not by any time, place, discipline, or field. This modernism, as Habermas argues, is incomplete, but it is not and never was the single project he mourns, which is why he struggles to see it in surrealism, let alone in Foucault.

While the modernist critical attitude is not a single position or arena of debate, contra Habermas, it is, or it can be, a "critical ontology of ourselves." This is both a negative moment of "historical investigation into the events that have led us to constitute ourselves and to recognise ourselves as subjects of what we are doing, thinking, saying" (Foucault [1978] 1984b: 46) and a positive movement of separating, "from the contingency that has made us what we are, the possibility of no longer being, doing, or thinking what we are, do, or think" (46). Kant's version of modernity is not the same as Foucault's, a fact made most obvious in Kant's invocation of God as the guarantor of correct reasoning. But the connection Foucault sees between Kant, Baudelaire, and himself is the emergence of modernism as both representation and experience of modernity. This critical attitude is not just characteristic of intellectuals, but rather is part of the demand modernity makes of everyone, compelling us "to face the task of producing" ourselves (42). The best questions for such a task will vary—they are, in that much maligned modernist parlance, relative. The modernist critical attitude is continually producing new areas of inquiry, such as "sexuality" in the nineteenth century, "subculture" in the mid-twentieth century, and "adolescence" in the decades therebetween.

Throughout this book I have repeatedly used the words "continuous" and "continuity," but it would in some respects be more helpful to think not of a continuous modernism but of a modernist refrain with many variations. While I have tried to avoid the refrain that tends to overshadow all others in discussions of Modernism—that is, the break—I have done so to better focus on others. The tensions between the popular and "Culture," between commodification and art, between the individual and the masses, the original and the copy, the banal and the spectacular, resistance and conformity, and subjective freedom and dependency are all modernist refrains. Such modernist refrains are not all binary propositions, however, and we can also find in Cultural Studies continual interrogation of the temporality of the present; of change and continuity at the level of popular culture or personal style; of the negotiations of cultural location, belonging, and community; of the fraught distinctions between expertise and taste; and of the relations between cultural economy, state institutions, and everyday life.

Modernism underpins Cultural Studies' resistance to a unifying disciplinary methodology and its attachment to both assemblage, or bricolage, and hermeneutics. As I explored in chapter 4, Cultural Studies foregrounds, as one of its central fields of inquiry, modernist critical reflection on the everyday. It insists, as I discussed in chapter 8, on relativity, context, and contingency in a demand that theory accommodate itself to the specificities of the objects being analyzed rather than the other way around. Even the elitist reassurance of much Cultural Studies analysis, deploying critical theory as a justification for attention to the popular or in order to mark itself off from everyday critical reflections that are less expert, is part of its modernism (see chapter 9). And its internal struggles over how specificity should be recognized in cultural analysis are always returning to the modernist debates that produced fraught disjunctions in what we now understand as the "human sciences." These refrains—together and separately—are considered by some to be Cultural Studies' great virtues and by others its great failings.

Cultural Studies' expansive attention to culture as well as its failure to resolve itself into properly territorial claims and agendas does single it out, not only as a critical target but also as a voracious consumer of other histories of innovation. But in such appropriations part of what Cultural Studies offers is the continuance of debates that have been closed off elsewhere. Such emphasis on continuity is in fact also, somewhat paradoxically, a characteristic of modernist studies, which has never been able to make strong disciplinary claims for itself. The range of disciplines and other interests seeking to have a stake in Modernism/modernity and the very fragmentation of modernism that has made it a key term in every field of contemporary academic work make such claims impossible. Both Cultural Studies and modernist studies, then, are vulnerable to claims that they do not adequately represent their object, but this vulnerability can also be a strength—an openness to diverse perspectives and tactics. It might even be easier for modernist studies to maintain such openness given that it is not constrained by disciplinary agendas, except that it is continually at risk of becoming Modernist studies instead and thus foreclosing on its own continuing relevance.

Taking Heidegger's critique of the closure of the experimental field seriously, disciplinarity transformed into both goal and justification undoubtedly limits any field's capacity to attend to the world. We can no more unmake the disciplinarity of Cultural Studies at this point than we can forget about postmodernism or jettison the canonical definition of Modernism. But it seems that the more certain Cultural Studies is about its disciplinary regime—at the points where it claims to be, for example, a unified field of "popular culture studies" or "High Theory" or "anti-capitalist critique"—the further it drifts from the tense contradictions needed to perpetually reestablish modernism's energy. At present, Cultural Studies' disciplinarity is incomplete and does not seem likely to be completed any time soon. As Stuart Hall puts it: "Cultural studies is not one thing, it has never been one thing" (277). In its multiplicity, and indeed in its role as the front of various "culture wars," Cultural Studies is a continuation of the broad field of debates that preoccupy modernism and, as such, Cultural Studies too must perpetually reestablish itself. Even if this can produce some rather tiresome refrains from the perspective of regular conference-goers—what has happened to Cultural Studies?, the death of Cultural Studies, what should Cultural Studies do now?—this continual reflection on the field is also at the same time its value for modernist studies today.

The institutionalization of Modernism as a clearly bounded conceptual field, and thus as a canon of great works, has limited modernist studies in two interrelated ways, both of which I think Cultural Studies needs to learn from. The first is its relegation to the past, its capture as Modernism, which forecloses on the importance of historical narratives about the ideas modernity has installed as certainties. While Cultural Studies must attend to the present it seems always more in danger of forgetting the past—including its modernism. Forgetting modernism may be, as Nietzsche suggests (see chapter 6), necessary to the continuity of our modernist experience, so that, for example, we forgetfully rediscover and thus learn afresh from the parameters of a new media experience or the tangle of identification with commodities. But at the level of scholarship some powerful connections and contexts are certainly lost. The second limitation that Modernism has imposed on modernist studies is that, in order to claim its canonized territory and thus be relegated to the past, Modernism had to nominate something complete and thus had to either exclude or extract from their common modernism works like *Battleship Potemkin* or artists like Chanel.

While Modernist scholarship undoubtedly gained a great deal of institutional credibility by the rapid invention of a coherent past object on which it is grounded, it has subsequently learned the usefulness of reconsidering the contents of Modernism, not just to keep making it "new" but sometimes also to respond to the way in which its object stubbornly refuses to die. But this false completion will never be redressed by adding works to the canon, or even by attending more closely to the context of such artifacts. What Cultural Studies has to learn from the dangers of canonical closure is partly obvious. Every discipline knows the difficulty of balancing advantages like departmental support and funding categories against the inertia of its own version of the "seventieth study of Keats and his use of Miltonic inversion which old Professor Z and his like are now inditing" (Woolf [1928] 1973: 90). But in continuing the irresolvable modernist refrains I am identifying here—there will always be some variation on the tension between aesthetics and commodification worth fresh attention—Cultural Studies is at particular risk of being stuck in reiteration. Popular culture is riddled with power. Capital pervades all aspects of everyday life.

It is not enough to see these refrains as "residual," taking up Raymond Williams' use of the term to denote that which is "formed in the past but [is] . . . still active in the cultural process, not only and often not at all as an element of the past, but as an effective element in the present" (1977: 122). Williams' distinction between the dominant, the residual, and the emergent was always somewhat problematic because even the most revolutionary formation is residual in just this sense and is named as emergent by being opposed to something it defines as dominant and thus on the verge of being passé. Postmodernism defines Modernism as residual, as something past on the one hand and as an official culture made terminally redundant by its success on the other. Setting this narrative aside seems useful because Cultural Studies has much to gain from acknowledging and engaging with its Modernist precursors and its place within what Williams understood as the critical force of modernism. I want more attention to be paid to the history of Cultural Studies in practice. But I also want the same thing for modernist studies, especially given the continued dominance of a now unhelpful strategic misprision by which modernism is aestheticized, relegated to the past, and thus closed off from considerations of ourselves today. Indeed, the fact that I have been able to use so many contemporary works of modernist studies to support my argument here demonstrates that this case is a compelling one. It is at the level of naming the field, and in its interaction with other fields, that modernist studies seems to exclude us.

Finally, if I want to have said one thing clearly in this book it is that the breadth of the objects and practices gathered into Cultural Studies does not merely resemble or continue the breadth of reference that established "culture" as a key concern of modernists and modernity—it is exactly the same thing. This is not to say that the present is merely an echo of the past. It is, rather, to pay attention to the set of changes that gave rise, in the wake of the canonization of Modernism, to both Cultural Studies and postmodernism as names for the continued energy of modernism. If there was no clear disciplinary context for Cultural Studies until the 1960s it is because only then, when Modernism seemed entirely relegated to the past even as the modernist model of culture continued to proliferate through established and emerging forms of cultural expertise, was a space created for a discipline that explicitly continued these critical refrains. Modernism became a thing of the past, but modernist reflection on a wide array of fields continued to seem imperative, and Cultural Studies appeared to fill a particular academic niche for modernism rather than Modernism. Perhaps at the forefront of Cultural Studies is the endless "what about now?" that drives the modernist refrain of the break. Neglecting the wider continuities that give this question shape and texture, however, has the effect of disconnecting Cultural Studies' interventions from its intellectual history and consigning the urgency of modernism's critical attitude to a past we can no longer access.

Notes

Introduction: The Critical Attitude

1. Johan Fornäs, for example, argues that the term "late modernity" provides a way out of both an "undifferentiated perspective on the whole modern epoch" and the "contradictions of postmodernity (which is neither opposite nor subsequent to modernity)" (36).

2. Berman also calls modernity "a mode of vital experience—experience of space and time, of the self and others, of life's possibilities and perils—that is shared by men and women all over the world. . . . People who find themselves in the midst of this maelstrom are apt to feel they are the first ones, and maybe the only ones, to be going through it. . . . however, great and ever-increasing numbers of people have been going through it for close to five hundred years" (53).

3. These "schools" are themselves not very coherent. The "Chicago School" refers to new work in urban sociology that specialized in adapting ethnographic method to urban contexts at the University of Chicago from the 1920s on. I will use "the Frankfurt School" more extensively, although usually with reference to individual authors rather than to a group. This term is commonly used to refer not only to members of the Institute for Social Research at the University of Frankfurt (1923–35), and then during their exile in the United States, but also to figures surrounding them at this time, such as Benjamin and Kracauer. I will similarly use "the Birmingham School" to name a movement in cultural analysis in the United Kingdom in the 1960s and 70s (during the earliest years of Cultural Studies' institutionalization) rather than restricting it to the CCCS at the University of Birmingham.

Chapter 1. Moving Pictures: Cinema as Modernism

1. Elza Adamowicz records the securely "visual art" frame in which this film was released and distributed: "*Un Chien Andalou* was previewed on 6 June 1929 at the Studio des Ursulines, and opened to the public on 1 October at Studio 28, where it ran for 8

months. Photogrammes of the film were reproduced in *Variétés* (July 1929), 209; *Cahiers d'art* (July 1929), 230; and *Bifur* (August 1929), 105."

2. See Hansen's work on American cinema, Weimar criticism, and Chinese silent film (Hansen 1987; 1991a; 2002); Gunning on cinema history (1994); and Thomas Levin's translations of Kracauer (1995). The mutual reconsideration of modernism and film studies can also be archival, as with Donald, Friedberg, and Marcus' collection *Close Up* (1998), or conceptual, as with Christine Gledhill's edited collection *Stardom* (1991).

3. As Barry Cullen summarizes the intersection between Eliot and the New Critics here, "Because the new philosophical realism had undermined the Victorian metaphysics of the subject, [I.A.] Richards and Eliot, in their varied responses, tried to re-locate poetics within a 'subject-free' zone, one that did not require validation through an appeal to expressive values. This resulted in a new emphasis upon 'impersonality'" (Cullen 155).

4. Vertov stressed that the "psychological" in film "prevents man from being as precise as a stop-watch and hampers his desire for kinship with the machine" (in Taylor and Christie 69). His "kinopravda" thus "made heroic efforts to shield the proletariat from the corrupting influence of fiction film dramas" (Vertov in Taylor and Christie 112).

5. Welles figures in Adorno and Horkheimer as an example of auteurism (although they don't use this term) construed as a commodified niche market. Welles' difficulties with the nexus of government and the studio system would make no difference to this. Adorno and Horkheimer's comments on the Hayes Code suggest that exceeding monitored studio norms did not mean evading the demands of the culture industry: "even the aesthetic activities of political opposites are one in their enthusiastic obedience to the rhythm of the iron system" (120).

6. For Deleuze and Guattari, the face constitutes both a cinematic style and certain cinematic reading practices. This face bounds and names the subject, framing identity through "the relation of the face to the abstract machine that produces it, and the relation of the face to the assemblages of power that require that social production. The face is a politics" (Deleuze and Guattari 181).

7. The French critics Christian Metz and Jean-Louis Baudry mark a turn in the 1970s toward specialized psychoanalytic analysis of film based on a parallel between film and the unconscious. In Baudry, this is integrated with a Marxist approach: "filmic productivity as 'a system of writing constituted by a material base and a countersystem (ideology, idealism) which uses this system while also concealing it'" (Stewart 84, quoting Baudry).

8. This essay is particularly interesting when juxtaposed with the discussions of "the collector" by both Nietzsche ([1876] 1997) and Benjamin ([1927–40] 2002), the latter of which also aligns "the interior" with detective fiction. Extending modernism as I argue we should, Benjamin's thoughts about the ambivalent relation between art and the space of collection are further unfolded, if in very different directions, by Bourdieu's discussion of the field in which art is produced as a "charismatic economy" (Bourdieu 1993: 40). It is also enriched by comparison to Benjamin's discussion of the bohème in particular and its allusion to Nietzsche's diatribe against art in the marketplace and Barthes' analysis of what Benjamin calls "the transfiguration of things . . . by taking possession of them" (Benjamin [1927–40] 2002: 9).

Chapter 2. Portrait of the Young Man as an Artist: Modernism
and Adolescence

1. As Rutter puts this, "the term adolescence was rarely used prior to the eighteenth century and although the characteristics of puberty were well recognized, little psychological significance was attached to them. The reaching of adulthood was determined by the acquisition of independence, a point having no direct connection with physiological maturity" (5).

2. The modernist "split subject" is an internalization of modernity's "subject/object split" (see Jameson 2002: 45 and chapter 7) and is now defined principally by Freud's model, although it was already (differently) integral to Hegel (see Hegel 313–21). At the forefront of Freud's model is the ego, which is the aspect of the self experienced as a coherent "I." But the ego represents mediation between the id and the superego (see Freud [1923] 1989a) and, at the same time, represents the self to the self, always in relation to an ego-ideal (see Freud [1914] 1953d).

3. This has been used to characterize *Finnegans Wake* as one of Deleuze and Guattari's schizo-texts. In this context, it is worth recalling Deleuze and Guattari's quite different placement of Joyce's *Ulysses* as a "fascicular" text that shatters "the linear unity of the word, even of language, only to posit a cyclic unity of the sentence, text or knowledge. . . . A strange mystification: a book all the more total for being fragmented" (Deleuze and Guattari 6).

4. Arnold's vision of "culture" grounds a call for education that might inspire and guide boys toward "sweetness and light"—a progress that is never finished because it comprises what a man is (Arnold [1869] 2006: 49; see chapter 8). Carroll's Alice stories dramatize the disciplines of proper development and recognize that "growing up" is defined (often arbitrarily) by the judgments and perceptions of others. And Mayhew's famous journalistic and sociological studies, in turn, elaborated ways of aiding the poor "by developing their powers of self-reliance, and certainly not by treating them like children" (Mayhew xviii).

5. The manifesto style has a long history, reaching back past Marx and Engels (1848), through Stephané Mallarmé's "Variations on a Subject: Crisis in Poetry" (1886–96)—"The pure work implies the disappearance of the poet as speaker, yielding his initiative to words, which are mobilized by the shock of their difference" ([1886] 1982: 75)—perhaps even to Blake, where prophecy and interdiction sometimes blend in a proto-manifesto style.

6. "The rise of women in English novel writing has spared no man: even those who pass for the most virile, the most phallocratic, such as Lawrence and Henry Miller, in their turn continually tap into and emit particles that enter the proximity or zone of indiscernibility of women. In writing, they become-women." (Deleuze and Guattari 276) Deleuze and Guattari leave an opening for this revision in the interchangeability of becoming-woman with other becomings (such as becoming-animal or imperceptible). Becoming-adolescent may in fact better capture the "intermezzo" Deleuze and Guattari extol in certain modernist writing, such as Woolf's (see chapter 6).

7. This is another as yet open debate. In 1983, Derek Freeman published a critique of

Mead's presumptions concerning both adolescence and "stress" in Samoan culture and, in 1994, James Côté published a further contribution, recontextualizing Mead's aims and conclusions in light of a nature-nurture debate he recognizes is still urgent sixty years later. (See Driscoll 2002a: 162–65.)

8. In the first issue of *Xin Qingnian* (1915–1926), Chen Duxiu wrote, "Youth is like early spring, like the rising sun, like trees and grass in bud, like a newly sharpened blade. It is the most valuable period of life. The function of youth in society is the same as that of a fresh and vital cell in a human body. In the processes of metabolism, the old and the rotten are incessantly eliminated to be replaced by the fresh and the living" (quoted in Chow 46; see also chapter 8).

9. Issy's romantic effusiveness is exemplary: "You know I'm tender by my eye. Can't you read by dazzling ones through me true? Bite my laughters, drink my tears. Pore into me, volumes, spell me stark and spill me swooning. I just don't care what my thwarters think. Transname me loveliness, now and here me for all times!" (Joyce [1939] 1989: 145).

Chapter 3. Modern Love: Sex Education, Popular Culture, and the Public Sphere

1. The "idyllic familial love Elizabeth represents" (Secomb 24) becomes a marginal motif in the early films Secomb refers to. In late twentieth-century adaptations, this idyllic family love is more likely to appear as a fantasy motif (for example, Scott's 1982 *Blade Runner*), be omitted entirely (for example, Warhol's 1973 *Flesh for Frankenstein*), or be present only in its absence or inversion (as in Tim Burton's 1990 *Edward Scissorhands*).

2. Rose coins the term "ethico-politics" to understand the contemporaneous relation between discipline and bio-power: "If discipline *individualizes and normalizes*, and bio-power *collectivizes and socializes*, ethico-politics concerns itself with the *self-techniques necessary for responsible self-government* and the *relations between one's obligations to oneself and one's obligations to others*" (Rose 1999: 188).

3. This is depicted in Fitzgerald's novel as "a new generation, shouting the old cries, learning the old creeds, through a revery [sic] of long days and nights; destined finally to go out into that dirty gray turmoil to follow love and pride; a new generation dedicated more than the last to the fear of poverty and the worship of success; grown up to find all Gods dead, all wars fought, all faiths in man shaken" (Fitzgerald 282).

4. Modern philosophies of love are also a story about constructing self. Beauvoir understands "the double aspect of the body as both the means by which we live in the world and also at the same time a limitation on our possible experience" (Secomb 44), but this is, via Freud, a sexualized embodied self. Beauvoir's love relation, in her picture of the modern woman's situation, is dominated by categorizations of sexual relations and experience (see Beauvoir [1949] 1988).

5. This claim is verified in this story by such an "absence of figure" enabling a male thief to pass as a girl and rob the Duchess. Sayers' own narration of the jazz age, aiming for a broad audience, provides a revealing insight into the generic rules of romance at the time, given the necessity of incorporating romance elements into her detective stories with as few but as recognizable cues as possible.

Chapter 4. The Life of a Shopgirl: Art and the Everyday

1. Vertov also understood his films as critiques of both commodification and the consciousness proper to it. Annette Michelson reports that, during a "polemical statement . . . made during a [1929] colloquium on Art and Everyday Life" in Moscow, Vertov declared, "we need conscious men, not an unconscious man submissive to any passing suggestion. Long live the class consciousness of healthy men with eyes and ears to see and hear with. Away with the perfumed veil of kisses, murder, doves and prestidigitation. Long live the class vision. Long live the cinema eye" (quoted in Michelson 66).

2. The form and method of the "convolutes" has often been discussed, but in the context of this argument they most resemble Deleuzo-Guattarian assemblage, or bricolage as it is manifest in texts like Barthes' *Mythologies* and at least rhetorically embraced by contemporary Cultural Studies. Each convolute is a framed mosaic, sometimes having an argumentative introduction but always composed of recurring themes, motifs, or colors. In the case of the convolute labeled, by editors, "The Flâneur," these colors include: American Indians, Balzac, Baudelaire, buses, cities, commodities, the crowd, detectives, Dickens, dreams, the flâneur, journalism, London, motion, observation, Paris, Poe, Proust, streets, traffic, travel, walking, and windows.

3. It is worth comparing this to the riveting moment in the trial of *Ulysses* when Judge Woolsey declares himself convinced of the book's significance because it realistically represents the double stream of consciousness that both he and the defense lawyer agree characterizes even their courtroom experience on that day (see "U.S. v. Ulysses").

4. Across Michael Grant's survey of Eliot criticism, the typist is depicted as low, dismal, tired, and sodden: "a poor little typist" subject to a tawdry, mechanical seduction. The clerk himself seems to stand for something more substantial—"the secularization of the humane and qualitative values in the modern world" (Middleton Murry in Grant 276). But the typist is herself a type, one of the "essential" human things Eliot "isolates . . . from all its infinite varieties of manifestations" (Morgan in Grant 215).

5. In 1915, Wyndham Lewis also reported, in the avant-garde "little magazine" *Blast*, on seeing "every day in a certain A. B. C. Shop at least three girls who belong to a new and unknown race. They would furnish an artist looking for an origin with a model of a new mankind" (Lewis quoted in Symons 7).

Chapter 5. Chanel: The Order of Things

1. Summarizing from Wilson and others: textile industries were among the first to be industrialized and further technological changes in the mid-nineteenth century made the mass production of more complex patterns possible. Union and feminist campaigns on behalf of clothing trade employees also spurred further development of machinery for complicated work. While the simplification of women's wear enabled more diversely active women's lives, it also opened up women's wear to mass production. Many of the major changes in the clothing industry in the early twentieth century can be linked to this expansion of ready-to-wear clothing.

2. Chanel's working-girl look seems to fit particularly well with the exceptional stylishness of some working girls on screen and thus to the makeover plots of Hollywood

film. But there was no enormous gulf to be articulated by a transformation from one style of dress to another within the Chanel look and her one foray into Hollywood design (in 1931 for Metro-Goldwyn-Mayer Inc.) was largely unsuccessful.

3. In an essay on surrealism, Benjamin places both Jacobus Johannes Pieter Oud and Corbusier as antitheses of surrealism—as boxing in its revolutionary potential ([1929] 1996c: 78). This essay was undoubtedly informed by the 1927 publicity around the Weissenhof Estate Exhibition of working class housing in Stuttgart, which featured both architects and is notable for its use of prefabrication and simplified facades (see chapter 7).

4. Though often critiqued as overly deterministic and unreflective (see Butler and Bohman's essays in Shusterman's collection), habitus does not conceptually exclude the possibility of change or critique. As Charles Taylor explicates, "A bodily disposition is a habitus when it encodes a certain cultural understanding. The habitus in this sense always has an expressive dimension. It gives expression to certain meanings that things and people have for us, and it is precisely by giving such expression that it makes those meanings exist for us" (42).

5. A related frame of reference for thinking about fashion as a technology is Foucault's "Technologies of the Self" (1988b), which is clearly indebted to Heidegger's conception of technology. While it lacks the same relation to institutional power as "confession" and other technologies identified by Foucault, there are disciplinary effects disseminated by expertise on and normalization of fashion. Craik's chapter on "technical bodies and technologies of the self" explores some of these connotations.

6. As Jessica Glasscock notes, some of the "fashion photography" Sherman produced for Comme des Garçons breaks the genre's most predictable rules and even challenges editorially adventurous fashion composition by virtually concealing the clothes. But figure 12 could be a fashion editorial, with the clothes themselves central to the characterization of the hybrid of the human and the mannequin just as much as its exposure of gender performance echoes Butler.

7. "[W]orks that lack 'this kind of humour,'" Breton argues, "are unlikely to endure, whether in the realm of science, art, poetry, or philosophy" (Breton quoted in Suleiman 2003). Breton also connects surrealism to Hegel here, as he had done elsewhere, stressing that surrealist humor involves a complicated form of objectivity that never escapes subjectivity: "The fundamental principle of Romantic art . . . is the concentration of the soul upon itself. . . . [I]f that interest goes so far as to absorb the mind in external contemplation, and if at the same time humour, while maintaining its subjective and reflective character, lets itself be captivated by the object and its real form, we obtain in this penetration a humour that is in a certain sense objective" (Hegel quoted in Breton [1966] 1997: xvi; see chapter 7).

Chapter 6. Between the Acts: The Time of Modernism

1. Jameson accounts for Lyotard's strategic claims about postmodern history as follows: "Lyotard found himself obliged to reinvent one of the oldest models of temporality on the books, namely the cyclical one, which alone could authorize the suitably outrageous position that postmodernism does not follow, but rather precedes, true modern-

ism as such, whose return it prepares" (Jameson 2002: 5). However, given the influence of Giambattista Vico on a range of modernist writers, including Benjamin, W. B. Yeats, and Joyce, and the popularity of "cyclical" historicity (whether in the style of Frazer, Jung, or Dunne), a cyclical model still does not break from the array of modernist narratives on history.

2. The popular circulation of classical and other mythologies were newly invigorated as mass culture by *Bulfinch's Mythology* (1881) in the United States, by the prose translations of Homer produced by Samuel Butler in England (1898, 1900) and by literary-historical texts like Jessie Weston's *From Ritual to Romance* (1920).

3. As Chadwick discusses, *Noire et Blanche* indexes a range of uses of the "primitive" and primitivism, juxtaposing the "African" mask with the first publication of Man Ray's photography in French *Vogue* (Chadwick 1995). On anthropology, see chapters 7–8. On primitivism and modernism, see Torgovnick's excellent *Gone Primitive* (1990), which covers more aspects of this complex set of momentums than I can here.

4. In dialogue with William Connolly, Butler insists that dialectics are not necessarily teleological (Butler and Connolly 38). Butler's insistence that "what comes of certain dialectical crises is 'the new,' a field of possibility which is not the same as an order of possibility" (39) is especially relevant to considering whether the new of modernism should be located in a particular period.

5. This distinction in many ways lines up with Elizabeth Grosz's distinction, for feminist philosophy, between "Cartesian" and "non-Cartesian" traditions (Grosz 8–13), although it is not in fact a rigid dichotomy. Many influential writers are much harder to place on one or the other side of such an opposition. Butler, after all, addressing a similar audience, wants to keep Foucault in the camp of "dialecticians," although she is happy to set aside Deleuze as a "romantic" opposed to dialectical analysis (see Butler and Connolly 2000).

6. The controversies surrounding Foucault's historiography are in fact an example of this. The issue with Foucault's lack of concern about certain dates is a matter of the scale at which he discusses change. In his "archaeological" texts, Foucault sets out to uncover "the episteme in which knowledge . . . manifests a history which is not that of its growing perfection, but rather that of its conditions of possibility" ([1966] 1973: xii). Foucault scholars often distinguish this approach from the later "genealogies," which are instead thought to unfold a discourse in relation to other institutions and discourses. But Foucault is consistently concerned with the historical conditions that produce a particular "present." Some of this complexity might be glossed by Jameson's reading of *The Order of Things*, where he argues that while Foucault carefully critiques the given-ness of modern understandings of language, economy, and biology, he avoids addressing "historicism" itself in the same archaeological fashion (Jameson 2002: 70–71), leaving historicism as the unexamined substratum of modernity. This seems neither incidental nor a matter of neglect but rather a proposition about the relation between history and modernity that is consistent with Foucault's discussion in "What is Enlightenment?"

7. Flaubert's *Madame Bovary* includes early signs of how this everyday history works. Details of clothing and food (Flaubert 6, 38, 63), for example, are used to distinguish between classes but also to anchor the narrative in a world anyone could experience as

an observer rather than as a judge. Flaubert's meticulous, almost clinical, cataloguing of such details is part of a new understanding of the everyday precisely because these elements can only have narrative weight by reference to how use gives them meaning and context.

8. Deleuze's summary of Bergson's theory stresses its overlap with cinema: "not only is the instant an immobile section of movement"—like frame to shot—"but movement is a mobile section of duration, that is, of the Whole or of a whole"—like shot to film. This implies "that movement expresses something more profound, which is the change in duration or in the whole" (Deleuze [1983] 1986: 9). See chapter 1.

9. This quotation is from Kristeva's essay "Women's Time" (1979), which also discusses feminism's relation to the past. Kristeva applauds here a new generation of feminists who refuse insertion into the historically-constituted subject of history (Kristeva 193–95), which suggests an interesting conjunction with Woolf's imagination, in *Three Guineas*, of a world in which the term feminist is no longer necessary. See also Jardine (1985) and Braidotti (1994).

10. Let me stress that I mean modernism and not Modernism here. Jane Austen, Aphra Benn, George Eliot, Lou Andreas-Salomé, George Sand, and Mary Wollstonecraft, to take only a few famous examples, should not be excluded from this—and nor, of course, should the suffragettes who formed, in many respects, another transnational modernist dialogue on modernity.

Chapter 7. The Age of the World Picture

1. In an interview, Foucault stressed that "Heidegger has always been for me the essential philosopher. . . . I began to read Heidegger in 1951 or 1952. . . . I still have the notes I took . . . I have tons of them! . . . My whole philosophical development was determined by my reading of Heidegger" (Foucault 1989: 326). Jameson crucially acknowledges, in an account that should be more widely read, that Foucault and Heidegger both "have more in common with modernism as such" than "with anything postmodern that might conceivably lay claim to some more fundamental and decisive break with modernity as such" (2002: 73).

2. The terms are tied together in many scholarly texts that position postmodernism as the globalized or globalizing phase of modernity. See, among many examples, Featherstone (1995) and Giddens (1990).

3. The term "The International Style" was coined in 1932, in Hitchcock and Johnson's guide to the exhibition of the same name, organized by Johnson to promote Mies van der Rohe, Corbusier, and Gropius. Corbusier's most famous contribution to this exhibition was his Villa Savoy, while Mies' contribution included a Weissenhof Estate building.

4. One example of a Disney attraction thought to be particularly postmodern is the "It's a Small World" ride, which Muschamp notes was "commissioned from Disney by the Pepsi-Cola Company for the 1964–65 New York World's Fair," thus being as much a product of Exposition culture as the EPCOT globe.

5. According to Benjamin, the Expositions were another form of utopian thinking that "modernize[d] the universe" ([1927–40] 2002: 18). His comparison of the Expositions to the caricatures of Grandville (aka Jean Ignace Isidore Gérard) is particularly

telling for this chapter. Grandville's famous image of lamp-lit Parisian bridges stretching across the solar system—"the ring of Saturn becomes a cast-iron balcony on which the inhabitants of Saturn take the evening air" (Benjamin [1927–40] 2002: 18)—might also now remind us of figure 14.

6. Malinowski claims that the "principles of method can be grouped under three main headings; first of all, naturally, the student must produce real scientific aims, and know the values and criteria of modern ethnography. Secondly, he ought to put himself in good conditions of work, that is, in the main, to live without other white men, right among the natives. Finally, he has to apply a number of special methods of collecting, manipulating and fixing his evidence" (6).

7. Heidegger does not value just any experience over experiment as verification of the known world. He distinguishes sensation (*erleben*, to live/feel)—discrete experiences that cannot form a self because they are insufficiently continuous—from the experience of self/being, which is *erfahren* (to learn/undergo/look for) (see Inwood 62). With a different set of modernist references, Williams distinguishes "experience past" (lessons or "processes of consideration, reflection and analysis") from "experience present" (innovations or experiment with "unquestionable authenticity and immediacy"). But for Williams these are linked by the kinds of "action and consciousness which they both oppose" (Williams 1985: 127–28).

Chapter 8. The Invention of Culture

1. Ten years later such education became compulsory for all children under thirteen and in conjunction with the legislation restricting child labor and, subsequently, with the introduction of still-recognizable sexual consent legislation (1881–1885), this must be seen as the simultaneous development of training for citizenship and the modernist adolescence discussed in chapter 2.

2. Bennett recalls being required to read Williams and Hoggart in 1962 for secondary school teaching. This negotiated, he says, "our assent to working on and with popular texts, and with our own everyday experience, as a means of provoking classroom discussion about contemporary social, political and moral issues" (Bennett 50). See chapter 9.

3. There are several snapshot histories of this Exposition (for example, Bolotin and Laing), called the World's Columbian Exposition to mark 400 years of "American" cultural development. Such popular histories are an important context for the place of the Fair in anthropological history.

4. Hoggart accounts for his method as follows: "Where it is presenting background, this book is based to a large extent on personal experience, and does not purport to have the scientifically-tested character of a sociological survey. There is an obvious danger of generalization from limited experience. I have therefore included, chiefly in the notes, some of the findings of sociologists where they seemed necessary, either as support or as qualification of the text. I have also noted one or two instances in which others, with experience similar to mine, think differently" (xli).

5. The cross-cultural trade in modernism and modernist Orientalism is important here, but it is not the origin of modernism in China or Japan. Lee quotes a story about Hong Kong, by Eileen Chang, published in a Shanghai journal in 1943, in which the nar-

rator comments on the "presence of" a "touch of oriental color . . . obviously meant for foreigners. The English came from far away to take a look at China, and we much give them a China to look at—a China in Western eyes: exotic, delicate, ludicrous" (in Lee 324). At the same time, Eisenstein's "The Cinematographic Principle and the Ideogram" (1929) and Ernest Fenollosa and Pound's "The Chinese Written Character as a Medium of Poetry" (1918) are contemporary with, rather than precursors to, Lu's work on the modernization of Chinese language and culture.

6. Lee elaborates: "the very word 'new' (xin) became the crucial component of a cluster of new word compounds denoting a qualitative change in all spheres of life" (Lee 44): reform movements, "new policies," "new schools," "new people," "new literature," and "new culture" (44). This "new vocabulary," in China, as in Europe, the United States, or Australia, was not confined to elite publications but was a "regular feature" of the popular press (Lee 45) and "middlebrow" publications, like the journal Dongfang zazhi (see Lee 47ff), and their "construction of a modern lifestyle through commodity advertisement" (82; see chapter 5). Although Lee's study focuses on Shanghai, which he and others acknowledge to be a "special cultural matrix" (82), the broader May Fourth movement embraced the idea that a "sense of living in a new era . . . was what defined the ethos of modernity" (44).

7. Naming himself "O'Reilly Tzu," and his supporters "T-Warriors" (T for tradition), Bill O'Reilly's Culture Warrior indicates much of what is at stake in the U.S. label "culture wars." What is at stake turns out to be largely defined by that modernist standard, relativism (O'Reilly 2007). It is not that the two polarized sides of "the culture wars" in O'Reilly's sense are both doing Cultural Studies. But both sides claim to speak of and for and as "culture" in ways shaped by the modernist installment of the cultural expert.

8. This suggests a break with prior certainty but turns on specialization: "As specialists, none of us claims to speak in the name of 'reality.' The good days of that assurance are long gone. We now have to recognise in every scientific result the value of a product—such as what comes off the conveyor belt of a factory—relative to institutions, to axioms and to procedures. Far from uttering truths, it is thus inscribed in one functioning among others. It refers to a specific place and to its own causes. It is inscribed in the logic of a technical production" (Certeau 1997: 125).

9. Marx's conception of ideology was centered on a "false consciousness" by which subjects consent to social structures and ideological practices they do not fully understand or are distracted from reflecting on. But Althusser positions ideology instead as representing "the imaginary relationship of individuals to their real conditions of existence" (Althusser [1971] 1994: 153). Because "Ideological State Apparatuses" necessarily allude to reality they "need only be 'interpreted' to discover the reality of the world behind their imaginary representation of that world" (154), but Foucault's "regions" are perhaps more complex in that such interpretation of the first region might take place in either science (the second) or culture (the third).

10. Butler's account of this situation stretches from Hegel through Lacan and Althusser to Foucault. This is the kind of philosophical and theoretical argument that is made difficult for Cultural Studies precisely because of the force attributed to distinctions between modernity, modernism, and "postmodernism" by the institutionalized

closure of Modernism. In much Cultural Studies writing on ideology, Foucault and even Butler, despite her own texts, are bluntly opposed to any discussion of ideology by the insistence on a major break that makes them "postmodern."

Chapter 9. On Popular Music

1. The Middletown studies note that marketing to cultural aspirations in book clubs and other mass-produced formats expanded in the 1920s (Lynd and Lynd 232). But insofar as they were seen to mimic a cultural maturity they did not possess, book-club consumers were ranked very low in the cultural critic's hierarchies of taste and consciousness. How this poor-taste consumption of culture might be aligned with the value of Allen Lane's Penguins is worth pursuing, because it can only lead us to the importance of expert evaluation. Criticism of the "vicarious" satisfaction achieved through book clubs also defined consumption as not so much opposed to production or imagination as productive of the wrong kind of imagination. As Janice Radway argues, such "standardized and feminized consumer-subjects" incited alarm because they responded to "culture" as a commodity, and if culture could be purchased "then it would no longer function as the uniquely unmarked mark of human distinction" (Radway 887).

2. The distinction between postmodernism and modernism is often construed as the emergence of "post-structuralist theory," citing texts that are often, paradoxically, not theories about postmodernism at all. Michael Drolet's *The Postmodernism Reader* (2004), for example, opens with Foucault's essay "What is Enlightenment?," followed by Berman's famous introduction to his "study in the dialectics of modernization and modernism" (Berman 16). Post-structuralist theory that does not refer to postmodernism dominates the collection: four pieces each by Foucault and Derrida, three by Deleuze and one by Luce Irigaray. Five pieces by Lyotard and one each by Bauman, Baudrillard, and Jameson are left to represent postmodernism as an *ism*.

3. Readings argues that "Cultural Studies does not propose culture as a regulatory ideal for research and teaching, so much as seek to preserve the structure of an argument for redemption through culture, while recognizing the inability of culture to function any longer as such an idea. . . . Cultural Studies, in its current incarnation as an institutional project for the 1990s, proceeds from a certain sense that no more knowledge can be produced, since there is nothing to be said about culture that is not itself cultural" (17). Readings compares this to the Leavisism discussed in chapter 8, but its particular map of nationalism, literature, and Cultural Studies owes more to the New Critics of the United States who were Leavis' interlocutors.

4. Adorno acknowledges that all art works are limited by the fully historical material available to them "including words, colors, sounds, associations of every sort and every technique ever developed" and, indeed, the constraints of taste (Adorno [1970] 1984: 195): "The choice of the material, its use, and the limitations of that use, are an essential element of production" (194).

5. A "Futurist" experimentalist, Russolo proclaims: "In the nineteenth century, with the invention of machines, Noise was born. . . . We will amuse ourselves by orchestrating together in our imagination the din of rolling shop shutters, the varied hubbub of train stations, iron works, thread mills, printing presses, electrical plants, and subways. . . . We

want to give pitches to these diverse noises, regulating them harmonically and rhythmically" (23).

Conclusion: Modernist Cultural Studies

1. In this respect, modernism is the ground, as Heidegger would suggest, of modern research culture, premised always on proving the innovation of a particular project against something prior to it. Heidegger decries—long before the solidification of practices now mourned in very similar terms—"the decisive development of the modern character of science as ongoing activity [that] also forms men of a different stamp. The scholar disappears. He is succeeded by the research man who is engaged in research projects. These, rather than the cultivating of erudition, lend to his work its atmosphere of incisiveness. The research man no longer needs a library at home. Moreover, he is constantly on the move. He negotiates at meetings and collects information at congresses. He contracts for commissions with publishers. The latter now determine along with him which books must be written" ([1938] 1977: 125).

2. This might be compatible with Matei Calinescu's argument, in *Five Faces of Modernity* (1987), that there are "two conflicting and interdependent modernities," one that is progressive and rationalist and one that is critical and self-reflexive and "bent on demystifying the basic values of the first" (265), or indeed with Friedman's quite similar argument discussed in the introduction. Calinescu understands "modernism" and "postmodernism" respectively as these two modernities. The other three "faces," although weighted equally by the book's structure, are rather relations between the fields of modernity, Modernism, and postmodernism.

Bibliography

Adamowicz, Elza. 2003. "Exquisite excrement: the Bataille-Breton polemic." *Aurifex* (2), http://www.goldsmiths.ac.uk/aurifex/issue2/adamowicz.html.

Adorno, Theodor W. 1976. *Introduction to the Sociology of Music.* Translated by E. B. Ashton. New York: Seabury. Originally published 1932.

———. 1984. *Aesthetic Theory.* Translated by C. Lenhardt. London: Routledge & Kegan Paul. Originally published 1970.

———. 2001. "The Culture Industry Reconsidered." In *The Culture Industry: Selected Essays on Mass Culture*, 98–105. New York: Routledge. Originally published 1967.

———. 2002. *Essays on Music.* Edited by R. Leppert. Berkeley: University of California Press.

———. 2005a. "Looking Back on Surrealism." In *Modernism: An Anthology*, edited by L. Rainey, 1113–16. Originally published 1956.

———. 2005b. "Trying to Understand *Endgame*." In *Modernism: An Anthology*, edited by L. Rainey, 1116–37. Originally published 1961.

Adorno, Theodor W., and Max Horkheimer. 1997. *Dialectic of Enlightenment.* London: Verso. Originally published 1944.

Aldridge, Brad. 2002. *Disneyland History.* JustDisney.com [cited 12 February 2007]. Available from http://www.justdisney.com/disneyland/history.html.

Althusser, Louis. 1994. "Ideology and Ideological State Apparatuses." In *Cultural Theory and Popular Culture*, edited by J. Storey, 151–63. Hemel Hempstead: Harvester Wheatsheaf. Originally published 1971.

Anderson, Benedict. 1991. *Imagined Communities: Reflections on the Origin and Spread of Nationalism.* London: Verso.

Appadurai, Arjun. 1996. *Modernity at Large: Cultural Dimensions of Globalization.* Minneapolis: Minnesota University Press.

———. 2000. "Grassroots Globalization and the Research Imagination." *Public Culture* 12 (1): 1–19.

Arnold, Matthew. 1962. "The Function of Criticism at the Present Time." In *Lectures and Essays in Criticism*, 258–90. Ann Arbor: University of Michigan Press. Originally published 1864.

———. 2006. *Culture and Anarchy: An Essay in Political and Social Criticism*. Oxford: Oxford University Press. Originally published 1869.

Attridge, Derek. 1988. "Joyce and the Ideology of Character." In *James Joyce—The Augmented Ninth: Proceedings of the Ninth International James Joyce Symposium, Frankfurt 1984*, edited by B. Benstock, 152–57. Syracuse: Syracuse University Press.

Austen, Jane. 2004. *Northanger Abbey*. New York: Collector's Library. Originally published 1818.

Badger, Clarence G. 1927. *It*. Starring C. Bow. U.S.A.: Famous Players-Lasky Corporation.

Bair, Deirdre. 1986. "Simone de Beauvoir: Politics, Language, and Feminist Identity." *Yale French Studies—Simone de Beauvoir: Witness to a Century* 72: 149–62.

Barthes, Roland. 1973. *Mythologies*. Translated by A. Lavers. London: Granada. Originally published 1957.

———. 1982. *Camera Lucida: Reflections on Photography*. New York: Hill & Wang. Originally published 1980.

———. 1983. *The Fashion System*. Translated by M. Ward. New York: Hill & Wang. Originally published 1967.

———. 1999. "The Death of the Author," translated by S. Heath. In *Image-Music-Text*, 142–48. New York: Hill & Wang. Originally published 1977.

———. 2005. *The Language of Fashion*. Edited by A. Stafford & M. Carter. Sydney: Power Publications.

Baudelaire, Charles. 1995. *The Painter of Modern Life and Other Essays*. Translated by J. Mayne. London: Phaidon. Originally published 1863.

Baudot, François. 1992. *'Mademoiselle Chanel': Chanel*. New York: Universe.

Baudrillard, Jean. 1988. "Simulacra and Simulations." In *Jean Baudrillard, Selected Writings*, edited by M. Poster, 166–84. Stanford: Stanford University Press. Originally published 1981.

Bauman, Zygmunt. 1992. *Intimations of Postmodernity*. London: Routledge.

Beauvoir, Simone de. 1988. *The Second Sex*. Translated by H. M. Parshley. London: Picador. Originally published 1949.

Beebe, Roger. 2002. "Mourning Becomes. . . ?: Kurt Cobain, Tupac Shakur, and the 'Waning of Affect.'" In *Rock Over the Edge: Transformations in Popular Music Culture*, edited by R. Beebe, D. Fulbrook, and B. Saunders, 311–34.

Beebe, Roger, Denise Fulbrook, and Ben Saunders, eds. 2002. *Rock Over the Edge: Transformations in Popular Music Culture*. Durham: Duke University Press.

Benjamin, Walter. 1969. *Illuminations*. Translated by H. Zohn. Edited by H. Arendt. New York: Schocken Books.

———. 1996a. "Addendum to 'The Paris of the Second Empire in Baudelaire.'" In *Marxist Literary Theory: A Reader*, edited by T. Eagleton and D. Milne, 80–83. Oxford: Blackwell Publishing. Originally published 1938.

———. 1996b. *Selected Writings: 1927–34*. Edited by M. W. Jennings. 3 vols. Vol. 2. Cambridge, Mass.: Belknap Press.

———. 1996c. "Surrealism: The Last Snapshot of the European Intelligentsia." In *Marxist Literary Theory: A Reader*, edited by T. Eagleton and D. Milne, 70–80. Oxford: Blackwell Publishing. Originally published 1929.

———. 2002. *The Arcades Project*. Translated by H. Eiland and K. McLaughlin. Cambridge, Mass.: Belknap Press. Originally published 1982.

Bennett, Tony. 1998. *Culture: A Reformer's Science*. London: Sage.

Bergson, Henri. 1944. *Creative Evolution*. Translated by A. Mitchell. New York: Random House. Originally published 1911.

———. 2001. *Time and Free Will: An Essay on the Immediate Data of Consciousness*. Translated by F. L. Pogson. 3d ed. New York: Courier Dover Publications. Originally published 1899.

Berlant, Lauren, and Michael Warner. 1998. "Sex in Public." *Critical Inquiry* 24 (2): 547–66.

Berman, Marshall. 1988. *All That Is Solid Melts into Air: The Experience of Modernity*. New York: Viking Penguin.

Boas, Franz. 1911. *The Mind of Primitive Man*. New York: Macmillan.

Bolotin, Norman, and Christine Laing. 2002. *The World's Columbian Exposition: The Chicago World's Fair of 1893*. Chicago: Illinois University Press. Originally published 1992.

Boorman, John. 1972. *Deliverance*. U.S.A.: Warner Bros.

Bordwell, David. 1989. *Making Meaning: Inference and Rhetoric in the Interpretation of Cinema*. Cambridge: Harvard University Press.

Bornstein, George. 1999. "Ezra Pound and the Making of Modernism." In *The Cambridge Companion to Ezra Pound*, edited by I. B. Nadel, 22–42. Cambridge: Cambridge University Press.

Bourdieu, Pierre. 1986. *Distinction: A Social Critique of the Judgement of Taste*. Translated by R. Nice. Cambridge: Harvard University Press. Originally published 1979.

———. 1993. *The Field of Cultural Production*. New York: Columbia University Press.

Bowlby, Rachel. 1992. "Walking, women and writing: Virginia Woolf as flanêuse." In *New Feminist Discourses: Critical Essays on Theories and Texts*, edited by I. Armstrong, 26–47. New York: Routledge.

———. 1993. *Shopping With Freud*. London and New York: Routledge.

Braidotti, Rosi. 1994. *Nomadic Subjects: Embodiment and Sexual Difference in Contemporary Feminist Theory*. New York: Columbia University Press.

Breton, André. 1972. *The Manifestoes of Surrealism*. Translated by R. Seaver and H. R. Lane. Ann Arbor: University of Michigan Press. Originally published 1925.

———. 1997. *Anthology of Black Humour*. Translated by M. Polizzotti. 3d ed. New York: City Lights Books. Originally published 1966.

Brown, Denise Scott. 1998. "Learning From Pop." In *Architecture Theory Since 1968*, edited by K. M. Hays, 60–67. Originally published 1971.

Bryher. 1928. "In Defence of Hollywood." *Close-Up*, February 1928: 42–47.

Butler, Judith. 1995. "Contingent Foundations." In *Feminist Contentions: A Philosophical Exchange*, edited by S. Benhabib, L. Nicholson, N. Fraser, and J. Butler, 35–58. London: Routledge. Originally published 1992.

———. 1997. *The Psychic Life of Power: Essays in Subjection.* Los Angeles: Stanford University Press.

———. 1999. *Subjects of Desire: Hegelian Reflections in Twentieth-Century France.* New York: Columbia University Press. Originally published 1987.

Butler, Judith, and William Connolly. 2000. "Politics, Power and Ethics: A Discussion Between Judith Butler and William Connolly." *Theory & Event* 4 (2): 1–40.

Cahoone, Lawrence, ed. 2003. *From Modernism to Postmodernism: An Anthology*, 2d ed. Cambridge, Mass.: Blackwell Publishers.

Calinescu, Matei. 1987. *Five Faces of Modernity: Modernism, Avant-garde, Decadence, Kitsch, Postmodernism.* Durham: Duke University Press.

Carroll, Lewis. 1970. *Alice's Adventures in Wonderland and Through the Looking-Glass.* Edited by M. Gardner. London: Penguin. Originally published 1865/1887.

Caughie, Pamela L, ed. 2000. *Virginia Woolf in the Age of Mechanical Reproduction.* New York: Routledge.

Certeau, Michel de. 1988. *The Writing of History.* Translated by T. Conley. New York: Columbia University Press. Originally published 1975.

———. 1997. *Culture in the Plural.* Translated by T. Conley. Minneapolis: University of Minnesota Press.

———. 1998. *The Practice of Everyday Life.* Translated by L. Giard and P. Mayol: University of Minnesota Press. Originally published 1984.

Chadwick, Whitney. 1995. "Fetishizing Fashion/Fetishizing Culture: Man Ray's 'Noire et Blanche.'" *Oxford Art Journal* 18 (2): 3–17.

———, ed. 1998. *Mirror Images: Women, Surrealism and Self-Representation.* Cambridge, Mass.: The MIT Press.

Childs, Peter. 2000. *Modernism.* London: Routledge.

Chow, Tse-Tsung. 1960. *The May Fourth Movement: Intellectual Revolution in Modern China.* Cambridge: Harvard University Press.

Clarke, John. 1975. "Style." In *Resistance Through Rituals*, edited by J. Clarke, S. Hall, T. Jefferson, and B. Roberts, 175–91.

Clarke, John, Stuart Hall, Tony Jefferson, and Brian Roberts. 1975. *Resistance Through Rituals.* Birmingham: Centre for Contemporary Cultural Studies.

Clément, Catherine. 1987. *The Weary Sons of Freud.* Translated by N. Ball. London: Verso. Originally published 1972.

Comaroff, Jean, and John Comaroff. 2006. "Introduction to 'Of Revelation and Revolution.'" In *Anthropology in Theory: Issues in Epistemology*, edited by H. L. Moore and T. Sanders, 382–96. Oxford: Blackwell Publishing.

Conley, Tom. 2007. *Cartographic Cinema.* Minneapolis: University of Minnesota Press.

Corbusier, Le. 1947. *The City of Tomorrow.* New York: The Architectural Press. Originally published 1927.

Corbusier, Le, Jacques Guiton, and Margaret Guiton. 1981. *The Ideas of Le Corbusier on Architecture and Urban Planning.* Translated by M. Guiton. New York: G. Braziller.

Côté, James E. 1994. *Adolescent Storm and Stress: An Evaluation of the Mead-Freeman Controversy.* Hillsdale: Lawrence Erlbaum Associates.

Craik, Jennifer. 1994. *The Face of Fashion: Cultural Studies in Fashion.* London: Routledge.

Crimp, Douglas. 1983. "On the Museum's Ruins." In *The Anti-Aesthetic,* edited by H. Foster, 43–56.

Croll, Elisabeth J. 1978. *Feminism and Socialism in China.* London: Routledge.

Cullen, Barry. 2005. "The Impersonal Objective: Leavis, the Literary Subject and Cambridge Thought." In *F. R. Leavis: Essays and Documents,* edited by I. D. MacKillop, 149–73. London: Continuum.

Dali, Salvador, and Luis Buñuel. 1929. *Un Chien Andalou.* France. Ursulines Film Studio.

Davis, Fred. 1992. *Fashion, Culture, Identity.* Chicago: University of Chicago Press.

Deleuze, Gilles. 1986. *Cinema I: The Movement-Image.* Translated by H. Tomlinson and B. Hammerjam. 2 vols. Vol. 1. London: The Athlone Press. Originally published 1983.

———. 1989. *Cinema II: The Time-Image.* Translated by H. Tomlinson and R. Galeta. 2 vols. Vol. 2. London: Athlone Press. Originally published 1985.

———. 1988. *Foucault.* Translated by S. Hand. London: The Athlone Press. Originally published 1986.

———. 1990. *The Logic of Sense.* Translated by M. Lester. Edited by C. V. Boundas. New York: Columbia University Press. Originally published 1969.

Deleuze, Gilles, and Felix Guattari. 1987. *A Thousand Plateaus.* Translated by B. Massumi. 2 vols. Vol. 2, Capitalism and Schizophrenia. Minneapolis: University of Minnesota Press. Originally published 1980.

Dennehy, Annabella. 1899. "Women of the Future." *Westminster Review,* July 1899: 100.

Donald, James, Anne Friedberg, and Laura Marcus. 1998. *Close Up, 1927–1933: Cinema and Modernism.* Princeton: Princeton University Press.

Driscoll, Catherine. 2001. "The Moving Ground: Locating everyday life." *South Atlantic Quarterly* 100 (2): 381–98.

———. 2002a. *Girls: Feminine Adolescence in Popular Culture and Cultural Theory.* New York: Columbia University Press.

———. 2002b. "Joyce's Feminist Audiences." In *Joyce's Audiences,* edited by J. Nash, 179–200. Amsterdam: Rodopi.

Drolet, Michael, ed. 2004. *The Postmodernism Reader.* New York: Routledge.

Dunne, John William. 1942. *The Serial Universe.* London: Faber & Faber. Originally published 1934.

During, Simon. 2005. *Cultural Studies: A Critical Introduction.* New York: Routledge.

Eckert, Charles. 1991. "The Carole Lombard in Macy's Window." In *Stardom: Industry of Desire,* edited by C. Gledhill, 30–39. London: Routledge. Originally published 1978.

Eckley, Grace. 1985. *Children's Lore in* Finnegans Wake. New York: Syracuse University Press.

Eisenstein, Sergei. 1926. *Battleship Potemkin.* U.S.S.R.: Goskino.

———. 1969. *Film Form.* Translated by J. Leyda. New York: Cleveland World Publishing Co. Originally published 1949.

Eliot, T. S. 1998. *The Waste Land and Other Poems*. Edited by H. Vendler. London: Signet Classics. Originally published 1922.

———. 2005. "Tradition and the Individual Talent." In *Modernism: An Anthology*, edited by L. Rainey, 152–56. Originally published 1919.

Ellmann, Richard, ed. 1975. *Selected Letters of James Joyce*. London: Faber & Faber.

Engels, Friedrich. 1987. *The Condition of the Working Class in England*. Translated by V. G. Kiernan. Harmondsworth: Penguin.

Ewen, Stuart. 1976. *Captains of Consciousness: Advertising and the Social Roots of the Consumer Culture*. New York: McGraw Hill Book Company.

Fanon, Frantz. 1999. *Black Skin, White Masks*. London: Pluto Press. Originally published 1952.

Featherstone, Mike. 1995. *Undoing Culture: Globalization, Postmodernism and Identity*. London: Sage.

Felski, Rita. 1994. "Modernism and Modernity: Engendering Literary History." In *Re-reading Modernism: New Directions in Feminist Criticism*, edited by L. Rado, 191–208. New York: Garland.

———. 1995. *The Gender of Modernity*. Cambridge: Harvard University Press.

———. 2000. "The Invention of Everyday Life." *New Formations* 39: 15–31.

Ferrer, Daniel. 1985. "The Freudful Couchmare of ∧d: Joyce's Notes on Freud and the Composition of Chapter XVI of *Finnegans Wake*." *James Joyce Quarterly* 22 (4): 367–82.

Fink, Robert. 2002. "Elvis Everywhere: Musicology and Popular Music Studies at the Twilight of the Canon." In *Rock Over the Edge: Transformations in Popular Music Culture*, edited by R. Beebe, D. Fulbrook, and B. Saunders, 60–109.

Fiske, John. 1990. *Understanding Popular Culture*. London: Routledge. Originally published 1989.

———. 2000. *Reading Popular Culture*. London: Routledge. Originally published 1989.

Fitzgerald, F Scott. 1996. *This Side of Paradise*. London: Courier Dover. Originally published 1920.

Flaubert, Gustave. 2003. *Madame Bovary*. Translated by E. Marx-Aveling. New York: Collector's Library. Originally published 1857.

Fornäs, Johan. 1995. *Cultural Theory and Late Modernity*. London: Sage.

Foster, Hal, ed. 1983. *The Anti-Aesthetic: Essays on Postmodern Culture*. Washington: Bay Press.

———. 1985. "Postmodernism (a preface)." In *Postmodern Culture*, edited by H. Foster, vii–xiv. London: Pluto Press.

———. 1996. *The Return of the Real: Art and Theory at the End of the Century*. Cambridge, Mass.: The MIT Press.

Foucault, Michel. 1973. *The Order of Things: An Archaeology of the Human Sciences*. New York: Vintage Books. Originally published 1966.

———. 1977. *Discipline and Punish: The Birth of the Prison*, translated by A. Sheridan. London: Allen Lane. Originally published 1975.

———. 1984a. *The History of Sexuality: An Introduction*. Translated by R. Hurley. 3 vols. Vol. 1. Harmondsworth: Penguin. Originally published 1976.

———. 1984b. "What Is Enlightenment?" translated by P. Rabinow. In *The Foucault Reader*, edited by P. Rabinow, 32–50. London: Pantheon Books. Originally published 1978.

———. 1986. "Of Other Spaces," translated by J. Miskoweic. *Diacritics*, 16 (Spring): 22–27. Original text 1967.

———. 1988a. "The Masked Philosopher," translated by A. Sheridan et al. In *Politics, Philosophy, Culture: Interviews and Other Writings 1977–1984*, edited by L. D. Kritzman, 323–30. New York: Routledge. Originally published 1980.

———. 1988b. "Technologies of the Self." In *Technologies of the Self: A Seminar with Michel Foucault*, edited by H. G. Luther, H. Martin, and Patrick H. Hutton, 16–49. Amherst: University of Massachusetts Press.

———. 1989. "The Return of Morality," translated by J. Johnston. In *Foucault Live: Collected Interviews, 1961–1984*, edited by S. Lotringer, 317–32. New York: Semiotext(e).

Frampton, Kenneth. 1983. "Towards a Critical Regionalism: Six Points for an Architecture of Resistance." In *The Anti-Aesthetic: Essays on Postmodern Culture*, edited by H. Foster, 16–30.

———. 1992. *Modern Architecture: A Critical History*. 3d ed. New York: Thames & Hudson.

Fraser, Nancy. 1992. "Rethinking the Public Sphere: A Contribution to the Critique of Actually Existing Democracy." In *Habermas and the Public Sphere*, edited by C. Calhoun, 109–42. Cambridge, Mass.: The MIT Press.

Freeman, Derek. 1983. *Margaret Mead and Samoa: The Making and Unmaking of an Anthropological Myth*. London: Harvard University Press.

Freud, Sigmund. 1922. *Group Psychology and the Analysis of the Ego*. Translated by J. Strachey. London: The Hogarth Press. Originally published 1921.

———. 1953a. "Femininity," translated by J. Strachey. In *New Introductory Lectures*, edited by J. Strachey, 136–57. Harmondsworth: Penguin. Originally published 1933.

———. 1953b. "A Fragment of an Analysis of a Study in Hysteria," translated by J. Strachey. In *Case Studies I*, edited by J. Strachey, 31–164. Harmondsworth: Penguin. Originally published 1904.

———. 1953c. "Infantile Sexuality," translated by J. Strachey. In *Three Essays on the Theory of Sexuality*, 153–59. London: The Hogarth Press. Originally published 1905.

———. 1953d. "On Narcissism: An Introduction," translated by J. Strachey. In *The History of the Psycho-analytic Movement*, 73–102. London: The Hogarth Press. Originally published 1914.

———. 1989a. *The Ego and the Id*. Translated by J. Strachey. New York: W. W. Norton. Originally published 1923.

———. 1989b. *Introductory Lectures on Psychoanalysis*. Translated by J. Strachey. New York: Liverwright Publishing Co. Originally published 1917.

Friedman, Susan Stanford. 2001. "Definitional Excursions: The Meanings of Modern/ Modernity/Modernism." *Modernism/Modernity* 8 (3): 493–513.

Frith, Simon. 1987. "Towards an Aesthetic of Popular Music." In *Music and Society: The Politics of Composition, Performance and Reception*, edited by R. Leppert and S. McClary, 133–50. New York: Cambridge University Press.

————. 1996. *Performing Rites: Evaluating Popular Music*. Cambridge: Harvard University Press.

Frith, Simon, and Andrew Goodwin, eds. 1990. *On Record: Rock, Pop and the Written Word*. London: Pantheon.

Frow, John, and Meaghan Morris. 1993. "Introduction." In *Australian Cultural Studies*, edited by J. Frow and M. Morris, vii-xxxii. St Leonards, NSW: Allen & Unwin.

Gadamer, Hans-Georg. 2004. *Truth and Method*. Translated by J. Weinsheimer and D. G. Marshall. New York: Continuum International. Originally published 1960.

Galassi, Peter. 1997. *The Complete Untitled Film Stills: Cindy Sherman*. The Museum of Modern Art [cited 12 April 2007]. Available from http://www.moma.org/exhibitions/1997/sherman/index.html.

Gambrell, Alice. 1997. *Women Intellectuals, Modernism, and Difference: Transatlantic Culture, 1919-1945*. Cambridge: Cambridge University Press.

Giddens, Anthony. 1990. *Consequences of Modernity*. Cambridge: Polity Press.

————. 1992. *The Transformation of Intimacy: Sexuality, Love and Eroticism in Modern Societies*. Cambridge: Polity.

Giddens, Anthony, and Christopher Pierson. 1998. *Conversations With Anthony Giddens: Making Sense of Modernity*. Stanford: Stanford University Press.

Gillies, Mary Ann. 1996. *Henri Bergson and British Modernism*. Montreal: McGill-Queen's Press.

Glasscock, Jessica. 1985. *Bridging the Art/Commerce Divide: Cindy Sherman and Rei Kawakubo of Comme des Garcons*. New York University Grey Art Gallery [cited 12 October 2007]. Available from http://www.nyu.edu/greyart/exhibits/odysseys/index.html.

Glazebrook, Trish. 2000. *Heidegger's Philosophy of Science*. New York.

Gledhill, Christine, ed. 1991. *Stardom: Industry of Desire*. London: Routledge.

Grajeda, Tony. 2002. "The 'Feminization' of Rock." In *Rock Over the Edge: Transformations in Popular Music Culture*, edited by R. Beebe, D. Fulbrook, and B. Saunders, 233-254.

Gramsci, Antonio. 1971. *Selections from the Prison Notebooks of Antonio Gramsci*. Translated and edited by Q. Hoare and G. Nowell-Smith. London: Lawrence and Wishart.

Grant, Michael, ed. 1997. *T. S. Eliot: The Critical Heritage*. London: Routledge.

Greenberg, Clement. 1961. "Avant-Garde and Kitsch." In *Art and Culture*, 3-21. New York: Beacon Press. Originally published 1939.

Griffith, Gareth. 1993. *Socialism and Superior Brains: The Political Thought of Bernard Shaw*. London: Routledge.

Grossberg, Lawrence. 1992. *We Gotta Get Out of This Place: Popular Conservatism and Postmodern Culture*. New York: Routledge.

————. 1994. "The Deconstruction of Youth." In *Cultural Theory and Popular Culture: A Reader*, edited by J. Storey, 183-90. Hemel Hempstead: Harvester Wheatsheaf. Originally published 1986.

————. 1997. "Cultural Studies, Modern Logics, and Theories of Globalization." In *Back to Reality: Social Experience and Cultural Studies*, edited by A. McRobbie, 7–35. Manchester: Manchester University Press.

———. 2002. "Reflections of a Disappointed Popular Music Scholar." In *Rock Over the Edge: Transformations in Popular Music Culture*, edited by R. Beebe, D. Fulbrook, and B. Saunders, 25–59.

Grossberg, Lawrence, Cary Nelson, and Patricia Treichler. 1992. "Introduction." In *Cultural Studies*, edited by L. Grossberg, C. Nelson, and P. Treichler. New York: Routledge.

Grosz, Elizabeth. 1994. *Volatile Bodies: Toward a Corporeal Feminism*. St. Leonards, NSW: Allen & Unwin.

Gunning, Tom. 1994. "The Whole Town's Gawking: Early Cinema and the Visual Experience of Modernity." *The Yale Journal of Criticism* 7 (2): 189–201.

———. 2004. "Re-newing Old Technologies: Astonishment, Second Nature, and the Uncanny in Technology from the Previous Turn-of-the-Century." In *Rethinking Media Change: The Aesthetics of Transition*, edited by D. Thorburn and H. Jenkins, 39–60. Cambridge, Mass.: The MIT Press.

Habermas, Jürgen. 1983. "Modernity—An Incomplete Project." In *The Anti-Aesthetic*, edited by H. Foster, 3–15. Originally published 1981.

———. 1989. *The Structural Transformation of the Public Sphere: An Inquiry into a Category of Bourgeois Society*. Translated by T. Burger and F. Lawrence. Cambridge, Mass.: The MIT Press. Originally published 1962.

———. 1996. "Georg Simmel on Philosophy and Culture: Postscript to a Collection of Essays." *Critical Inquiry* 22 (3): 403–14.

Hall, G. Stanley. 1911. *Adolescence: Its Psychology and Its Relations to Physiology, Anthropology, Sociology, Sex, Crime, Religion, and Education*. 2 vols. New York: Appleton. Originally published 1904.

Hall, Radclyffe. 1929. *The Well of Loneliness, with a Commentary by Havelock Ellis*. New York: Covici Friede.

Hall, Stuart. 1996. *Stuart Hall: Critical Dialogues in Cultural Studies*. Edited by S. Hall, D. Morley, and K.-H. Chen. London: Routledge.

Halliwell, Martin, and Andy Mousley. 2003. *Critical Humanisms: Humanist/Anti-Humanist Dialogues*. Edinburgh: Edinburgh University Press.

Hansen, Miriam. 1987. "Benjamin, Cinema and Experience." *New German Critique* 40: 179–224.

———. 1991a. *Babel and Babylon: Spectatorship in American Silent Film*. Cambridge: Harvard University Press.

———. 1991b. "Pleasure, ambivalence, identification: Valentino and female spectatorship." In *Stardom*, edited by C. Gledhill, 259–82.

———. 2000. "Fallen Women, Rising Stars, New Horizons: Shanghai Silent Film as Vernacular Modernism." *Film Quarterly* 54 (1): 10–22.

Hartley, John. 2003. *A Short History of Cultural Studies*. London: Sage.

Harvey, David. 1989. *The Condition of Postmodernity: An Enquiry Into the Origins of Cultural Change*. Malden: Blackwell Publishing.

Hassan, Ihab. 1982. *The Dismemberment of Orpheus: Toward a Postmodern Literature*. 2d ed. Madison: University of Wisconsin Press.

Hawes, Elizabeth. 1938. *Fashion is Spinach*. New York: Random House.

Hays, K. Michael. 1998. *Architecture Theory Since 1968*. Cambridge, Mass.: The MIT Press.

Heath, Stephen. 1981. *Questions of Cinema*. Bloomington: Indiana University Press.

Hebdige, Dick. 1979. *Subculture: The Meaning of Style*. London: Methuen & Co.

Hegel, G. W. F. 1977. *Phenomenology of Spirit*. Translated by A. v. Miller. Oxford: Oxford University Press. Originally published 1807.

Heidegger, Martin. 1962. *Being and Time*. Translated by J. Macquarrie and E. Robinson. New York: Harper & Row. Originally published 1927.

———. 1971. *Poetry, Language, Thought*. Translated by A. Hofstadter. New York: Harper & Row. Originally published 1931.

———. 1977. *The Question Concerning Technology, and other essays*. Translated by W. Lovitt. New York: Harper & Row.

Hemingway, Ernest. 2006. *The Sun Also Rises*. New York: Scribner. Originally published 1926.

Henderson, Carole E. 2007. "Notes from a Native Daughter: The Nature of Black Womanhood in *Native Son*." In *Richard Wright's Native Son*, edited by A. M. Fraile, 55–72. Amsterdam: Rodopi.

Hetherington, Kevin. 1997. *The Badlands of Modernity: Heterotopia and Social Ordering*. London: Routledge.

Hitchcock, Henry-Russell. 1929. *Modern Architecture: Romanticism and Reintegration*. New York: Payson & Clarke Ltd.

Hoggart, Richard. 2004. *The Uses of Literacy*. 3d ed. New Brunswick: Transaction Publishers. Originally published 1957.

Hollander, Anne. 1999. *Feeding the Eye*. New York: Metropolitan Museum of Art, Yale University Press.

Holub, Renate. 1992. *Antonio Gramsci: Beyond Marxism and Postmodernism*. London: Routledge.

Hurlock, Elizabeth. 1929. *The Psychology of Dress: An Analysis of Fashion and Its Motive*. New York: The Ronald Press Co.

Huxley, Aldous. 1998. *Brave New World*. New York: Harper Perennial Modern Classics. Originally published 1932.

Huyssen, Andreas. 1986. *After the Great Divide: Modernism, Mass Culture, Postmodernism*. Bloomington: Indiana University Press.

Inwood, M. J. 1999. *A Heidegger Dictionary*. Oxford: Blackwell Publishing.

Jagodzinski, Cecile M. 1999. *Privacy and print: Reading and writing in seventeenth-century England*. Charlottesville: University Press of Virginia.

James, William. 1995. *Pragmatism*. Edited by T. Crofts and P. Smith. Toronto: Dover. Originally published 1907.

Jameson, Fredric. 1983. "Postmodernism and Consumer Society." In *The Anti-Aesthetic*, edited by H. Foster, 111–25.

————. 1991. *Postmodernism, or, the Cultural Logic of Late Capitalism*. Durham: Duke University Press.

————. 2002. *A Singular Modernity: Essay on the Ontology of the Present*. New York: Verso.

————. 2004. "The Politics of Utopia." *New Left Review* 25: 35–54.

Jardine, Alice A. 1985. *Gynesis: Configurations of Woman and Modernity*. Ithaca: Cornell University Press.

Jencks, Charles. 1998. "Post-Modern Architecture." In *Architecture Theory Since 1968*, edited by K. M. Hays, 306–17. Originally published 1977.

Jenkins, Henry, Tara McPherson, and Jane Shattuc. 2002. "Defining Popular Culture." In *Hop on Pop: The Politics of Popular Culture*, edited by H. Jenkins, T. McPherson, and J. Shattuc, 26–42. Durham: Duke University Press.

Jenks, Chris, ed. 2004. *Urban Culture: Critical Concepts in Literary and Cultural Studies*. Abingdon: Routledge.

Jones, Ellen Carol. 1989. "The Letter Selfpenned to One's Other: Joyce's Writing, Deconstruction, Feminism." In *Coping with Joyce*, edited by M. Beja and S. Benstock, 180–93. Columbus: Ohio State University Press.

Joselit, David. 1998. *Infinite Regress: Marcel Duchamp 1910–1941*. Cambridge, Mass.: The MIT Press.

Joyce, James. 1966. *Stephen Hero*. Edited by J. J. Slocum and H. Cahoon. Barnards Inn: The New English Library Ltd. Originally published 1957.

————. 1967. *Dubliners*. London: Jonathan Cape. Originally published 1914.

————. 1984. *Ulysses*. Edited by H. W. Gabler. Harmondsworth: Penguin. Originally published 1922.

————. 1988. "A Portrait of the Artist as a Young Man." In *The Essential James Joyce*, edited by H. Levin, 175–365. Harmondsworth: Penguin. Originally published 1916.

————. 1989. *Finnegans Wake*. London: Faber & Faber. Originally published 1939.

"Judge Ben Lindsay calls upon Colleen Moore and tells her the flapper type of motion picture is doing a lot towards teaching America that sex isn't a sin." 1927. *Photoplay*, November 1927: 29+.

Jung, Carl G. 1982. "The Love Problem of a Student," translated by R. F. C. Hull. In *Aspects of the Feminine: From the Collected Works of C. G. Jung*, 27–40. Harmondsworth: Penguin. Princeton: Princeton University Press. Originally published 1928.

Kant, Immanuel. 2003. "An Answer to the Question: 'What is Enlightenment?'" In *The Enlightenment: A Sourcebook and Reader*, edited by P. Hyland, O. Gomez, and F. Greensides, 55–58. London: Routledge. Originally published 1784.

Kayser, Rudolf. 1994. "Americanism." In *The Weimar Republic Sourcebook*, edited by A. Kaes, M. Jay, and E. Dimendberg, 395–97. Berkeley: University of California Press. Originally published 1925.

Kelly, Michael. 1994. *Critique and Power: Recasting the Foucault/Habermas Debate*. Cambridge, Mass.: The MIT Press.

Key, Ellen. 1918. "The Right of Motherhood." In *The Woman Question*, edited by T. R. Smith, 116–36. New York: Boni & Liverwright.

Kline, Katy. 1998. "In or Out of the Picture: Claude Cahun and Cindy Sherman." In *Mirror Images: Women, Surrealism and Self-Representation*, edited by W. Chadwick, 125–33.

Koda, Harold. 2005. "Introduction." In *Chanel: Catalogue for the Metropolitan Museum of Art exhibition*, edited by H. Koda and A. Bolton, 11–12.

Koda, Harold, and Andrew Bolton. 2005. *Chanel: Catalogue for the Metropolitan Museum of Art exhibition*. New York, New Haven: Metropolitan Museum of Art, Yale University Press.

Kracauer, Siegfried. 1994. "Girls and Crisis." In *The Weimar Republic Sourcebook*, edited by A. Kaes, M. Jay, and E. Dimendberg, 565–6. Berkeley: University of California Press. Originally published 1931.

———. 1995. *The Mass Ornament*. Translated by T. Y. Levin. Cambridge: Harvard University Press.

Krauss, Rosalind. 1985. *The Originality of the Avant-Garde and Other Modernist Myths*. Cambridge, Mass.: The MIT Press. Originally published 1981.

Kristeva, Julia. 1986. *The Kristeva Reader*, edited by T. Moi. Oxford: Basil Blackwell.

Laing, Dave. 1994. "Review Essay." *Popular Music* 13 (2): 223–27.

Lawrence, D. H. 1960. *Lady Chatterley's Lover*. Harmondsworth: Penguin. Originally published 1928.

———. 1989. *Women in Love*. Hardmondsworth: Penguin. Originally published 1920.

Leavis, F.R. 1930. *Mass Civilisation and Minority Culture*. Philadelphia: R. West.

Leavis, F. R., and Denys Thompson. 1964. *Culture and Environment: The Training of Critical Awareness*. London: Chatto & Windus. Originally published 1933.

Lee, Leo Ou-fan. 1999. *Shanghai Modern: The flowering of a new urban culture in China, 1930–1945*. Cambridge: Harvard University Press.

Lefebvre, Henri. 1991. *A Critique of Everyday Life*. Translated by J. Moore. London: Verso. Originally published 1961.

———. 2005. *Everyday Life in the Modern World*. Translated by S. Rabinovitch. New Jersey: Transaction Publishers. Originally published 1971.

Loos, Adolf. 1966. "Ornament and Crime." In *Adolf Loos: Pioneer of Modern Architecture*, edited by L. Münz and G. Künstler. New York: Thames and Hudson. Originally published 1908.

Lukács, Georg. 1969. *The Meaning of Contemporary Realism*. Translated by J. Mander and N. Mander. London: Merlin. Originally published 1962.

Lusty, Natalya. 2007. *Surrealism, Feminism, Psychoanalysis*. Aldershot: Ashgate.

Lynd, R. S., and H. M. Lynd. 1929. *Middletown: A Study in American Culture*. New York: Harcourt, Brace & Co.

Lyotard, Jean-François. 1984. *The Postmodern Condition: A Report on Knowledge*. Translated by G. Bennington and B. Massumi. Minneapolis: University of Minnesota Press. Originally published 1979.

MacCabe, Colin. 2006. "Foreword." In *Cinema and Modernism*, by D. Trotter, ix–xii.

MacCannell, Dean. 2005. "The Fate of the Symbolic in Architecture for Tourism: Piranesi, Disney, Gehry." In *Learning From The Bilbao Guggenheim*, edited by A. M. Guasch and J. Zulaika, 21–36. Reno: University of Nevada Press.

Malinowski, Bronislaw. 1999. *Argonauts of the Western Pacific. An Account of Native Enterprise and Adventure in the Archipelagoes of Melanesian New Guinea*. New York: E.P. Dutton. Originally published 1922.

Mallarmé, Stephané. 1982. *Selected Poetry and Prose*. Edited by M. A. Caws. New York: New Directions.

Marchant, J. R. V., and J. F. Charles, eds. 1957. *Cassell's Latin Dictionary, Latin-English and English-Latin*. 28 ed. London: Cassell.

Marcus, Stephen. 1985. "Freud and Dora: Story, History, Case History." In *In Dora's Case*, edited by C. Bernheimer and C. Kahane, 56–92. London: Virago.

Marinetti, Fillippo Tommaso. 2003. "Founding and Manifesto of Futurism." In *From Modernism to Postmodernism: An Anthology*, edited by L. Cahoone, 118–21. Originally published 1909.

Marvin, Carolyn. 1988. *When Old Technologies Were New: Thinking about Electric Communication in the Late Nineteenth Century*. New York: Oxford University Press.

Marx, Karl. 1990. *Capital: A Critique of Political Economy*. Translated by B. Fowkes. 3 vols. Vol. 1. Harmondsworth: Penguin. Originally published 1867.

Marx, Karl, and Friedrich Engels. 1962. *Selected Works*. London: Lawrence & Wishart. Originally published 1859.

Mayhew, Henry. 1985. *London Labour and the London Poor: Selections*. Harmondsworth: Penguin. Originally published 1851.

McClary, Susan, and Robert Walser. 1990. "START MAKING SENSE! Musicology Wrestles with Rock" In *On Record: Rock, Pop and the Written Word*, edited by S. Frith and A. Goodwin, 237–49. Originally published 1988.

Mead, Margaret. 1943. *Coming of Age in Samoa: A Study of Adolescence and Sex in Primitive Societies*. Harmondsworth: Penguin. Originally published 1928.

Michelson, Annette. 1972. "The Man With the Movie Camera: From Magician to Epistemologist." *Artforum* (March): 60–73.

Molesworth, Helen. 1998. "Work avoidance: The Everyday Life of Marcel Duchamp's Readymades." *Art Journal* 57 (4): 50–61.

Morley, David. 2006. *Modernity, Media, Technology*. London: Routledge.

Morris, Meaghan. 1990. "Banality in Cultural Studies." In *The Logics of Television*, edited by P. Mellancamp, 14–43. Bloomington: Indiana University Press.

———. 1997. "A Question of Cultural Studies." In *Back to Reality?: Social Experience and Cultural Studies*, edited by A. McRobbie, 36–57. Manchester: Manchester University Press.

———. 1998. *Too Soon Too Late: History in Popular Culture*. Bloomington: Indiana University Press.

———. 2006. *Identity Anecdotes: Translation and Media Culture*. London: Sage.

Moxcey, Mary. 1916. *Girlhood and Character*. New York: The Abingdon Press.

Mulhern, Francis. 2000. *Culture/Metaculture*. London: Routledge.

Murphie, Andrew. 2001. "Computers Are Not Theatre: the machine in the ghost in Gilles Deleuze and Felix Guattari's thought." In *Deleuze and Guattari: Critical Assessments of Leading Philosophers*, edited by G. Genosko, 1299–332. London: Taylor & Francis. Originally published 1996.

Muschamp, Herbert. 1998. "Disney: Genuinely Artificial, Really Surreal." *New York Times*, October 4, 1998, AR41.

Nabokov, Vladimir. 1989. *Lolita*. New York: Vintage. Originally published 1955.

Nietzsche, Friedrich. 1974. *The Gay Science: With a Prelude in Rhymes and an Appendix of Songs*. Translated by W. Kauffmann. New York: Vintage Books. Originally published 1887.

———. 1997. "On the Uses and Disadvantages of History for Life," translated by R. J. Hollingdale. In *Untimely Meditations*, 57–124. Cambridge: Cambridge University Press. Originally published 1876.

O'Reilly, Bill. 2007. *Culture Warrior*. New York: Broadway Books.

Olsen, Liesl M. 2003. "Virginia's Woolf's 'cotton wool of daily life.'" *Journal of Modern Literature* 26 (2): 42–66.

Ortega y Gasset, José. 1985. *The Revolt of the Masses*. Translated by A. Kerrigan. Notre Dame: University of Notre Dame Press. Originally published 1932.

Pagnattaro, Marisa Anne. 2001. "Carving a literary exception: The obscenity standard and *Ulysses*." *Twentieth Century Literature* (Summer 2001): 217–42.

Parkes, Adam. 1996. *Modernism and the Theater of Censorship*. New York: Oxford University Press.

Poggioli, Renato. 1968. *The Theory of the Avant-Garde*. Translated by G. Fitzgerald. Cambridge, Mass.: Belknap Press. Originally published 1962.

Pound, Ezra. 1972. "A Few Don'ts by an Imagiste." In *Imagist Poetry*, edited by P. Jones, 130–34. Harmondsworth: Penguin. Originally published 1913.

Radway, Janice. 1994. "On the Gender of the Middlebrow Consumer and the Threat of the Culturally Fraudulent Female." *South Atlantic Quarterly* 93.4 (Fall 1994): 871–94.

Rainey, Lawrence, ed. 2005. *Modernism: An Anthology*. Oxford: Blackwell.

Readings, Bill. 1996. *The University in Ruins*. Cambridge: Harvard University Press.

Reich, Wilhelm. 1978. *The Mass Psychology of Fascism*. Translated by V. R. Carfagno. 3d ed. Harmondsworth: Penguin. Originally published 1942.

Rhys, Jean. 1975. *Good Morning Midnight*. Harmondsworth: Penguin. Originally published 1939.

Rilke, Rainer Maria. 1994. "Dolls: On the Wax Dolls of Lotte Pritzel." In *Essays on Dolls*, edited by I. Parry. London: Penguin. Originally published 1913.

Riviere, Joan. 1986. "Womanliness as Masquerade." In *Formations of Fantasy*, edited by V. Burgin, J. Donald and C. Kaplan, 35–44. London: Macmillan.

Rose, Nikolas. 1999. *Powers of Freedom*. Cambridge: Cambridge University Press.

Rose, Nikolas, and Paul Rabinow. 2003. "Thoughts on the Concept of Biopower Today." *The Molecular Sciences Institute* [cited 12 June 2008]. Available from http://www.molsci.org/research/publications_pdf/Rose_Rabinow_Biopower_Today.pdf.

Rosenberg, Beth Carole. 2000. "Virginia Woolf's Postmodern Literary History." *MLN* 115 (5): 1112–30.

Rousseau, Jean Jacques. 1911. *Émile*. Translated by B. Foxley. 1955 ed. London: Dent. Originally published 1762.

Russolo, Luigi. 2005. "The Art of Noises: A Futurist Manifesto." In *Modernism: An Anthology*, edited by L. Rainey, 23. Originally published 1913.

Rutter, Michael. 1980. *Changing Youth in a Changing Society: Patterns of Adolescent Development and Disorder*. Cambridge: Harvard University Press.

Sass, Louis A. 1987. "Introspection, Schizophrenia and the Fragmentation of Self." *Representations* 19 (Summer 1987): 1–33.

Sayers, Dorothy L. 2002. "The Entertaining Episode of the Article in Question." In *The Complete Stories*, 24–35. New York: Perennial. Originally published 1925.

Scott, Bonnie Kime. 2000. "The Subversive Mechanics of Woolf's Gramophone in *Between the Acts*." In *Virginia Woolf in the Age of Mechanical Reproduction*, edited by P. L. Caughie, 97–114. New York: Routledge.

Scott, Ridley. 1982. *Blade Runner*. U.S.A.: Blade Runner Partnership.

Secomb, Linnell. 2007. *Love and Philosophy: From Plato to Popular Culture*. Edinburgh: Edinburgh University Press.

Showalter, Elaine, ed. 1978. *These Modern Women: Autobiographical Essays From the Twenties*. New York: Feminist Press.

Shusterman, Richard, ed. 1999. *Bourdieu: A Critical Reader*. Oxford: Blackwell.

Simmel, George. 2000. *Simmel on Culture: Selected Writings*, edited by D. Frisby and M. Featherstone. London: Sage.

Spacks, Patricia Meyer. 1981. *The Adolescent Idea: Myths of Youth and the Adult Imagination*. New York: Basic Books, Inc.

Stanton, Henry. 1922. *Sex: Avoided Subjects Discussed in Plain English*. New York: Social Culture Publications.

Steele, Valerie. 1998. *Paris Fashion: A Cultural History*. 2d ed. Oxford: Berg.

———. 2000. "Fashion: Yesterday, Today and Tomorrow." In *The Fashion Business: Theory, Practice, Image*, edited by N. White and I. Griffiths, 29–44. Oxford: Berg.

Stewart, Garrett. 2000. *Between Film and Screen: Modernism's Photo Synthesis*. Chicago: University of Chicago Press.

Suleiman, Susan Rubin. 1998. "Dialogue and Double Allegiance: Some Contemporary Women Artists and the Historical Avant-garde." In *Mirror Images: Women, Surrealism and Self-Representation*, edited by W. Chadwick, 128–55.

———. 2003. "Surrealist Black Humour: Masculine/Feminine." *Papers of Surrealism* [cited 18 August 2008]. Available from http://www.surrealismcentre.ac.uk/papersof-surrealism/journal1/acrobat_files/Suleiman.pdf.

Symons, Julian. 1987. *Makers of the New: The Revolution in Literature 1912–1939*. London: Andre Deutch Ltd.

Tamagne, Florence. 2006. *History of Homosexuality in Europe, 1919-1939*. New York: Algora Publishing. Originally published 2000.

Taylor, Charles. 1999. "To Follow a Rule . . ." In *Bourdieu: A Critical Reader*, edited by R. Shusterman, 29–44. Oxford: Blackwell.

Taylor, Richard, and Ian Christie, eds. 1994. *The Film Factory: Russian and Soviet Cinema in Documents, 1896–1939*. London: Routledge.

Thalberg, Irving. 1964. "The Modern Photoplay." In *Film and Society*, edited by R. D. MacCann, 44–47. New York: Charles Scribner's Sons. Originally published 1929.

Torgovnick, Marianna. 1990. *Gone Primitive: Savage Intellects, Modern Lives*. Chicago: University of Chicago Press.

Tratner, Michael. 2000. "Why Isn't *Between the Acts* a Movie?" In *Virginia Woolf in the Age of Mechanical Reproduction*, edited by P. L. Caughie, 115–34. New York: Routledge.

Trilling, Lionel. 1962. "Science, Literature And Culture A Comment On The Leavis-Snow Controversy." *Universities Quarterly* 17 (1): 9–32.

Trotter, David. 2006. *Cinema and Modernism*. London: Blackwell.

Troy, Nancy. 2003. *Couture Culture: A Study in Modern Art and Fashion*. Cambridge, Mass.: The MIT Press.

———. 2005. "Chanel's Modernity." In *Chanel: Catalogue for the Metropolitan Museum of Art Exhibition*, edited by H. Koda and A. Bolton, 18–21.

Tungate, Mark. 2004. *Media Monoliths: How Great Media Brands Thrive and Survive*. London: Kogan Page.

Turner, Graeme. 2003. *British Cultural Studies*. 3d ed. New York: Routledge.

Tylor, Edward Burnett. 1964. *Primitive Culture*. 2 vols. Vol. 1–2. New York: Brentano's. Originally published 1871.

"United States v. One Book Called 'Ulysses' 5 F.Supp. 182." 1933. Southern District of New York.

Veblen, Thorstein. 1965. *The Theory of the Leisure Class*. New York: The Macmillan Co. Originally published 1899.

Venturi, Robert, Denise Scott Brown, and Steven Izenour. 1977. *Learning from Las Vegas: The Forgotten Symbolism of Architectural Form*. Cambridge, Mass.: The MIT Press.

Vertov, Dziga. 1929. *Man with a Movie Camera*. U.S.S.R.: Vutku.

———. 1984. *Kino-Eye: The Writings of Dziga Vertov*. Translated by K. O'Brien. Edited by A. Michelson. Berkeley: University of California Press.

Welchman, John C. 2005. "Architecture :: Sculpture." In *Learning from the Bilbao Guggenheim*, edited by A. M. Guasch and J. Zulaika, 235–58. Reno: University of Nevada Press.

West, Rebecca. 1928. *The Strange Necessity: Essays and Reviews*. London.

———. 1994. *Black Lamb, Grey Falcon*. Harmondsworth: Penguin. Originally published 1941.

White, Cynthia L. 1971. *Women's Magazines from 1693–1965*. London: Michael Joseph. Originally published 1970.

Wicke, Jennifer. 1993. "Modernity Must Advertise: Aura, Desire and Decolonization in Joyce." *James Joyce Quarterly* 30–31 (4–1): 593–613.

Wigley, Mark. 2001. *White Walls, Designer Dresses*. Cambridge, Mass.: The MIT Press. Originally published 1995.

Williams, Raymond. 1967. *Culture and Society*. London: Chatto & Windus. Originally published 1958.

———. 1975. *The Country and the City*. London: Chatto & Windus.

———. 1977. *Marxism and Literature*. Oxford: Oxford University Press.

———. 1985. *Keywords: A Vocabulary of Culture and Society*. New York: Oxford University Press. Originally published 1976.

———. 1989. "When Was Modernism?" In *The Politics of Modernism*, 31–35. London: Verso.

———. 2002. "Culture is Ordinary." In *The Everyday Life Reader*, edited by B. Highmore, 92–100. New York: Routledge. Originally published 1958.

Williams, Raymond, R. J. Kaufman, and Alun Jones. 1959. "Our Debt to Dr Leavis." *Critical Inquiry* 1 (3): 245–56.

Wilson, Elizabeth. 2003. *Adorned in Dreams: Fashion and Modernity*, 2 ed. New York: Rutgers University Press.

Witkin, Robert W. 2003. *Adorno on Popular Culture*. London: Routledge.

Woolf, Virginia. 1966. *Three Guineas*. London: Harcourt Brace. Originally published 1938.

———. 1973. *A Room of One's Own*. Harmondsworth: Penguin. Originally published 1928.

———. 1981. *The Diary of Virginia Woolf*. 3 vols. Vol. 2. Harmondsworth: Penguin. Originally published 1978.

———. 1984. "Modern Fiction." In *The Common Reader*, edited by A. McNeillie, 146–54. London: The Hogarth Press. Originally published 1925.

———. 1990. "Mr. Bennett and Mrs. Brown." In *The Gender of Modernism: A Critical Anthology*, edited by B. K. Scott, 634–41. Bloomington: Indiana University Press. Originally published 1924.

———. 1992. *Between the Acts*. London: Penguin. Originally published 1941.

Index

Catherine Driscoll is chair of gender and cultural studies at the University of Sydney. She writes and teaches across a range of fields, including modernist studies, cultural studies and cultural theory, new media, rural studies, and youth culture. She is the author of *Girls: Feminine Adolescence in Popular Cultural and Cultural Theory*, as well as numerous essays and articles.